CIVILIZING CONTENTION

CIVILIZING CONTENTION

International Aid in Syria's War

Rana B. Khoury

CORNELL UNIVERSITY PRESS
ITHACA AND LONDON

Copyright © 2025 by Cornell University

All rights reserved. Except for brief quotations in a review, this book, or parts thereof, must not be reproduced in any form without permission in writing from the publisher. For information, address Cornell University Press, Sage House, 512 East State Street, Ithaca, New York 14850. Visit our website at cornellpress.cornell.edu.

First published 2025 by Cornell University Press

Library of Congress Cataloging-in-Publication Data

Names: Khoury, Rana B. author
Title: Civilizing contention : international aid in Syria's war / Rana B. Khoury.
Other titles: International aid in Syria's war
Description: Ithaca : Cornell University Press, 2025. | Includes bibliographical references and index.
Identifiers: LCCN 2025003328 (print) | LCCN 2025003329 (ebook) | ISBN 9781501784101 hardcover | ISBN 9781501784118 paperback | ISBN 9781501784125 epub | ISBN 9781501784132 pdf
Subjects: LCSH: Humanitarian assistance—Political aspects—Syria | Humanitarian assistance—Syria—International cooperation | Humanitarian assistance—Syria—History—21st century | Civil war—Protection of civilians—Syria | Nonviolence—Syria—History—21st century | Civilians in war—Syria—History—21st century | Syria—History—Civil War, 2011—Civilian relief
Classification: LCC DS98.6 .K478 2025 (print) | LCC DS98.6 (ebook) | DDC 361.2/6095691—dc23/eng/20250408
LC record available at https://lccn.loc.gov/2025003328
LC ebook record available at https://lccn.loc.gov/2025003329

To my everything—Alex and Sumi

تذكرون لماذا بدأتم وكيف؟ اذكروني جيدا، واعلموا أنكم ستبلغوني حين تعرفوني، أنا الثورة: روحي ستبقى ولن تموت في صدوركم

Do you remember why you began and how? Remember me well, and know that you will reach me when you know me. I am the Revolution: My spirit is eternal and will live on in your hearts.

—Banner displayed by community members identifying as the Syrian Revolution in Kafr Nabl, October 16, 2014

Contents

Preface ix
List of Abbreviations xiii

Introduction: Contention in War 1
1. How Aid Civilizes Contention 21
2. Contention, Conflict, and Crisis in Syria 41
3. The Facilitating Process 63
4. The Formalizing Process 81
5. The Filtering Process 106
6. Comparative Cases 127
Conclusion: Contention, Civilized 142

Acknowledgments 157
Notes 161
References 167
Index 189

Preface

"This is the hardest question you can ask," replied a thoughtful Syrian man during a June 2024 interview in southern Turkey. My question had been: "Do you have a country?" He proceeded to cry. I had been interviewing Syrians about their resilience or vulnerability after a decade of displacement and about their sense of political belonging—or lack thereof. He gathered himself. "My country is Syria. I love it," he said. "But I don't think of returning." This profound sense of loss pervaded my visit. The conflict had since 2020 been at a stalemate—territory still divided, but the regime apparently victorious. Most Syrian refugees did not think they could go back home. As he explained: "I wish to return. . . . We didn't want to leave. The regime forced us to."

That would be the regime of Bashar al-Asad, who in 2000 inherited Syria from his father, Hafez, who had ruled since 1970. My interviewee, older than his thirty-two years, was forced to flee because of a war that took hundreds of thousands of lives, drove millions from their homes, and created enormous humanitarian needs as it destroyed and deprived a people and a land. But he also fled for more particular political reasons. He had marched in protests during the 2011 Syrian uprising, part of a wave of "Arab Spring" movements across the region, and he had remained in Syria as that nonviolent uprising, met with regime repression, escalated into armed conflict. Throughout the war he labored on behalf of cause and community at great risk, in a way that resembles many civil actors in this book. Living in a rebel-held area, he worked in emergency medical response for a hospital operating underground due to regime shelling. He eventually fled into refuge in Turkey, passing through other rebel-held areas to avoid either detainment or conscription by the regime. From there he worked with humanitarian programs that had international support in the rebel-held northwest. All of these actions closed Asad's Syria off to him.

Asad controlled more than just the Syrian people. The regime in Damascus had, from the start of the conflict, also politicized international aid and blocked it from reaching opposition strongholds. In response, many international organizations found ways to work from across the Turkish and Jordanian borders to achieve humanitarian and other objectives. Yet they would not assume the risks of operating inside Syrian or rebel-held territory, nor did they enjoy the necessary knowledge, connections, or access to do so. For that, as this book demonstrates, they relied on Syrians, who in turn found ways to persist in wartime activism—building something like a civil society in a place where one had never existed and against the odds of a brutal war. They documented daily events, fed and sheltered people in need, advocated for detainees, prepared transitional justice processes for a peace that seemed ever more improbable, distributed public goods, and sought protection for their own human rights. This book, through an analysis of Syria's war, theorizes that international aid, through institutional processes, facilitates, formalizes, and filters wartime activism—enabling civil action but constraining its politics and collectivity. It also contends that as international aid imposes its structures and routines, it leaves activists unprotected from the violence of war and its aftermath.

Civil actors like the young man with whom I spoke lived with a deeply unsettling feeling of insecurity by 2024. His Turkish refuge was becoming overtly hostile, Europe was an impenetrable fortress, and Syria was a rehabilitating member of its regional community. He was haunted by nostalgia as he continued to consider to what country he belongs. "Maybe one day," he said. "In the future," he dared imagine, "if the regime falls, if there is a new government in Syria . . . a free country like we want. I will return."

On December 8, 2024, the regime did fall, after an eleven-day rebel offensive that set frozen conflict lines ablaze and awed the country and the world. Only once the regime's rule crumbled did its vulnerability become apparent: it had existed underneath a fierce, but brittle, façade. The regime had been enriched as the country regressed; survived as sanctions impoverished it; remained triumphant as rebels grasped at the corners; and relied on Russia, Iran, and Lebanon's Hezbollah, while each fought their own battles and Israel's military assaults reshaped the order of the Middle East.

Hope is desperately felt in this moment of change. Yet the path forward is fraught for Syria's new authorities. The challenges include divisions along lines of control, ethnicity, and region that are at risk of exploitation by spoilers from the old regime, aggravation by genuine fears among minorities, and exacerbation by geopolitical rivalries and interventions. Their task is to bring a host of rebel groups into one national project that is inclusive of an array of societal interests and to do so in an authoritarian region and in a world backsliding on democracy as majoritarianism threatens individual rights, while millions of refugees risk losing protection in their host countries even as conditions for voluntary return remain uncertain.

Civil society cannot overcome all these obstacles. But the assets of civil organizations built in crisis—the perseverance and experience of those nonviolent actors recounted in this book—hold the potential to mitigate them. These activists can hold power to account, advocate for inclusivity, articulate grassroots demands, and mobilize the masses. They can use their skill sets to address issues of transitional justice, reconstruction and development, and representative institution building. And they can help serve the immense material needs that face the country and that will undermine stability if ignored. What was something like a civil society during the war, dispersed as it was abroad and squeezed into rebel-held areas at home, stands the chance in a post-Asad Syria to be a genuine civil society for the whole country. These Syrians have mobilized under challenging conditions for years. They do have a country—and now their country *may* have them too.

Abbreviations

3RP or RRRP	Regional Refugee and Resilience Plan
ACU	Assistance Coordination Unit
CSO	civil society organization
CVE	countering violent extremism
DFID	Department for International Development, United Kingdom
FSA	Free Syrian Army
GIZ	Deutsche Gesellschaft für Internationale Zusammenarbeit, Germany
GONGO	government-organized nongovernmental organization
HNAP	Humanitarian Needs Assessment Programme
HTS	Hay'at Tahrir al-Sham
ICRC	International Committee of the Red Cross
IDP	internally displaced person
IGO	intergovernmental organization
INGO	international nongovernmental organization
IS	Islamic State
JN	Jabhat al-Nusra (later Hay'at Tahrir al-Sham)
KDP	Kurdistan Democratic Party
KNLA	Karen National Liberation Army
KNU	Karen National Union
LC	local council
LCC	local coordination committee
M&E	monitoring and evaluation
MB	Muslim Brothers association, or Muslim Brotherhood
MSF	Médecins Sans Frontières (Doctors Without Borders)
NGO	nongovernmental organization
OCHA	United Nations Office for the Coordination of Humanitarian Affairs
OLS	Operation Lifeline Sudan
OTI	Office of Transition Initiatives of USAID
PSS	psychosocial support
SIG	Syrian Interim Government
SNAP	Syria Needs Analysis Project
SOC	Syrian Opposition Coalition

SPLM/A	Sudan People's Liberation Movement/Army
SRRA	Sudan Relief and Rehabilitation Association
UN	United Nations
UNHCR	United Nations High Commissioner for Refugees (UN refugee agency)
UNRWA	United Nations Relief and Works Agency for Palestine Refugees in the Near East
USAID	United States Agency for International Development

INTRODUCTION
Contention in War

Ahmed grew up in Dar'a, a bucolic province in southern Syria. His mother, like others in their agricultural town, encouraged him to study, "because the parents are tired and want their kids to get educated."[1] So after high school Ahmed moved to "the center of it all," the bustling capital city of Damascus, to pursue a technical business degree. While there he saw more money, development, cars, and alcohol than he ever had. Exposed to inequality, Ahmed began to think about politics. Mandatory grueling military service deepened his thinking: The severe institution seemed to spare only those with connections. After these stints in the city and army, he eagerly returned to a "cleaner life" in the countryside, where he got married. Ahmed was working two jobs to support his new wife and their budding family when the Syrian uprising began in March 2011.

He joined his town's first demonstration, alongside just fifteen others who dared to defy the notoriously fierce regime. As he put it, "Us youth, we were taking to the streets against oppression." Security forces showed up and the protesters went home. Yet that night hundreds of people in the town came out—for Ahmed, it was a revelation. He and a group of trusted friends began coordinating contentious actions. From his conversations with community members he developed the sense that a long road lay ahead—most Syrians lacked experience in democratic participation or independent organizing. It was a prescient, if understated, impression.

Ahmed was shocked and disturbed the first time he saw a nonviolent activist injured and bleeding. "I didn't expect that the army would actually shoot us!" he recalled. Still, he persisted. Within the coordinating committee, Ahmed was tasked with documenting events and disseminating footage to raise awareness of the movement and of the repression it faced. Although he was new at this, he progressed from sending cell phone videos to a contact in Jordan to producing direct broadcasts for international satellite TV stations. Another group of Darawis (people from Darʻa) was coordinating the efforts of local committees across the province that helped organizers like Ahmed acquire information such as the location of army checkpoints. The protests continued for months and in the beginning, Ahmed asserts, they were not sectarian. The Islamists and extremists, he says, came later.

When the opposition movement took up arms, initially in self-defense, Ahmed remained committed: "If you were on the side of the demonstrations, you also had to be on the side of the arming." He joined a Free Syrian Army (FSA) rebel unit as media coordinator, carrying weapons for his own protection. A few months in, however, Ahmed was disappointed. The rebels weren't always upholding the democratic and participatory ideals that had originally motivated the movement. He laid down his arms.

Yet Ahmed continued to act on behalf of the cause. He converted his house to a shelter for activists; a tile in his floor served as the opening to an underground hiding place that could fit as many as fifteen people. This was a risky undertaking, but it maintained his influence in the movement while he considered his next move. In a town surrounded physically by armed groups and ideologically by burgeoning Islamist currents, Ahmed had ruled out participation in violent rebellion. But he wasn't ready to stop participating altogether.

During war, civil activists confront hard choices under harder circumstances. Government repression can quash protest. Individuals can rule out the use of violence. Collective exhaustion can undo a social movement. As options for nonviolent action narrow, risks grow: cleavages harden, territory is divided, and armed actors target real and perceived opponents. The odds are stacked against people like Ahmed. Indeed, a common narrative tells us that Syria's social movement failed and violence prevailed. An encyclopedia entry captures this view: "The regime's harsh military crackdown escalated tensions, and by September 2011 the peaceful protests had become an armed insurgency" (*Britannica* 2023).

This book challenges that narrative. While some activists joined the insurgency and others capitulated to governmental repression, many others embarked on wartime activism. Even as refugees were escaping violence and needs inside the country surged, it was Syrians themselves who delivered the vast majority of emergency relief in their country. In the depths of war and without experience in independent organizing, Syrians founded countless organizations to advocate for detainee rights, document daily events, distribute public goods, and provide psychosocial support to displaced people. In short, something like a civil society emerged during Syria's war. How did this happen, with what resources, in which areas, and to what ends?

Perhaps one explanation for this surge in civil organization among Syrians is that these novel forms of nonviolent action were safe compared to mass protests that make for easy targeting. Yet existing research suggests otherwise. Syrians who engaged in post-protest activism were detained, violently targeted, or forcibly displaced throughout the war (Becker and Stolleis 2016; El-Helou and Antara 2018; Martínez and Eng 2018). Humanitarians were not spared from these risks. The Syrian regime, according to Physicians for Human Rights, "strategically targeted health facilities and health workers" and "branded health workers as enemies of the state" (Koteiche et al. 2019, 3). Indeed, Syria became one of the "deadliest places for aid workers in the world" at the height of its civil war, according to an international humanitarian organization (CARE 2018).

Why did militarization not quell activism altogether? How did nonviolent action persist alongside the violent offshoots of the anti-regime movement? How did activists remain engaged while in neighboring countries despite the precarity of forced displacement? In this book, I argue that to give a satisfactory answer to these questions, we should look toward a common element of crisis contexts: international aid, or humanitarian and other nonmilitary assistance deployed by outside actors to achieve certain objectives.

International aid organizations arrived to help in and around Syria beginning in 2011 as the clashes between the regime and its opponents escalated. In the decade that followed, hundreds of thousands perished while millions fled internally and to neighboring countries as the war wrought unfathomable destruction on the country. The Syrian regime blocked aid to rebellious regions, leading many international aid organizations to set up operations in neighboring countries, including Turkey and Jordan, where they had more autonomy to pursue humanitarian and other objectives in areas outside governmental control in Syria and among refugees. To execute cross-border aid operations from neighboring countries into rebel-held regions like Darʻa, international actors would turn to locals like Ahmed. People like Ahmed—facing multiplying challenges and risks—would in turn find a way to participate in nonviolent action on behalf of the Syrian cause by working with and for international aid organizations.

These convergences between international and local actors lead to this book's primary research question: How does international aid shape civil action in war? To answer it, I develop a framework to understand the interactions between international and local actors in the nonviolent action that unfolds alongside military action during war. My framework applies when humanitarians and other nonmilitary aid actors, such as those working in development or conflict resolution, have the autonomy to respond to crises relatively unhindered by state or nonstate armed actors. Under such conditions, international actors work with and through local actors to achieve their objectives. The primary takeaway from the study is that international aid can support, train, and reward some local activists during war, but not without costs for the cadres involved. In short, international aid both enables and constrains civil action in war.

My argument proceeds in three parts that track with the institutional qualities of contemporary international aid. Each of these qualities is associated with a process that shapes contention into something quite different than the informal and transgressive action that characterized Ahmed's first uprising year. First, international aid actors forge relations with civil actors in conflict zones to enact their crisis responses; these linkages can create the means and opportunities for local actors to participate in the framework of crisis response despite the violence around them. Second, aid organizations impose rules that establish their authority over the response; these rules can equip local activists with technocratic skills that can be deployed to monitor and evaluate problems in their country, but not to transgress on the political structures that create them. And third, international humanitarians distribute resources based on needs but also on other institutional imperatives; these resources can favor the most fit, legible, and "legitimate" local actors, while introducing novel cleavages and hierarchies in a population of organizations that itself grew in response to the presence of international aid.

International aid, through these three processes, simultaneously enables and constrains local nonviolent action in war—shaping contention into a "civilized" population of organizations actively engaged in conflict processes. That is, in attempting to engage in and impose order on the parts of the conflict over which they can exert some influence, international aid organizations forge something like a civil society among local actors by supporting their active participation in crisis response in particular ways. International aid, however, cannot provide the protection that civil society needs; civil societies are defined in relation to—and need the protection of—states (Alagappa 2004). As a result, aid can leave local activists bare to the violence that unfolds during war and its aftermath.

This framework can explain how someone like Ahmed emerged from a kitchen floor foxhole to establish an educational organization in Darʿa with his brother that lightened the hardships of hundreds of children with the support of a managerial office staffed by fellow activists who had taken refuge across the border in Jordan. Then, Ahmed worked to advance "good governance" in his town, bringing in significant service programs like street cleaning. As he learned to adhere to stringent accounting protocols, Ahmed was also engendering the distrust of local leaders and the disdain of Islamist organizations. He had to battle accusations of secularism, escape shelling and armed clashes, and combat his own guilt about earning a comfortable salary amid such conditions of suffering—all concerns he shared with me during one of his capacity-building trainings in Jordan. Savvy and irrepressibly likeable, Ahmed earned and maintained grassroots community support to continuously pursue his goals until the Syrian armed forces reclaimed control of Darʿa in 2018 and all that civil action came to a crushing end. Ahmed was forced to leave.

International Aid and Civil Action in War

This book identifies the institutional processes through which international and local nonmilitary actors interact during war, rather than focus only on internal or on external drivers of change in Syria. The theoretical framework improves our understanding of how civilians and refugees engage in activism—particularly nonviolent action taken to bring change to the lives of others (Bayat 2002)—during war and despite violent targeting, generalized insecurity and displacement, and crises of resource-intensive needs. I contend that through its encounters with international aid organizations, civil action is both enabled and constrained during war. In the course of everyday interactions, international aid reconstitutes local nonviolent action and ultimately "civilizes" it: Aid forges something resembling a civil society, but one laid bare to risks and lacking protection. This book provides an explanatory framework for a civil war process that has been given little attention. Table 1 summarizes my theory of civilizing contention.

This theory of civilizing contention was built inductively. That means, I was informed by insights in relevant scholarly literature, but it was primarily in empirical observation of the case itself that I identified patterns and then generated

TABLE 1. Summary of theory of civilizing contention

Scope condition: International aid autonomy	INSTITUTIONAL QUALITIES OF AID	INSTITUTIONAL QUALITIES' COMPONENTS	CAUSAL PROCESS ACTIVATED BY AID	CAUSAL PROCESS MECHANISMS	EFFECTS ON CIVIL ACTION
	Relations	Social Infrastructural Material	Facilitating	Constitution and allocation	Enable participation
	Rules	Rationalism Moralism Professionalism	Formalizing	Coercive and normative pressures	Constrain politics
	Resources	Contracts Ideas	Filtering	Selection and legitimation	Constrain collectivity

theory to explain them. It begins with a scope condition (or circumstance in which I expect the theory to be relevant) that I call aid autonomy. International aid actors enjoy autonomy in "areas of limited statehood" (Risse 2011a) like rebel-held territory or weak states, and in contexts in which strong states choose not to restrict aid organizations.[2] Autonomy gives humanitarians and other aid actors leeway to interact directly with local actors to achieve their objectives. These interactions activate processes that generate change in nonviolent action. My approach does not take international aid as an exogenous or random variable that predictably shapes nonviolent action in a singular way. Instead, repeated international interactions with local actors are endogenous processes that generate change in nonviolent action, even while other factors affect both international aid and local nonviolent action, and they both affect each other.

The theory argues, first, that when international aid actors have a reasonable degree of autonomy, the relations they build with local actors to achieve their objectives can facilitate local participation in nonviolent action, even when violence is pervasive and risks are high. Second, aid organizations' institutional rules can formalize the orientation of local nonviolent actors, containing transgressive preferences or politics to which they might otherwise subscribe and which may, in any case, be attributed to them. Third, aid's institutional resources can filter the population of nonviolent organizations, elevating some while sidelining others and inducing or exacerbating cleavages between them.

When the relations, rules, and resources of international aid facilitate, formalize, and filter local activism in these ways, civilized contention results: Activists are enabled to participate in something like a civil society, in service of humanitarian governance that constrains their politics and their collectivity. The central claim of the theory is that international aid institutions induce changes in local action, which have consequential effects on contentious politics in places from which those international organizations will, eventually, withdraw.

Concepts and Contributions

This project differs from others in that it explores relationships between international aid organizations and local nonviolent actors in areas of conflict. Scholars have studied how international aid affects violent action in war. They have uncovered the effects of international aid on nonviolent action in post-conflict contexts (Berry 2018; Lake 2018; McMahon 2017). A large literature also addresses the effects of development aid in peaceful contexts, often documenting a phenomenon called NGOization, whereby local grassroots action transforms into formal, neoliberal, or donor-oriented forms (Ali 2018; Chahim and Prakash 2014; Hammami 1995; Hearn 1998; Jad 2004; Jamal 2012; Roy 2014). In contrast, this project attends to these relationships during war, but it offers more than a change in scenery.

This process-based theory of civilizing contention fills in explanatory gaps and answers lingering questions in existing research. For example, the idea of NGOization is often invoked in a derogatory fashion: Bad material incentives offered by outsiders sever good local movements from their grass roots. But it is not a given that international organizations cause harm despite their objectives; nor is it obvious why activists would repeatedly opt into processes that lead them away from their original trajectories. Acknowledging the needs of communities in conflict, as well as the risks undertaken by activists to serve them, should disabuse us of the idea that wartime activists lose their attachments to the grass roots. At the same time, this framework also identifies the power of international aid to inflect local activism even under the direst of circumstances, such as warfare. In other words, while the notion of NGOization suggests a trade-off between international subjugation and local political commitments, this theory suggests that sometimes contradictory and always complex outcomes are produced that can advance the interests of both international and local actors, even as trade-offs remain.

More importantly, this framework helps us better understand real-world processes that unfold during war. These include how local activists assume risks that international aid workers won't in feeding and sheltering hundreds of thousands of people; how rebels govern with, or beside, civilian counterparts; how events on the ground are documented when international media lacks access; and how activists who have been displaced become brokers for international interveners—and are changed through these interactions. I particularly seek to advance our understanding in three areas: contentious politics during war, connections between refugees and civilians who engage in wartime processes, and international interventions and interactions with local actors.

These contributions begin with enhancing our understanding of wartime activism, a term I use interchangeably with civil action and nonviolent action. I build on a burgeoning literature in civil war studies that takes civilians as people with politics and agency that can persist and transform during war (Avant et al. 2019a; Balcells 2017; Barter 2014; Steele 2017; Van Baalen 2024; J. Krause et al. 2023; Kreft 2019; Yadav 2020; Kasfir 2005; Wood 2008; Kaplan 2017; Jose and Medie 2015; Paddon Rhoads and Sutton 2020). I connect this literature to (otherwise unconnected) studies in forced migration scholarship that identify the ways refugees act as agents that can uplift themselves and their communities (Carpi and Fiddian-Qasmiyeh 2020; Clarke 2018; Fiddian-Qasmiyeh 2016; Holzer 2012; Horst 2013; Irfan 2020; Pincock et al. 2020; Ruiz de Elvira 2019)—including those in the civil war state (Banki 2024; Brynen 1990; Hamdan 2020; Horstmann 2011;

Jacobsen 2019; J. A. Mundy 2007). These insights on civil action are put into conversation with ideas from social movement literature about movement cycles and demobilization (Tarrow 1993, 2011) to reveal how nonviolent and violent contention can coincide during war (Brockett 2005; Parkinson 2023). This means that social movements may have afterlives in war that we miss altogether when we don't pay attention to the forms and motivations of wartime activism and the civil actors involved—many of whom may have fled into refuge.

Indeed, border regions can comprise subsystems of nonviolent (if also violent) conflict processes where local, refugee, regional, and international actors pursue political, diplomatic, humanitarian, development, and other objectives (Nordstrom 1997; Schneckener 2011). Such bustling areas have emerged across the border from southern Sudan in Kenya, where international aid organizations worked with local activists and rebel groups to provide relief during the Sudanese civil war (Riehl 2001; Karim et al. 1996; Mampilly 2011); in the border regions between Tunisia and Libya following the Libyan war and uprising (Moss 2021); in Algeria across from Moroccan-controlled Western Sahara where an entire nongovernmental government has risen and gained international support (J. A. Mundy 2007; Fiddian-Qasmiyeh 2014); in Nepal where Bhutanese activists forged an ecosystem of exile politics in demanding rights from their nearby home state (Banki 2024); and in the border regions between Thailand and Myanmar, where nonviolent activists, nonstate armed groups, and international aid actors have pursued their goals for decades (Fumagalli 2022; Callahan 2007; Horstmann 2011). From Afghanistan and Pakistan to Ukraine and Poland, the phenomenon of civil action among both refugees and civilians is common if strikingly underexplained.

Time and again, international aid organizations are also in these regions, connecting in the transnational spaces of civil wars (Andreas 2008; Autesserre 2010; Bob 2005; Campbell 2018; Kassimir et al. 2001; Lubkemann 2008; Nordstrom 1997). I conceive of international aid actors as intergovernmental and nongovernmental organizations, networks, and donor governments that provide nonmilitary material and immaterial assistance to achieve humanitarian and nonhumanitarian ends during war. Nonhumanitarian aid may advance development, political processes, stabilization to prevent violence, early recovery and reconstruction, and peacebuilding and conflict resolution. Humanitarian aid traditionally refers to efforts to save lives and alleviate suffering in line with certain principles including neutrality, impartiality, independence, and humanity; humanitarianism may also strive for more ambitious objectives to address root causes of crises or to advance foreign policy goals (Barnett 2013; Barnett and Snyder 2008; Bhungalia 2015; Carbonnier 2015; Cutts 1998; Duffield 2001; Fearon 2008; Weiss 1999).

Humanitarian and nonhumanitarian organizations both respond to contemporary crises, often at the behest of the same donor governments, who also support both intergovernmental and nongovernmental organizations. There are important differences between a United Nations (UN) agency that is delegated authority and funded by the consensus of governments, and an international nongovernmental organization (INGO) that can attain independent funding and act flexibly against state-imposed constraints, but in practice the boundary is penetrable. Intergovernmental organizations (IGOs) such as UN agencies and INGOs both engage in crisis response, in parallel and in partnership. The empirical analysis in the following chapters disentangles humanitarians from nonhumanitarians and governmental from nongovernmental organizations when relevant, but conceptually, and often on the ground, a unified framework is appropriate (Ahmed 2019).

These international actors matter because they insert material resources into conflict contexts, but their influence goes beyond the provision of raw assistance. They also matter because they hold constitutive power over social actors (Barnett and Finnemore 1999; Ferguson 1990; Mitchell 2002; J. Mundy 2015). That means they can shape the capacities and interests of those over whom they hold power (Barnett and Duvall 2005): They can affect who engages in crisis response, in which ways, for which beneficiaries, toward what ends, with whom, and to whose advantage—all while filling in log frames at their computers and professing principles like neutrality (M. Krause 2014). Chapter 1 will delve into the theorized processes that explain how this constitutive power affects local civil actors.

Suffice to say that it matters that international-local interactions change the actors involved, especially those on the weaker side of the power relationship who are all the while put at risk. International aid organizations, reflecting their logistical and operational needs and sometimes their "localization" and "participatory" objectives, often engage local actors in their undertakings (Mohan and Stokke 2000; Fiddian-Qasmiyeh 2018; Khoury and Scott 2024). Some scholars promote such international-local engagement as a normatively and practically desirable approach to intervention (Autesserre 2014; Konyndyk and Worden 2019); they contend that local actors can be key to the success of international actors seeking to resolve conflict and build peace (Autesserre 2021; Mac Ginty 2014).[3] Perhaps. But those interactions will have changed them.

What Civilizing Means

The cumulative outcome of the facilitating, formalizing, and filtering processes is "civilized contention." *Civilizing* is a potentially loaded word, associated with the "progress of man" or with the "civilizing mission" of colonizers and empires to make the subjects of their domination better, modern, and, as it happens, more like themselves. This normative connotation need not be based on superiority. "Civility" can refer to politeness and norms of everyday conduct that facilitate interactions between people (Bybee 2021). Scholars of civil action have adopted this mild conception, referring to "mere civility" as a basis for nonviolent action that maintains an openness to interacting respectfully even in disagreement (Avant et al. 2019b).

Yet the term *civil* may be descriptive rather than normative, referring simply to the Latin *civis*, or citizen. Citizens sometimes go to war with each other, as in "civil war." They often organize themselves into a "civil society." They are "civilians," the people who do not participate in hostilities in armed conflict. They may be people who adhere to nonviolence as they pursue contentious goals, as in "civil resistance" (Schock 2013) (although if they do so for moral reasons, we might consider civil resistance a norm-laden form of contention).

My use of the term *civilizing* straddles these approaches. *Civil* here is descriptive, focused on civilians (including those who flee across borders, that is, refugees) who engage in nonviolent action and who do so in interaction with international actors provisioning nonmilitary aid in a violent context. I also have in mind a set of processes that come together to civilize that nonviolent action: making it more organized and routine, separating it from the armed actors it might otherwise engage with, seeking order and rationality in an uncertain context.

In *The Civilizing Process*, sociologist Norbert Elias describes and theorizes a process that unfolded slowly but surely in the Western world from the thirteenth to eighteenth centuries. Through norms like shame and repugnance, people and societies became more internally restrained; they ceased spitting in public and improved their table manners, while also refraining from fatal duels and deferring to central authorities. An internal "pacification" corresponded with growing interdependence of people within a territory, even if these emergent states unleashed violence on external foes (2000 [1939]).

In this ambivalent approach set by Elias, *civilizing contention* refers to a set of processes that impose structures and routines to address crises through those actors whose conduct can be moderated and restrained even amid war. These processes unfold through everyday interactions and institutional mechanisms more than through deliberate intent, specific actors, or even explicit notions of superiority. International organizations, in this sense, aim to pacify war—or the parts of it over which they can exert control.

Research Design

This book studies the case of Syria's conflict to build a theory and infer causal processes through which international institutions generate change in wartime activism. For decades the country's ruling authoritarian regime heavily circumscribed independent organizing and proscribed dissent altogether. In 2011, Syrian activists began to protest amid a wave of "Arab Spring" uprisings. The repression and militarization that ensued unleashed a war that killed hundreds of thousands and displaced half of the country's prewar population. The outcome identified in this book, of something like a civil society, was far from given.

At the same time, international responses to the crisis epitomized the institutional structure of contemporary aid. Civilians and refugees received record amounts of international assistance from a plethora of contracted and contracting organizations that undertook efforts to shelter and feed Syrians in need, educate children, electrify villages, equip hospitals, model good governance, protect women, stabilize local conditions, and combat violent extremism. The complex aid response was built for government- and rebel-held territories and refugee host states, followed lines of armed control and the politics of states, and was reliant on Syrians for information, implementation, risk-taking, and monitoring. The Syrian war is thus a crucial lens through which to ask how international aid affects local nonviolent action during war, or how ostensibly impartial actors transform activists' wartime engagements.

FIGURE 1. Map of Syria. Source: OCHA.

Analytical Approach

To answer these questions, I adopt an analytical approach that foregrounds causes, mechanisms, and interpretation. First, I start with the case and outcome I seek to explain and "move backward toward the causes," adopting a "causes-of-effects" approach to explanation (Mahoney and Goertz 2006, 230). The outcome and case here are something like a civil society in Syria's war, and the causes I have identified are the institutional characteristics of international aid. (This contrasts with an "effects-of-causes" approach common to quantitative methods, which focuses on identifying average effects across a population of cases more than on explaining specific outcomes in particular cases.) Second, I infer mechanisms, or the "causal pathway or process" leading from cause to effect (Gerring 2008, 166). These mechanisms (which come together as a set of three causal processes) are more or less activated under certain conditions, even in the absence of researcher control or randomization of the cause (Beach and Pedersen 2019). Third, interpretation allows me to understand what matters in these international-local interactions in war and the often subtle and sensitive manner in which they unfold through the meanings that involved actors attribute to them.

To uncover and infer meaning-laden causal processes, I undertake process tracing, or the examination of evidence within a case to infer causal processes that explain the case (Bennett and Checkel 2015). Process tracing begins with collecting as much information as possible to develop an explanation against which additional evidence can be examined (Bennett and Checkel 2015). It also involves identifying the role of sequence and temporality in these explanations (Bennett 2010). For instance, in the Syrian case, the facilitating, formalizing, and filtering processes are activated in close succession rather than simultaneously. Process tracing is also central in the arbitration of complementary and alternative explanations. For example, a social preference for nonpartisan undertakings likely explains the contained political expression of some Syrian activists at all times, but that explanation does not capture the temporal and spatial variation in political expression identified in the empirical analysis of chapter 4. Finally, this version of process tracing also involves interpretation. In addition to using my data as diagnostic evidence, I also use it to "tell the whole story," as Crasnow puts it. I use narratives of involved individuals to do the "cognitive work" that identifies which parts of the case are "causally salient" (Crasnow 2017).

I process trace through a within-case analysis focused on nonviolent action across the war over time, beginning in late 2011, when aid actors began to intervene in Syria. I do not aim to explain the onset of the Syrian uprising. Instead, I analyze those times and places when aid was part of the conflict context and process trace to explain its interactions with and effects on civil action in war.

Within-case process tracing enables claims about causality between explanatory and outcome variables, even if alternative variables are also at play (Collier et al. 2004). One such compelling alternative variable, for instance, would be activists' own tactical adaptation to conflict conditions, which helps explain why activists undertook mutual aid to assist victims in their communities; it does not, however, explain the surge in formal civil organization and other changes in the scale and substance of local efforts.

Still, variation can provide additional analytical leverage if we disaggregate a case, for example, temporally or spatially (Gerring 2004). I leverage variation in international aid autonomy to explore differing causal pathways. These are not clean comparisons uninfluenced by other factors: The Syria of 2012 was different than the Syria of 2017 in many ways besides the influx of aid, as were its northern and southern provinces, leaving aside the distinct international response to each. Rather than treat variation in aid across the war zone as a source of robust causal identification, I instead think of it as an opportunity to build a theory, infer the mechanisms underlying change, and explore counterfactual analyses.

For temporal variation, I note that international aid to Syria and Syrians, at first minimal, increased over time until it surpassed historical and global levels, as visualized in figure 2. Aid to Syria also varied across space, reflecting territorial control, patterns of nonviolent and violent contention, and the politics of refugee host states. For example, international actors enjoyed substantial autonomy for a significant stretch of the war (about 2011 to 2017) in Turkey and indirectly across the border into northwest Syria. They had relatively less autonomy in Jordan and indirectly across the border into southern Syria due to the Jordanian government's caution and preoccupation with its own security. (Despite large quantities of aid, they had virtually no autonomy in government-held territory and civil organizing was a nonstarter; the situation in northeast Syria and across the border with Iraq followed a different pattern still, but is outside the scope of this project.) This spatial variation is described at length in chapter 2.

My analytical approach has at least two limitations. First, a concern common to within-case analysis is its generalizability, or lack thereof. This book does not test probabilistic predictions based on cross-national data. Yet it is informed by global and historical cases. For example, I have found that humanitarian autonomy is not uncommon and is in fact common to cross-border operations in places like Myanmar, southern Sudan, and numerous other cases. Because this is a process-based argument, its insights can also be extended to contexts with very different starting points on the causal pathway. For instance, I find that international humanitarians focus on connecting with the most seemingly professional local actors, no matter how distinct the educational systems or the level of development of civil society are in places like Afghanistan and Ukraine.

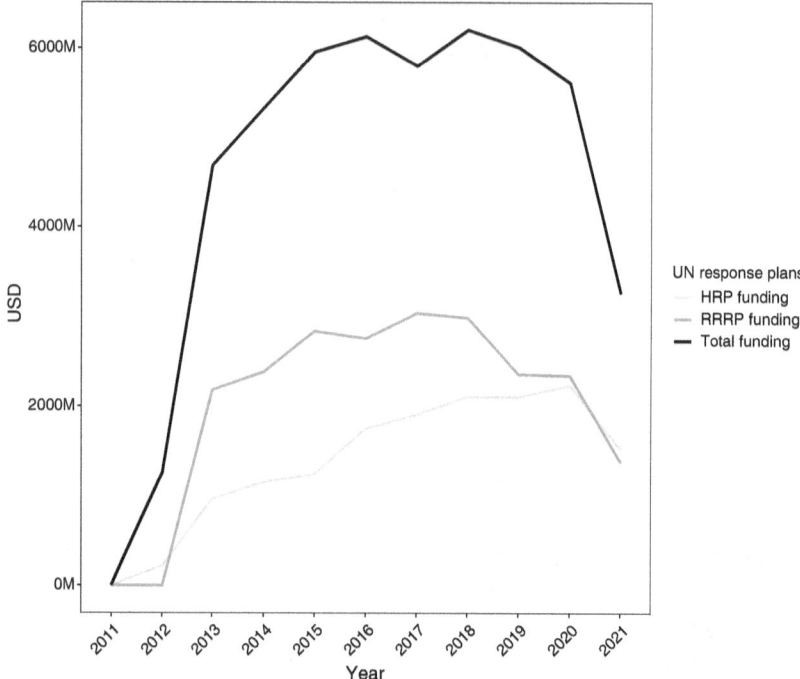

FIGURE 2. UN funding for the Syria crisis. Humanitarian Response Plans (HRP) were directed internally; Regional Refugee and Resilience Plans (3RP or RRRP) were directed to refugees and host communities in neighboring countries. Source: Public data from OCHA Financial Tracking Service, compiled by author. Website: https://fts.unocha.org.

Chapter 6 is dedicated to exploring how the theory and its component processes apply in other parts of the world.

A second limitation of this account is that I consider international aid to be largely the purview of institutionalized intergovernmental and nongovernmental aid organizations headquartered in Western capitals and funded by governments in the global North. Donors in the global South, as well as diasporas—who have local origins but are based abroad—have become increasingly involved in humanitarian efforts around the world.[4] Such nontraditional aid deserves attention, has informed the theory, and appears throughout the case analysis. At the same time, however, such aid has often flowed through the channels of the northern-dominated humanitarian system, or been outpaced and outspent by traditional aid actors as conflicts drag on. Therefore, institutionalized international aid—though its dominance may be impermanent—is at the core of this project, as it was core to the Syria response.

Data

For the fine-grained empirical detail critical to process tracing (Collier 2011), I rely primarily on field-based research conducted in Jordan, Turkey, and Lebanon. Semi-structured and in-depth interviews and immersive observation with Syrian activists and international aid workers provide insight into action and meaning-making among actors in the war. For additional evidence, I analyze an original dataset of Facebook pages representing Syrian organizations.

The analytical value of immersion is in "highlighting insiders' views, performances, and understandings of membership; it privileges interlocutors' experiences of the organizational worlds that they inhabit rather than relying on external categorizations" (Parkinson 2021, 66). Interviews, for their part, reveal individuals' trajectories and interpretations of their own position and those of others in these organizational worlds (Fujii 2018; Soss 2015). They also generate data for identifying recurrent themes or the empirical footprints of causal mechanisms, as well as information about how events unfolded and who was involved (J. Lynch 2013). To these ends, I conducted 136 semi-structured and in-depth interviews with displaced Syrians and international aid workers in Jordan, Turkey, and, less centrally, in Lebanon over ten months in multiple trips from 2014 to 2017. During my months in the field, I often shadowed and lived with American staff and Syrian refugees engaged in elements of the international response and in activism.[5] Through this immersion I learned of the "everyday elements of life and work" in what Autesserre calls "Peaceland, inhabited by the transnational community of interveners" (2014, 6). In this story, Peaceland is inhabited by local actors as well.

Some of my interviews with activists and aid workers ran for less than one hour, others lasted many hours, and a few stretched over the years. Interviews with Syrians were generally conducted in colloquial Syrian Arabic. I have taken efforts to protect my interview subjects and their confidentiality.[6] Rather than arbitrate whether some individuals can be identified, for example those figures who are publicly known or who hold power, I have retained everyone's anonymity. Accordingly, I cite them with a non-identifying number, year of the interview, and usually the country in which the interview took place. I do not share subnational location information or exact dates of interviews because I believe this would pose undue risks to participants who may be of interest to intelligence agencies in the region, and the analytical benefits would be negligible. I do provide relevant contextual information in the prose.

I adopted protocols that would respect participants' preferences and protect their privacy and data.[7] I conveyed to participants the risks, benefits, and purposes of participation, and obtained their verbal consent for interviews, most of which

I recorded on audio with their explicit permission.[8] I expect that I made mistakes despite my intentions, but I am not aware of any repercussions faced by my interlocutors or research participants. During research trips I sought to remain within the boundaries of political sensitivity. I did not explicitly investigate Turkish or Jordanian domestic politics, extremist groups, refugee legal status, or traumatic events such as torture and detainment. Most of the time, interviewees volunteered this information on their own. One Syrian, relaying his uprising narrative, which included detention in a regime prison, noted to me: "You've met enough people to know what happened during that month."[9] He was, sadly, correct.

I coded interview data using a self-directed, iterative, and manual process. I read the hundreds of pages that constituted my typed interview transcripts multiple times, each time identifying and coding across four spreadsheets to capture substantive themes and subthemes, international and Syrian organizations and initiatives, localities within Syria, and quotes that were representative or revelatory of key ideas. Although my research questions and subjects of concern were driven by increasingly coherent hypotheses during my fieldwork, I did not grasp the overarching puzzle, story, and explanation that came to constitute this project until after this rather laborious coding process that I carried out before writing. This iterative sequence is appropriate to "theory-building process-tracing," which involves "a wide-ranging search of the empirical record, with material collected without knowing what it is evidence of yet," followed by inferring that the material is evidence of "empirical fingerprints" left by the operation of plausible causal mechanisms, and then by evaluation of the material against hypothesized processes (Beach and Pedersen 2019, 10–11).

I did not travel to Syria for field research. I have firsthand knowledge of the country as a Syrian-American and because I spent one year based in Damascus, from 2008 to 2009, during which I traveled to thirteen of the country's fourteen provinces, volunteered as an English instructor to displaced Palestinian adolescents and medical personnel, and studied formal Arabic. I remain in active contact with people inside the country and have occasionally conducted interviews with activists in rebel-held territory through secure messaging applications, but I refrained from traveling to the country for this research to protect my interlocutors, my relatives, and myself. I regret that conditions of authoritarian reprisal and general insecurity inside Syria prevented more firsthand accounts of a country that, for more than a decade, writhed in violence and destruction. To minimize any resultant bias caused by this physical distance, I have not sought to explain nonviolent action in government-held areas. That said, my theory and case knowledge suggest that the way the government blocked international aid autonomy led to limited development of independent civil organizations. A post-Asad Syria may be a safer site for research, and for civil organizing alike.

I also draw on an original dataset of public Facebook pages of Syrian organizations that I constructed after building the foundations of my theory. Because this dataset did not inform the theory-building, it is well-suited to the evaluation of the observable implications of my argument (Bennett and Checkel 2015). In the period of the Arab uprisings beginning in late 2010, Syrian activists emerged on Facebook to organize their dissent.[10] Syria's became one of the most "socially mediated" conflicts in history (Lynch et al. 2014), and 97 percent of Syrian social media users turned to Facebook at that time, far above any other platform (TNS 2015). Public Facebook pages became a way for various groups to represent their existence, messages, and activities to Syrians and to the outside world. Such "virtual civil societies" might not cohere into organized and sustained challenges against autocratic regimes (Beissinger 2017); I do not study the dataset with this expectation. Rather, organizations commonly created Facebook pages as a matter of representation, if not substance.

With a Syrian research assistant, I audited public Facebook pages using preexisting lists of Syrian nonstate media and civil society organizations (Issa 2016; Alzouabi and Iyad 2017), keyword searches, and snowball sampling of "related pages."[11] The 1,362 pages included are outward-facing representations of formal organizations and informal groups of Syrians in the country, in refugee-receiving states, and in the wider diaspora. They include community-based, faith-based, and nongovernmental organizations, as well as coordination committees, opposition governance bodies, media outlets, art collectives, human rights advocates, and so forth.

The Facebook dataset is well suited to capturing trends among the population of civil organizations that have emerged since 2011, but it does not distinguish between groups that received international aid and those that did not. The more modest application of this dataset is to evaluate the observable implications of the theory with "large-n" data that was not used in the building of that theory. In this way, it complements the qualitative data that provides granular insights into the everyday experiences of aid actors and activists. The project is also informed by primary sources, including the reports and public data of aid organizations, Arabic media, Syrian social media activity, and secondary sources such as historical and contemporary accounts and analyses.

Layout of the Book

Chapter 1 is dedicated to concepts and theory. I draw connections between existing ideas in the study of civilian agency and forced migration and in international aid-based interventions in contexts of conflict and limited statehood.

Then, I build a theory of how aid affects civil action during war. I delve into the institutional qualities of contemporary international aid (relations, rules, and resources), the causal processes that these qualities activate (facilitating, formalizing, filtering) and the mechanisms that animate those processes, and finally the outcomes they produce for local nonviolent action in war. The takeaway is that international and local interactions transpire during war that generate change in nonviolent action; aid does more than provide relief.

Chapter 2 is an analytic narrative of contention, conflict, and crisis response in Syria. It begins with a brief historical overview of independent organizing—or lack thereof—in the country. Then, using the voices of my research participants, I describe the creative and courageous actions of civil activists during Syria's 2011 uprising and their adaptations after repression and escalation to armed conflict. I turn next to describe that civil war and trace spatial connections between the nonviolent movement, rebel-held territory, and patterns of displacement. The international aid response to the war, with its variations in aid autonomy, reflected these spatial configurations.

The first process-based empirical chapter, chapter 3, begins with the puzzle of persistent participation in civil action during war. Allowing that adaptation is a key internal explanation of persistence, it is an insufficient explanation on its own. For the full story, we need an account of international aid and an explanation for the relationships that emerge between international and local actors during war. Establishing connections from highly divergent starting points in violent contexts is not easy; making them productive is harder still. Yet I find that through constitutive and allocative mechanisms, international aid facilitated participation in local nonviolent action by deeming Syrians to be potential crisis responders and affording them the capacity to act as such. I identify multiple pieces of evidence that suggest that growth in the population of local organizations was often connected—sometimes dramatically so—to international aid. Analysis of the Syrian case reveals that international and local actors both stood to gain from interacting, even as power imbalances between them were stark.

Chapter 4 moves to the next process connecting international aid to local activism—a formalizing process that is activated by the rules of international aid and that generates change in the politics of civil action. Local activists assume significant risks by participating in nonviolent action during war. Despite that political context, international aid compels local actors to obey rules for producing and provisioning knowledge, for outward presentations of neutrality, and for acting professionally in the crisis response sector. The Syrian case reveals that these rules operate through coercive and normative mechanisms—they are imposed from above and often embraced from below. I trace the ways Syrians knowingly navigated bureaucratic labyrinths and find spatial evidence that is difficult to explain in the absence of international aid. The empirical analysis also reveals serious and risk-inducing tensions in rule-following for local actors, whose adoption of technocratic and humanitarian principles do not protect them from generalized violence or even targeted reprisals.

The third and final process-based chapter, chapter 5, infers a filtering process that elevates some local organizations above others, even as the overall population of local organizations broadly responded to the same resource environment structured by international aid. Collective action is notoriously difficult to initiate and sustain and Syria's civil actors suffered many cleavages unrelated to international aid. Yet granular empirical analysis shows that ideas of what makes for a "good" local partner induced novel sources of division and exacerbated existing ones, while analysis of the financial reports of international aid organizations reveals built-in inequities. Through selection and legitimation mechanisms, Syrians learned what it took to scramble for organizational survival, even at times compromising their physical safety, while international actors favored some and limited collectivity among all.

Chapter 6 explores how the theory and its component processes apply to contexts around the world. It delves most deeply into the Myanmar-Thailand borderlands, but also journeys to southern Sudan and elsewhere. Throughout, I find that when aid actors enjoy autonomy—often through cross-border operations that enable their entry into areas of limited statehood—they activate facilitating, formalizing, and filtering processes among local actors. I then return to Syria for one final probe of the theory by investigating the extreme situation of an area with no aid autonomy: that territory held by the Islamic State.

Finally, the conclusion considers what it means for international aid to have civilized contention. Aid's presence and autonomy are volatile, inherently limited, and subject to military, geopolitical, and domestic shifts in the country in conflict and in donor states. When an earthquake struck Turkey and northwest Syria in 2023, the same spaces where something like a civil society had emerged during the war, a "civilized" society was left almost entirely unprotected. A post-Asad Syria may offer this civil society the chance to function in relation to and with the protection of a state. The book's contributions include attention to the phenomenon of civil action in the Middle East, a region where violence and international intervention so frequently converge with such devastating consequences. The chapter concludes the book by considering implications for international aid actors, activists, and the people who study them.

International aid saves lives by sheltering the displaced, feeding the hungry, and treating the ill. Its contemporary features also create effects beyond the provision of relief. This project theorizes and assesses these effects; it is *not* an evaluation of the efficacy of aid for people in need. Aid today is used by a multitude of actors deploying technocratic approaches to resolve what are fundamentally political problems. In Syria, as elsewhere, aid had clear limits. Humanitarianism did not protect civilians from government shelling nor generalized violence. It did not resolve the conflict between the regime and its opponents. It did not provide relief to civilians in areas controlled by the Islamic State, let alone protect them from a brutal social order. It did not create conditions for millions of people to remain in their homes rather than flee, nor force rich countries to resettle them in new ones. It did not prevent already displaced Palestinians from being displaced again. It barely overcame sieges imposed by armed actors; it certainly could not have lifted them. Humanitarianism is simply not equipped to address the political problems that give life to conflict.

Yet the practices that characterize contemporary aid did have other, at times paradoxical, and perhaps unintended effects on the Syrians who engaged in nonviolent conflict processes. It enabled their participation in these processes despite the violence around them, even while constraining their politics and collectivity. Without international aid, civil activists may have demobilized (or ceased to act altogether), or they may have taken up arms; they may have engaged in more informal, small-scale, and diffuse ways akin to mutual aid. However, their story unfolded with international aid. In the pages that follow, I seek to explain what happened.

1
HOW AID CIVILIZES CONTENTION

Ali was a recent Aleppo University graduate working as a mechanical engineer when the Syrian uprising reached the country's northern metropolis.[1] Having kept his dissent buried in his heart for years, he eagerly "participated from day one in the revolution, thank God." He joined two local committees coordinating nonviolent resistance, one in Aleppo City and one at the university, and was partaking in as many as three or four demonstrations per day some weeks. When he witnessed the shooting of a protest participant, Ali was awed that people not only came out again the next day, but their numbers increased. However, popular support did not prevent more regime repression and violent escalation. Aleppo's largely nonviolent uprising soon gave way to the dynamics of civil war that were taking hold throughout the country.

Yet Ali, like other civil activists, remained committed. When Free Syrian Army rebels took control over areas of eastern Aleppo City in mid-2012, he supported the nearest unit by crossing lines of control and delivering food and medical supplies, fixing electrical lines, and the like. But fear caught up with Ali when a friend's family was targeted by regime security forces. He traveled with his parents to Turkey in August 2012, leaving them in refuge and crossing back into Aleppo where civilians were establishing governance councils in "liberated" (rebel-held) areas. A general committee elected a local city council for Aleppo and Ali served as a member in the engineering department. Basic services, like waste management, had been absent since state forces withdrew from the area.

To get a handle on public service provision, Ali began looking for donors, writing proposals, and soliciting advice. This was 2013, when the international aid response was still emergent. "We didn't know who NEA, OTI, DFID, GIZ were," Ali explained. "We knew the Americans, the British, the Germans, or Gulf individuals."[2] He wrote over thirty proposals and received negligible support in return. Meanwhile, the regime was continuously shelling the city and a new Islamist council was competing with the local council. In his fifth month on the council, he resigned.

Ali found a position with an international nongovernmental organization (INGO) distributing food aid in rural Aleppo and progressed quickly through the ranks, from assistant coordinator of the food security project, to coordinator for the project as a whole, to senior coordinator for security in general, and then to overseeing "cross-border between Turkey and Syria." Remuneration was impressive, starting at $800 USD per month compared to the $120 per month he had made on the city council. "See the difference?" he explained: "This was the case with the organizations. . . . How [could] we keep talent in the local council?"

That salary would support his family and parents in Turkey but Ali was not driven by the money. He saw the enormity of need all around him and he wanted to help. Distributing tens of thousands of food baskets across Aleppo Province was useful and meaningful: "It was beautiful, how much we were distributing." Ali had his frustrations, however.

The INGO sidestepped the local councils in their distribution areas, wary of political bodies, but Ali knew the councils had the best data on needs and perhaps more legitimacy than the local relief organizations the INGO preferred. He also felt it was incumbent on field-workers to offer some of the distribution to rebel groups, who were in need and, frankly, in control—an instinct the INGO didn't like to indulge explicitly. Working his connections among Syrian activists in southern Turkey, Ali found a new position on a UK-backed stabilization project promoting good governance in local councils. After years of danger and displacement, Ali ultimately returned—from across borders—to the local councils in rebel-held areas where he had begun. This time, he was a development professional remotely monitoring and evaluating their performance.

This position sat easily on Ali's heart: Here the goal was empowering local councils to implement the kinds of rules and services that governance institutions (rather than organizations, as he avers) should be focused on, or at the very least to develop procedures for such work. For instance, they created a census project for a rebel-held town in rural Aleppo and transparently hired people to conduct assessments and track the statistics. "It was really good," he explains, until "there was shelling, and people were displaced." Running a census on people running for their lives, as it happens, is difficult.

Indeed, imposing structures and routines during war—the work associated with civilizing contention—is arguably inherently elusive. At least it was for Ali, who had been working on projects in Aleppo City until December 2016, three months before our conversation. "Now, we're not," he said. "There is no Aleppo City." Following months of brutal siege and desperate warfare, the Syrian regime had regained control over his home city by the end of 2016. Rebels, as well as civil activists—and the something like a civil society they had become—all left Aleppo behind them.

Ali's story illuminates the evolving trajectory of a single activist who participated in the Syrian uprising, insurgency, humanitarian crisis, and oppositional political response that unfolded beginning in 2011. Like many of his counterparts in Turkey and to a lesser extent in Jordan, he engaged in rebel-held territories, in cross-border response, and from refuge. His experience demonstrates the drive and adaptability of Syrians against the odds of a brutal conflict. Ali navigated challenges of repression, armed conflict, and displacement, and adapted his nonviolent action all the while.

At the same time, Ali's narrative reveals that international actors played a key role in facilitating civilian and refugee participation in large-scale and complex engagements in the depths, and across the borders, of the civil war. His story provides a view into the nature of the relationships that international aid actors entered into within the conflict zone, the rules through which they asserted their authority over the response, and the resources they distributed to achieve their objectives. For instance, international humanitarian organizations rebuffed oppositional local councils, but they supported the provision of relief. They set the terms of remuneration, but fairly rewarded those who advanced humanitarian priorities. They worked with and through local actors like Ali to enact the international aid response in an area of limited statehood, at least until the state came back. While international aid organizations worked with and through local civil actors to feed the hungry, shelter the displaced, extend public services in war-wrecked localities, and so on, they altered the course of a contentious social movement.

Civil Action, International Aid, and Conditions for Their Connection

For all its distinctive characteristics, the Syrian conflict shares important traits with other civil wars: civilians navigating survival, organized international aid response, and divisions in territorial control. When international aid organizations enjoy access and autonomy unconstrained by powerful governing actors, like in areas of limited statehood or in permissive host states, they carry their institutional qualities—relations, rules, and resources—into their interactions with nonviolent actors on the ground who can help pursue international objectives. They activate processes that interact with and alter nonviolent action by facilitating, formalizing, and filtering it—they civilize contention. *Civilizing contention* refers to a set of processes that impose structures and routines on conflict processes, particularly those actors whose conduct can be moderated and restrained even amid war. It manifests, among local activists, as something like a civil society, or a population of civil organizations participating in nonviolent processes, but without the state that civil society needs. To move us toward those theorized processes that constitute civilizing contention, I first conceptualize civil action in war, international aid, and the conditions under which they intertwine. In the second half of the chapter, I will unpack the theory.

Civil Action in War

War can provide civilians with new means for extending their agency (Nordstrom 1997). To acknowledge as much is not to understate the centrality of armed actors in war and the destruction that violence unleashes on regular people, yet it is to suggest that civilian and refugee-driven social and political processes persist and are reinvented in war's course, even amid violence (Parkinson 2023; Wood 2008). In war, regular people adopt ways of coping with violence and uncertainty (Nordstrom 1997). Agential acts—including displacement—are not exclusively forced reactions to violence, but can also be calculated choices that enable the pursuit of social agendas and life projects (Lubkemann 2008).

Political scientists have identified agential civilian responses to armed actors, ranging from defection and resistance to cooperation and participation in governance (Kasfir 2005; Kalyvas 2006; Parkinson 2013; Arjona 2016, 2017; Finkel 2017; Kaplan 2017). Some focus on explicitly political, active, or mobilized segments of the civilian population (Barter 2014, 2015; Van Baalen 2024). For example, studies of civil action in violent contexts conceive of a range of ways that civil actors can affect and even quell violence (Avant et al. 2019a). Some have identified how political mobilization and loyalties that precede the outbreak of war remain relevant in its course—specifically insofar as they become a reason for armed groups to target opponents (Balcells 2017; Balcells and Steele 2016; Steele 2017). In other words, politics does not wholly give way to violence during war (Kalyvas 2006), but interacts with it in meaningful, if dangerous, ways.

These insights indicate connections between war and social movement trajectories. Some suggest that violent conflict represents an escalation of nonviolent contentious politics, or that the reverse amounts to de-escalation (McAdam et al. 2001; Tarrow 2007). Along these lines, a "civil resistance" research agenda has sought to unify the study of nonviolent and violent strategies, described as "alternatives" to each other and to institutional politics (Chenoweth and Cunningham 2013). But can nonviolence and violence coincide, rather than alternate? From Guatemala to Lebanon, scholars have found that nonviolent contention can cycle in and out during war rather than cease or demobilize altogether and that unarmed and armed groups often overlap or have ties between them (Brockett 2005; Parkinson 2023).

If civilians can remain actively engaged in nonviolent action during war, what is the range of ways they may do so? If protest declines, for example, it may be possible for civilians to pursue political, social, or other non–rebel facing agendas through other means. War can alter gender roles in ways that have enabled women's participation in post-conflict politics in Rwanda (Berry 2018) and Colombian women responded to threats of sexual violence with protest and engagement in civil society organizations, even during war (Kreft 2019). Wartime activism can be taken up by a range of participants who are navigating new realities while maintaining their commitment to a cause. For example, Shane Barter has discovered that both urban activists and Islamic leaders in rural Indonesia found pathways to pursue their social and political objectives while at the same time cooperating with rebels in governance during the Aceh insurgency (2015).

Though generally operating in a separate disciplinary silo, scholars of displacement have also found a range of action among refugees—victimized as they may be. Displacement can spur social mobilization and politicization: The experience of flight leads some to take "transformative action" ranging from photography to anti-racist advocacy (Horst 2019). Refugees may act on behalf of refugee communities, including through relief and service provision (Pincock et al. 2020), as well as protest (Murshid 2013; Clarke 2018). In some cases refugees work on behalf of a home state cause or conflict (Banki 2024; Jacobsen 2019), including in the cases of Palestinian and Sahrawi refugees who have formed unions, popular organizations, and service institutions in their host countries and advanced their nationalist cause (Brynen 1990; J. A. Mundy 2007).

In sum, connections across literatures and conflict contexts point toward the potential for nonviolent action in war by both civilians and refugees, who can pursue social and political agendas that do not exclusively pertain to violence or relations with rebel groups. This civil action, or wartime activism, can be affected by outside actors.

International Aid in War

Local actors reside in or originate from the conflict state, while international actors are those not based or founded in the conflict state. These ideal types are, in practice, transmutable. Diaspora organizations, for instance, can both originate in and operate outside of a conflict state. Yet I adopt them as useful, if flawed, operationalizations of important concepts, and I leave space for narrative detail to capture relevant nuances. International aid actors are intergovernmental and nongovernmental organizations, networks, companies, and donor governments that provide nonmilitary material and immaterial assistance to achieve humanitarian and nonhumanitarian ends. Such assistance includes money, in-kind contributions, labor, infrastructure, services, and technical assistance, as well as information, leadership, and symbolic capital. Traditionally, humanitarian aid seeks to "save lives and alleviate suffering of a crisis-affected population in accordance with humanitarian principles" (ReliefWeb 2008). Those humanitarian principles include humanity (suffering must be addressed), neutrality (without taking sides), impartiality (according to needs), and independence (autonomously). Nonhumanitarian aid promotes social and economic development; political processes, participation, and authority; stabilization to prevent violence; early recovery, transition, and reconstruction; and peacebuilding and conflict resolution.

Wars elicit both humanitarian and nonhumanitarian aid. Sometimes, these forms of aid are funded, coordinated, or implemented separately from one another. For instance, the UN Office for the Coordination of Humanitarian Affairs, OCHA, relies on humanitarian aid organizations to coordinate its assistance clusters, like food security and health, led by the World Food Program and the World Health Organization respectively. Yet political or stabilization aid actors can operate outside of humanitarian coordination bodies in the same crisis response, often with funding from the same donor governments, and working toward similar ends. For instance, development companies funded by a US government agency may support an educational system in rebel-held territories, in coordination with oppositional governance institutions, in order to achieve stabilization objectives (to prevent violence and extremism). At the same time, Save the Children, a humanitarian INGO, also receiving funds from the United States, might coordinate OCHA's education cluster and implement education projects in those same territories based on a humanitarian imperative.

While humanitarians might hold fast to the boundaries between themselves and nonhumanitarians, the very existence of an "education cluster" in an OCHA-coordinated response points to humanitarianism's substantive expansion in the post–Cold War era. Beyond food and shelter, humanitarians have pursued objectives that may have been previously thought of as "developmental" by supporting longer-run social and economic well-being and not just lifesaving relief. Mark Duffield has coined the term "new humanitarianism" to describe the aid-based responses to post–Cold War wars that have included development and security objectives that aim to address root causes and transform social processes (2001;

also Fearon 2008; Barnett and Snyder 2008). Of course, there is important organizational diversity in the international humanitarian sector and conflicting views on the what, when, where, why, and how of response (Barnett 2011; Cutts 1998; Rieff 2002; Weiss 1999), yet it has been broadly common for new humanitarians to consider how their aid affects war (for example by entrenching it) and therefore how they can positively affect ground-level processes where they intervene (Duffield 2001). Preventing a "lost generation" of children by educating them is one such new humanitarian approach that aims to do more than save lives.

In pursuit of these many objectives, international aid in general and humanitarianism in particular are likely to shape local, nonviolent processes in war. Existing research has mostly focused on international aid's effects in post-conflict or peacetime contexts, or in conflict contexts with a focus on armed groups. At least three key insights emerge from these literatures. First, a distance often exists between the experiences and approaches of international actors—especially bureaucratic organizations—and those of local actors embedded in particular contexts, networks, and ways of doing things (Autesserre 2010; Campbell 2018; Mitchell 2002; J. Scott 1998). Second, the generally technocratic approaches of those international organizations can depoliticize or obfuscate the processes and complexities that they subject to intervention (Barnett 2001; Bush 2015; Ferguson 1990; J. Mundy 2015). Third, and despite this depoliticization, international interventions produce political effects—by the very essence of their everyday routines. James Ferguson has compellingly written about development aid as an "anti-politics machine" that goes about "depoliticizing everything it touches, everywhere whisking political realities out of sight, all the while performing, almost unnoticed, its own pre-eminently political operation of expanding bureaucratic state power" (1990, xv). While principles like humanitarian neutrality should be taken seriously, it is often through everyday routines and bureaucratic processes, not larger strategies or normative commitments, that aid's effects can be produced, including effects on political processes, such as contentious social movements, that are underway in the contexts into which they enter.

Conditions of Connection: International Autonomy

Under what conditions might we expect international aid to produce effects beyond the provision of relief, and on civil action in particular? I posit international autonomy as a scope condition, wherein international aid actors are relatively unconstrained by governing actors (akin to the humanitarian principle of independence). Autonomy is commonly achieved in at least two ways. First, it can occur in areas of limited statehood where aid organizations are unlikely to be impeded by powerful state authorities. Second, autonomy can be acquired when states or other governing authorities allow aid actors to operate without undue obstruction or constraints. These two conditions shape the scope in which international aid organizations are likely to interact closely with local-level nonviolent actors to achieve their objectives in conflict contexts.

International autonomy is far from given. The international humanitarian system is intimately tied to the modern state system—donor governments fund it, intergovernmental organizations dominate it, and those aid organizations generally rely on the consent of a host state to operate within its sovereign territory. To achieve access to people in need or other targets of their aid, therefore, aid organizations often make operational compromises or accept some state control over their actions—even at the cost of humanitarian principles. In the US-led interventions in Afghanistan and Iraq, the primary belligerent was simultaneously the largest donor to the many humanitarian and development organizations involved (Donini et al. 2004; Benelli et al. 2012). The close association between US forces and NGOs (nongovernmental organizations), the latter famously called "force multipliers" by Secretary of State Colin Powell, had operational consequences including the targeting of aid actors by various armed groups, the inability of aid organizations to hold governments accountable, and the diversion of resources from other conflicts to that in which the donor was engaged as a belligerent (Torrenté 2004). In these cases, international aid organizations gained access to crises at the cost of autonomy. That is because access is precious to aid organizations.

Access is a persistent and evolving challenge for humanitarian and nonhumanitarian international aid actors. In conflict settings they deal with everything from physical insecurity, like attacks on field-workers, to logistical issues like obtaining registration permits (Smirl 2015; Krause 2014). When they perceive that insecurity poses severe risks to themselves, international aid actors may find alternative means to achieve or maintain access.[3] Some of these means decrease their autonomy, like the political instrumentalization described above, but also like quotidian logistical measures of physical securitization such as the erection of gated compounds and use of muscular vehicles (Smirl 2015; Duffield 2012).

Yet a brief look at the history of international crisis responses suggests that humanitarians and other aid actors often wield more autonomous power than we might think. Kate Pincock and coauthors show that even in relatively strong states a "dominant logic" of international superiority often prevails in situations of humanitarian crisis; in refugee response, for instance, international organizations are given leeway by states that would rather not deal with the issue themselves (2020). Such stances coincide with ideas of "standoffish" policymaking or "strategic indifference" attributed to governments dealing with refugee crises (Mourad 2017; Norman 2020), who would rather have international organizations deal with (and foot the bill for) refugee response.

When governments do get in the way, measures to achieve or maintain access include clandestine, cross-border, and conflict actor–aligned operations (Scott 2022). These measures can also increase autonomy. Their use may suggest that aid organizations are intervening in areas outside a central government's control, that is, in areas of limited statehood, often in peripheral or border regions of the affected country. Thomas Risse defines areas of limited statehood as "those parts of a country in which central authorities (governments) lack the ability to implement and enforce rules and decisions or in which the legitimate monopoly over the means of violence is lacking, at least temporarily" (2011a, 4).

Autonomy, especially in areas of limited statehood, can allow aid organizations to pursue their objectives more freely. Milli Lake reveals this in her scholarship on international efforts to promote gender justice in post-conflict contexts; she finds that INGOs have fashioned strong judicial practices for prosecuting gender-based violence in contexts of state fragility, like in the Democratic Republic of Congo, but have achieved less in stronger states like South Africa (Lake 2018). The logic here is that international aid actors can be strong where states are weak. They can also be strong where otherwise strong state and nonstate actors are permissive.

Cross-border operations can afford aid organizations autonomy from obstructive central governments in the conflict state; they also generally rely on permissive neighboring states or other governing authorities like armed groups. During the Ethiopian conflict in the 1980s, some aid actors overlooked the government's politicization of aid and maintained access by operating from the capital, compromising their autonomy in favor of access. Others, however, set up cross-border operations from Sudan in cooperation with autonomy-granting Eritrean and Tigrayan rebel groups. Hugo Slim and Emanuela-Chiara Gillard document historical cross-border aid operations that have entailed varying configurations of consent from state and nonstate actors (2013). For example, while the Nigerian government rejected (and targeted) a cross-border air bridge into its rebellious Biafra region, São Tomé enabled international aid actors operating from their territory by hosting the air bridge. The UN has, elsewhere, been part of and authorized cross-border efforts, such as those from Kenya into southern Sudan in the 1990s and from Turkey and Iran into northern Iraq that same decade (Slim and Gillard 2013). In these instances, aid organizations gain autonomy in areas of limited statehood in border regions, as well as from permissive neighboring states or armed groups, even if their access remains imperfect.

All that said, in some times and places, aid actors do give up their efforts if impediments are too numerous. During the war in Yemen in the 2010s, for instance, the World Food Program periodically suspended operations in response to efforts by Houthi rebels to control and divert aid. At times, the dynamics of war might simply be so violent that international aid actors refrain from trying to achieve access at all, as in their lack of effort to break through the Russian-imposed siege of Grozny during their second war in Chechnya (Andreas 2008). Finally, the anti-terror laws of donor governments can constrain aid organizations even in spaces where armed groups might permit them to operate. In general, though, aid actors want access and they try to find ways to achieve it—sometimes in ways that compromise their autonomy, but other times in ways that maintain or enhance it.

It is what autonomous aid organizations *do* in the areas of their intervention that implicates local nonviolent actors. Humanitarians distribute goods, like food baskets and tent shelters. They provide services, like vaccinations and safe drinking water systems, and they promote rules, like safeguarding child protection and countering gender-based violence. Goods, services, and rules are the domains of governing authorities, even in the absence of governments (Risse 2011a). It is an implication of the theory of civilizing contention that humanitarians govern when they enjoy autonomy (Barnett 2013).

Humanitarians and other aid actors certainly do not control territories in areas of limited statehood, as rebels might, but by providing goods and services and creating rules, international aid organizations engage in governance—not *over* territory, but *in* it (Latham 2001). The UN agency tasked with providing relief to Palestinian refugees, UNRWA (United Nations Relief and Works Agency for Palestine Refugees in the Near East), for instance, may be considered a "quasi-state" as it provides services like education, health care, and identification documents to refugee camp residents. UNRWA is not stronger than the host governments in whose terrain it works; rather, those host governments have historically opted to limit their own interventions in the camps to security and policing (Irfan 2023). When international aid organizations enjoy autonomy, they enact their (governance) objectives with and through local actors. It is under these conditions that international aid in general, and humanitarianism in particular, operates in a manner that civilizes contention—enabling civil actors to participate in nonviolent action while simultaneously constraining their political and collective character.

How Aid Civilizes Contention

International aid to contemporary crises shapes nonviolent action, particularly where international actors enjoy autonomy, which is common in areas of limited statehood or where these actors are otherwise not constrained by strong governments, and which allows international aid organizations to pursue their objectives with and through local nonviolent actors. The processes they activate when so doing reflect efforts to bring order to conflict processes; these efforts civilize contention.

Civilizing contention occurs through repeated interactions between international aid and domestic actors. International aid does not produce change in wartime activism through one-off encounters, nor through some automatic structural change that occurs across an entire war zone wherever an international aid organization might be found. Rather, through repeated interactions, international aid actors gradually generate changes in local nonviolent action in concert with those local actors who bring their own experiences, adaptations, and preferences to the field of action. Through these interactions, the institutional qualities of aid—relations, rules, and resources—enable the participation of civil actors in nonviolent processes, but also constrain their politics and collectivity. In other words, international aid creates something like a population of civil society organizations, but one that exists in the service of international interveners and without the state protection that civil society needs. It is thus that contentious action may transform—without entirely demobilizing—in conflict contexts.

These theorized processes are grounded in insights from institutionalism, organization theory, and constructivism, but they do not follow a single paradigm or grand theory. The project is oriented by the empirical problems to be explained, and infers mechanisms that make sense of them (Davis and Marquis 2005; McAdam et al. 2001). Given that international aid, social movements, civil wars, and civil societies are all domains constituted by institutions and organizations, it follows that these mechanisms often reflect insights from these schools of thought. In particular, this study focuses on resource-endowed bureaucratic institutions that govern the provision of relief and other aid-based interventions in contemporary crises, that is, international aid. James March and Johan Olsen define an institution as "a relatively enduring collection of rules and organized practices, embedded in structures of meaning and resources that are relatively invariant in the face of turnover of individuals and relatively resilient to the idiosyncratic preferences and expectations of individuals and changing external circumstances" (2008). This definition contains three pertinent qualities of institutions: (1) the identities and belongings that they structure, (2) the rules and practices that prescribe appropriate behavior, and (3) the resources that create capabilities for action (March and Olsen 1984, 1989, 2008), qualities that can be described as relations, rules, and resources.

These core institutional qualities of international aid enable and constrain possibilities for nonviolent action in war, where aid actors enjoy autonomy and pursue their objectives with and through local actors. When they do so, their institutional qualities shape and reshape multiple dimensions of nonviolent action. Relations facilitate the participation of nonviolent actors; rules formalize their politics; and resources filter the population of organizations that engage. These three processes are jointly necessary, sequential, and mutually reinforcing in the production of civilized contention (see table 1 in the introduction).

International Aid Relations Facilitate Nonviolent Action

Interactions between international aid organizations and local nonviolent actors begin with the relationships that are forged between them. International actors pursue these relations to achieve their objectives; they produce change in participation in nonviolent action among local activists. The relationships develop along three dimensions: social, infrastructural, and material. Jointly, these three forms of relationship facilitate participation in nonviolent action through constitutive and allocative mechanisms. These relations shape actors and their capacities: They constitute identities for social beings and allocate material and immaterial capacities to them to enact those identities. In the case of international aid, local actors are constituted as crisis responders and allocated channels and resources through which to act as such. Through these constitutive and allocative mechanisms, international aid organizations facilitate local participation in crisis response. Understanding this process is important for grasping how activists can persist in their engagements as time passes, needs mount, and crises deepen over the course of a war.

First, international actors forge social linkages to local actors to achieve access and information to implement their objectives, whether enhancing sanitation in displacement shelters or supporting a political opposition faction. Carolyn Nordstrom contends that the interactions "among those populating the massive transnational flow" of warscapes lead their concerns to become "enmeshed in the cultural construction of the conflict": International and local actors inform and construct each other's actions, strategies, antagonisms, and responses to a war (1997). That is, international and local actors shape each others' experiences and opportunities. International aid actors will constitute locals as potential aid actors to avail themselves of knowledge related to community, context, and conditions (Autesserre 2014). Activists, for their part, might aim to realize objectives that coincide with those of international actors, be they political, tactical, or technical in nature. In such scenarios, local and international actors can converge on areas of mutual gain, yet this relationship is structurally imbalanced (Bob 2005), as international actors will direct local capacities to particular interests and actions—constituting activists as crisis responders in the process.

Second, international aid actors forge infrastructural linkages through which local actors can engage in crisis response. International humanitarian institutions are complex and have become increasingly so in the post–Cold War period. Alex de Waal has noted the UN's introduction of new categories of people to assist, the "invention" of concepts like "complex emergency," and the passage of resolutions that affirm the right to relief (de Waal 1997). Others have referred to the "task expansion" and "institutional proliferation" of the international refugee regime (Betts 2009; Fearon 2008). Atop these developments is a "growing superstructure of coordination" that includes the UN Office for the Coordination of Humanitarian Affairs, established in 1991 (Kent et al. 2016). This expansive infrastructure opens channels within which international, national, and local organizations can operate during crisis response, and includes channels geared directly toward local organizations such as the UN's country-based pooled funds.

Allocating channels for local participation within international infrastructure builds on ideas related to institutions in social movement theory. In contention, "moderate" local actors facing repression are expected to break from extremists and institutionalize (Tarrow 2011). But in some contexts, channels between domestic groups and their governments are blocked or ineffective; in these cases, institutional channels can manifest at the international level instead (Keck and Sikkink 1998). Moreover, institutions can potentially provide opportunities for mobilization by integrating people, providing means of communication, and standardizing frameworks for participation (Tarrow 2011; Brooke and Ketchley 2018; Zeira 2019). In international institutions, international aid and interventions allocate infrastructural frameworks within which local activists can organize. Local action is channeled, through this infrastructural linkage, into international frameworks.

Third, international actors forge material linkages with local actors that allocate resources to them. Local actors can provision movements with communication networks, leadership, ideas, and participants (Chenoweth and Stephan 2011; Cunningham et al. 2017; McAdam 1999), yet resources that originate outside movements can be decisive (Jenkins and Perrow 1977; McCarthy and Zald 1977). Material resources are an important, even if not singular, source of capacity that enables civil action in violent contexts (Avant et al. 2019b). Although humanitarian budgets are almost always limited, international actors generally bring relatively greater material resources to bear on domestic arenas than do local constituents. International resources tend also to be sustained longer than those of local actors and others like diasporas, even if the latter are on the ground before and after any international presence (Moss 2021).

Donor funding of humanitarianism grew substantially in the post–Cold War era. OECD spending on international humanitarian assistance more than tripled in the 1990s and doubled in the 2000s. From 2011 to 2018, rich donor governments directed an average of $12.7 billion per year to crises around the world

(OECD 2020). More comprehensive estimates bring these figures to $29 billion in 2018 (Urquhart 2019). Contracting practices have also increased: Aid is contracted to intergovernmental and nongovernmental organizations that, in turn, subcontract to each other and to smaller organizations (Cooley and Ron 2002; Duffield 1997; Hulme and Edwards 1997; Roberts 2014). By allocating resources, even if indirectly, international actors can increase activists' material capacity.

Organizations respond to such resource environments (Hannan and Carroll 1992; Hannan and Freeman 1977). In the study of INGOs, scholars have found that when an organizational form is new and competition over resources is limited, that new form grows rapidly (Abbott et al. 2016; Bush and Hadden 2019). In post-conflict contexts, top-down support can create a "boom" in local NGOs (Berry 2018; Jad 2004; McMahon 2017). We should expect downstream resource flows in countries during conflict, as well. Thus, despite inequities and risks, such resources are likely to spur local organizational growth.

The social, infrastructural, and material relations of international aid consist of constitutive and allocative mechanisms that generate a facilitating process: International aid organizations identify locals as potential aid actors, channel their actions into international frameworks, and grow their capacity and organizations. In the aggregate, international aid relations facilitate local participation in nonviolent action in war and refuge.

International Aid Rules Formalize Nonviolent Action

As international aid organizations pursue their objectives with and through local actors with whom they develop relations, they base their interactions on rules. As Michael Barnett and Martha Finnemore argue, "Impersonal rules are the building blocks of a bureaucracy" (2004, 18). The conditions of autonomy under which international organizations sometimes operate amplify their rules-based authority. In these spaces, the presence of "humanitarian governance," or "the organized effort to reduce human suffering," is likely (Barnett 2013; also Fassin 2012). What makes that effort organized is its rule-based structure. The rules of international bureaucratic organizations rest on three bases: rationalism, moralism, and professionalism.[4]

Aid's rules produce change in the politics of nonviolent actors through coercive and normative mechanisms. Coercive pressures are not coercive in the physical sense, but rather are the "imposition of organizational models on dependent organizations" through "pressures, mandates, standards, and ritualized controls" (DiMaggio and Powell 1983). Normative pressures operate through attraction: Dependent organizations adopt the rules and scripts of existing institutional structures because they are attracted to, or persuaded by, them (Beckert 2010).[5]

Through these two mechanisms, international aid rules formalize nonviolent action during war and contain its politics.

First, international actors will orient local actors toward producing and provisioning knowledge in order to collect information and data that will enhance international authority over the response. Nonviolent actors' time and energy becomes occupied by creating knowledge according to the rules of international organizations; less time and energy remains for other—potentially more political—action. Rational rules are advanced through coercive organizational pressures. As bureaucracies, international organizations enjoy and are even constituted by rational authority (Barnett and Finnemore 2004). Knowledge is central to rationality in a Weberian sense: Knowledge is a means to achieving rational ends (Swidler 1973). Thus, those international humanitarians that come to help, including through development and conflict management, construct their countries of intervention as objects of knowledge (Ferguson 1990; J. Mundy 2015). Yet in the muddled contexts of conflict, that knowledge can be difficult to construct.[6] How do humanitarians acquire knowledge of their objects of intervention, make that knowledge legible and, through it, retain their authority?

To acquire knowledge, international actors will incorporate locals into their responses to avail themselves of information related to community, context, and conditions that locals generally have and internationals often lack (Autesserre 2014). To make that local knowledge understandable and useful, they will impose rules on its production and provision. Through the imposition of rules, international actors will "harness" civil society organizations "to the task of governing" by orienting their actions toward practices and techniques supportive of governmental rationality (Sending and Neumann 2006). Donor governments do so vis-à-vis international aid organizations whom they contract, prioritizing evidence-based procedures, quantifiable indicators, and measurable outcomes (Bush 2015; Heiss and Kelley 2017; Henderson 2002; Kelley and Simmons 2015). Rational rules should do the same at lower levels of organization and thereby occupy the time and energy of activists that may have been oriented elsewhere.

Second, international actors will also orient local actors toward "moral" and "neutral" claims-making. In addition to their rational authority, international organizations enjoy moral authority; their apparent embodiment of principles like impartiality is a basis for their power (Barnett and Finnemore 2004). Thus, local actors will generally adopt outward presentations of objectivity as they are brought into the frameworks of international response. Moral authority may be especially relevant for those international actors who see their mission as helping others. For Didier Fassin, the very definition of "humanitarian government" is the "deployment of moral sentiments in contemporary politics" (2012, 1). Indeed, humanitarians have overseen the enshrinement of principles—humanity, impartiality, neutrality, and independence—into international law, and celebrated the twentieth-century expansion of humanitarianism as "one of humanity's great moral achievements" (Slim 2015). Nonhumanitarian interveners, though not bound by humanitarian principles, also deploy moral authority as a basis of their power. Peacekeeping interventionists "claim the moral high ground" through their elevation of neutrality and impartiality (Autesserre 2014, 237). Development agencies and NGOs operate as though technical approaches are neutral ones (Ferguson 1990; Fisher 1997).[7] These morals and principles contribute to the "network of routines, symbols or scripts providing templates for behavior" (Hall and Taylor 1996, 948) that characterize crisis responses and other institutional frameworks.

Moralistic rules operate through coercive and normative pressures that push or encourage local actors to present themselves as neutral crisis responders. International actors view local actors as potentially risky partners unless the latter can demonstrate their adherence to the rules (Barbalet 2019; Fast and Bennett 2020), yet local actors may also be "attracted" to these normative templates (Beckert 2010). That is, the internal preferences of local actors can explain the "pull" of some local actors toward moral and neutral scripts, but the rules and material incentives of international actors provide the coercive "push."

Third, international actors will favor those local actors that acquire, or already possess, technical qualifications and expertise, and they will build the capacity of those who do not. Expertise, like rationalism and moralism, is a basis of authority among international organizations (Barnett and Finnemore 2004). Expertise, in this understanding, is based on technical knowledge and professional training (Ferguson 1990; J. Mundy 2015). International humanitarians have since the 1990s generally moved from voluntarism to professionalism—in the global North humanitarianism and development are learned through educational tracks and careers (Barnett 2011; Calhoun 2004; DuBois 2018; Hopgood 2008; James 2015; Kent et al. 2016; Slim 2020). Although no singular accreditation or professional association is in place for humanitarians (Walker and Russ 2010), the intervention sector has professionalized (Bush 2015). While degrees and trainings in humanitarianism and development have trickled down to the global South, in the latter local actors are often learning on the job, tactically responding to needs around them. In this context, international organizations privilege those locals who can "speak the international language" of "technical terms and acronyms, understand the logic of the international aid system, are familiar with its values, and know how to navigate complex international processes" (Autesserre 2014, 88). Often, professionalism will operate through normative "attraction"; that is, activists' own preferences can coincide with an explanation based on international rules, though the latter also exert coercive pressures.

The rationalism, moralism, and professionalism of international aid organizations, which are built on their rules-based authority as bureaucracies, operate through coercive and normative pressures that constitute a formalizing process. They consume the time and energy of local actors, orient them toward outward presentations of neutrality, and elevate those with technical qualifications. In the aggregate, aid's rules formalize nonviolent action in war and contain its politics.

International Aid Resources Filter Nonviolent Action

A third fundamental quality of all institutions, including international aid, is resource distribution. Aid resources are disbursed through contracts and directed toward the priorities (that is, the ideas) of donors and major aid organizations. Contracted and idea-based resources filter their organizational recipients: Some local nonviolent actors participating in crisis response meet the contracting demands and ideational preferences of international aid, others do not.

International assistance is disbursed based on needs, but not exclusively so. The contemporary rise in humanitarian resources also reflects the politics of aid, including the ambitions of donors or aid organizations that that seek to resolve—or govern—global problems (Duffield 2001; Fearon 2008). At the same time, these resources are finite. Humanitarian responses are almost always underfunded. Given financial constraints, aid resources filter the population of nonviolent organizations—portending survival for some and decline for others—while discouraging collectivity among all.

Contract and idea-based resources operate through selection and legitimation mechanisms that produce winners and losers among local nonviolent organizations. To fit and survive their resource environments (Aldrich and Pfeffer 1976; Hannan and Freeman 1977; Pfeffer and Salancik 1978; Hannan and Carroll 1992), organizations can select into success: Individual organizations or their leaders seek to reduce uncertainties and enhance their position within their wider economic context (Baum and Amburgey 2017; Pfeffer and Salancik 1978), often by learning from competition with their peers (Bush 2015). At the same time, the resource environment legitimizes organizational forms based on how well they "incorporate the practices and procedures" of the wider institutional context (Meyer and Rowan 1977). Legitimation mechanisms filter organizations that reflect institutional priorities and not necessarily those that are most efficient or productive in the work they have set out to do (Meyer and Rowan 1977). The institutional resources of international aid activate these selection and legitimation mechanisms and, by filtering organizations in and out, induce and exacerbate novel and existing sources of cleavage among the population of local organizations.

The concept of contracted resources combines existing theories in the new economics of organizations with insights about international aid in particular. International aid is disbursed through a supply chain, or what has been called the "aid chain" (Watkins et al. 2012). States channel aid to intergovernmental organizations and INGOs that themselves contract to national-level organizations, which in turn subcontract to more local organizations. In this chain, local nonviolent actors are subcontracted and tasked with accessing beneficiaries and implementing projects on behalf of suppliers (Watkins et al. 2012). Barnett has referred to local aid actors as the "hired help" (2021)—highlighting an imbalance of power that concepts like brokers or intermediaries fail to invoke.

Contracting practices activate a "scramble" among recipient organizations. Alexander Cooley and James Ron's (2002) essay on the "NGO scramble" was groundbreaking in its focus on donors' marketization of transnational activities, especially the adoption of contracting and competitive bidding. The consequences of these trends, as experienced by INGOs otherwise driven by liberal norms and values, include uncertainty, competition, and insecurity that force a focus on survival as a primary organizational imperative (Cooley and Ron 2002). Observable implications of this mechanism follow from the material incentives and principal-agent problems created by contractual relations between donors and organizations (Bush 2015). These include recipient organizations' focus on securing and renewing contracts, competition between them over the same projects, inefficiencies, and tensions with normative objectives (Cooley and Ron 2002).[8]

Organizations at the bottom of the chain scramble over the limited resources that trickle down, through subcontracts, from above. These local organizations in a conflict context—whose very existence may be new in part due to international crisis response—are unlikely to enjoy the developed practices and personnel, such as professional grant writers, of their international counterparts when navigating the resource environment of the NGO scramble. What's more, they operate in violent contexts rife with unique sources of uncertainty, such as shifts in territorial control and physical insecurity. The local nonviolent organizations able to survive through these contractual filters are likely to do so based on their sheer adaptability in fitting their environment and the legitimation of organizational forms able and willing to pass through these multiple contractual hoops.

In contexts of war in particular, humanitarian contracting practices revolve around projects. Krause contends that the "project" is the primary commodity or "unit of production" in humanitarianism. Projects are allocated based on needs, but also on access, added value, and mundane managerial logics (Krause 2014). As project decisions are made, only some local organizations will be tasked with implementing them. Organizations delivering goods and services—especially emergency relief—are poised to survive relative to those pursuing less tangible or more political projects. The contract filter is animated by selection and legitimation mechanisms. To obtain projects, local organizations might engage in "competitive learning," which Sarah Bush describes as the process by which some new organizations come to understand and select into strategies for success (2015). At the same time, legitimation mechanisms should generate winners based on who best models the organizational structures suited to surviving international project processes.

Ideational resources reflect and reward certain ideas, beliefs, and preferences. At first glance, it might seem odd to suggest that bureaucratic organizations hold beliefs and preferences, or to think that we can observe them. However, local interpretations of aid's ideational filters provide a rich and at times devastating view into the process through which some local action is legitimated. In order to navigate their resource environments, organizations "enact" that environment: They interpret, perceive, and, essentially, construct it; enacting the resource environment allows organizations to grapple with their position of dependence within it (Pfeffer and Salancik 1978). Parkinson uses the term "money talk" or "'everyday' discourse that uses the social meaning of money to express deeper moral critiques and judgments," which makes it a useful indicator for how organizations enact their resource environments (2016, 977). In particular, she posits two critical ideas: (1) that money talk is a vehicle for discourse around norms, values, and morals, and (2) that it can create and reproduce cleavages within organizational structures. For instance, her examination of external material aid to rebels finds that it can introduce "a potential source of organizational schism" because it can be perceived as a moral affront to political ideals and a diversion from recipients' trajectories and loyalties (Parkinson 2016, 977).

Insights related to money talk should extend to those engaged in nonviolent action, where activists' discourse can reveal underlying grievances that have material and ideational components that relate to local cleavages (Simmons 2014). In the context of a resource environment dominated by international aid, resources like remuneration and donor funding are salient and potentially laden with meaning that filters for organizational survival. For example, given that the bulk of funding to local NGOs in developing countries comes from INGOs and donors (Barr et al. 2005), scholars have observed that this external support creates a separation between modern, donor-oriented NGOs and "grassroots" or "community-based" associations in the developing world (Gugerty and Kremer 2008; Chahim and Prakash 2014; Dupuy et al. 2015). Do local actors perceive and interpret this separation in the same way? The enactment of the resource environment's ideational filters should be observable in money talk.

The contracted and ideational resources activated by aid consist of selection and legitimation mechanisms that favor local organizations that are fit to participate in crisis response based on the demands and notions of international aid. In the aggregate, international aid's resources filter the population of organizations involved in nonviolent action in war and refuge.

Contemporary conflict responses are complex with many actors on both the demand and the supply side and others mediating between and against them. Yet the conditional framework of civilizing contention suggests that if international actors are able to pursue their objectives without undue obstructions from state and nonstate actors, it is possible to gain a relatively predictable understanding of the mechanisms aid will activate even in complex and uncertain conflict contexts. When they enjoy autonomy, international aid actors work with and through local actors to achieve their objectives. As they seek to feed the hungry, shelter the displaced, educate the children, protect the women, and combat the extremists, among many other objectives, international aid organizations connect with, impose rules on, and select from among local actors. In aiming to pacify war—or the parts of it over which their structures and routines can be exerted—international actors will enable and constrain local civil activists. They create something like a population of civil society organizations, allowing civilians and refugees to play meaningful roles in conflict processes and civic life, rather than exit the conflict or take up arms. Thus contentious action may transform in conflict contexts. At the same time, the action that persists is altered in other ways too: The skills, motivations, politics, and collectivity of these actors are all transformed, as well. Ultimately, that something like a civil society, lacking a state with which to relate and from which to receive protection, is left bare to war's violence. These processes are visible in the contention and conflict that characterized Syria before and during its civil war.

2
CONTENTION, CONFLICT, AND CRISIS IN SYRIA

Nahla was one of just a handful of women at the first big protest in the central city of Homs in March 2011.¹ A master's student preparing a thesis on contemporary literature, Nahla had been involved in small-scale oppositional activity for years and had long awaited this moment. She was astonished when she saw demonstrators tear down one of the ubiquitous posters of Syria's former president Hafez al-Asad, which kept watch over the country controlled by his son, Bashar. This was a revolution of the youth, she felt, of her generation. When others tried to shepherd the movement, including old elite families (oppositional "aristocrats," as she called them) and Muslim Brothers affiliates with backing from Gulf donors (the "Jeddah Treasury," she quipped), Nahla understood the need for coordinating from below.

She joined a local coordination committee (LCC) connecting activists in the city center with those in the Homs periphery. She drew on her connections in other regions of the country as well in order to establish an alternative media network; she spent hours on Skype, with finicky internet connectivity, training activists in journalistic practices. Next, she and her friends took on violations documentation to record the names of the casualties of repression. This dynamo dissident also oversaw the founding of the "first liberated newspaper" and a cross-province student organization.

When the movement took up arms, Nahla accepted this development. That was because in Homs, at least, they were the same young men who had partaken in demonstrations. "We said: we each play our roles. You [with arms] defend, but we [unarmed] have control over you. We are the ideas, we are those who started the revolution," Nahla explained. But divisions deepened. External actors with Islamist ideologies were putting their weight behind both nonviolent and violent groups. The independence and self-financing that Nahla exalted were difficult to sustain. Then, in 2012, Baba Amr, a rebel-held neighborhood in Homs, was besieged by the regime. Nahla's family fled to Damascus for safety, while she went north to join a burgeoning nonviolent movement in Aleppo. By March, the regime had regained control of Baba Amr. A few days later, Nahla was detained during a visit to her family in Damascus. She spent a torturous six months in prison. She doesn't like to talk about it. Because Nahla was a prominent figure in the movement, many advocated for her release, including in the West. This inequity made her feel ashamed, for her arrest "was very ordinary," as were the beatings. Regardless, those six months did not stop Nahla.

Upon her release she sought out activists in Damascus but, to her "great surprise," most were engaged in humanitarian work. Moreover, it appeared that the political opposition abroad was funding these relief-based endeavors. She protested: "Humanitarianism can never bring down a regime!" Instead, she fears, it leaves the square empty, relieves the regime of responsibility for its own people, and relies on external funds that could end at any moment. Nahla traveled to the northwest of the country where "liberated" rebel-held territory offered the promise of an ongoing revolution. Her disappointment intensified. First, there were the battalions, many Islamist-oriented, that tried to restrict activities and control attire. Second was the preoccupation of civil activists with administration—particularly from within local administrative councils (LCs). "When we transformed from a revolution of coordinating committees to local councils, we transformed to an administration. Administration has nothing to do with a revolution," Nahla lamented.

Nahla's story tells of many turning points that boded ill for Syria's social movement. Regime repression presented an immediate and intransigent threat to the persistence of protests. The violent response of Bashar al-Asad's forces and emerging paramilitaries catalyzed the arming of the opposition, which justified further the regime's deployment of military might. But regime repression was not the movement's only challenge. Because they lacked experience in independent organizing and collective action, activists had to "mobilize from scratch" (Pearlman 2021). Diasporic and older opposition actors, many with resources, sought influence over the grass roots and the cleavages among them were renewed. As Syrian territory was carved up by state and nonstate armed actors, several rebel groups leaned into, or were prevailed upon by, extremist ideologies. Many nonviolent actors, responding to the fallout of militarization all around them, made a tactical turn toward humanitarianism or participated in the administration of local institutions in rebel-held territory. Nahla, for her part, survived the regime's prisons only to emerge disillusioned by all that had unfolded in her absence. This was the scene into which international aid organizations entered.

In this chapter, I describe the contention and conflict in Syria to which international aid actors began to respond in 2011. Civilians continuously engaged in nonviolent action from 2011 onward, driven to some extent by domestic drivers of change, such as tactical adaptation to wartime conditions, that are sometimes coincidental, but incomplete explanations for producing something like a civil society during war. Violent dynamics also developed from the 2011 uprising, and exhibited a particular spatial distribution that related to nonviolence and to the international aid response. Patterns in the geographic distribution of nonviolent and violent contention fed into distinct configurations of international aid autonomy and responses to the crisis. Activists like Nahla did not merely demobilize or give up in the face of these many challenges, nor were the changes they underwent driven by internal factors alone. Many persisted in nonviolent action for years after and international aid provided an important pathway for so doing, a pathway that would alter this action—and civilize it.

A Very Brief History of Nonviolent Action in Syria

For more than half a century, the Asad dynasty shaped the opportunities, restrictions, and impulses of civil society and dissent in Syria. President Hafez al-Asad controlled Syria from 1970 until his death in 2000. His son, Bashar, succeeded him and remained in power until the sudden collapse of his regime in December 2024. Over these decades Syria operated under emergency rule, without free opposition or elections, and with callous control and coercion (Munif 2020). Hafez al-Asad did not only prohibit dissent, he also expected public dissimulation and reverence of leadership (Wedeen 1999). While sustaining this personalistic form of authoritarianism, Bashar al-Asad would continue his father's legacy in at least two additional ways, economic and coercive, that shaped civil action in Syria.

First was his continuation of a long-term shift from socialism toward private capital (Dahi and Munif 2012). In the late 1980s, income from oil revenues, remittances, and foreign aid from Arab states was interrupted and a severe financial crisis ensued (Perthes 1997). In response, Asad began a gradual move from full economic control toward inclusion of a networked and privileged public-private elite (Haddad 2012). Over time, this transformation led Syria's civil actors away from incorporated populist groupings and toward charitable bodies, which grew "in number and scale" in the 1990s and 2000s (Pierret and Selvik 2009). Toleration of charities was a practical move: the regime sought to compensate for inequitable economic growth and the degradation of its social bases by loosening restrictions on faith-based charitable associations (Ruiz de Elvira and Zintl 2014). However, these shifts did not empower civil society. Rather, up until the 2011 uprising, "political restrictions . . . maintained Islamic associations in a somewhat 'primitive' state, most of them remaining simple administrative structures involving few human resources . . . they cannot be considered a locus of political mobilization and socialization but are mere functional agencies" (Ruiz de Elvira and Zintl 2014, 597).

Asad the son, together with his wife Asma, also supported the development of a handful of apparently modern, development-oriented and government-organized NGOs, or GONGOs. Laura Ruiz de Elvira and Tina Zintl argue that both the traditional charitable associations—a "noncontentious civil society"—and the elitist GONGOs—a "loyalist" one—were reflections of the authoritarian political system's abandonment of its socialist social contract (2014). This abandonment was, in the first decade of the twenty-first century, compounded by surging costs of living, drought in agricultural areas, and labor force and housing pressures compounded by rural to urban migration.

Second, Bashar al-Asad persisted in proscribing political dissent and pushing opponents into prison or exile (Lefèvre 2013; Ismail 2018). Urban uprisings emerged in the late 1970s, during the father's reign, especially in the cities of Aleppo and Hama. These cities were bases for Syria's Muslim Brothers association (MB) and home to landed Sunni elites who had been politically excluded under a rural-oriented socialism. During the uprising, the MB engaged in competitive outbidding with a militant splinter group. Insurrection escalated and fed into cycles of violence and repression with the state's security forces (Lefèvre 2013). Events peaked with an armed insurgency in Hama in 1982 that ended with Asad's forces killing (perhaps tens of) thousands; the casualty count is unknown. Thereafter, Hafez al-Asad decreed MB membership a capital offense and the organization dispersed into exile. The group renounced the use of violence but, weakened, continually suffered from strategic and ideological disagreements between its factions, their respective host states, competitive personalities, and younger and older members (Lefèvre 2013).

The accession in 2000 of Bashar the son inspired hope for political reform and events in the first decade of his reign opened up political opportunities, although coercion soon closed them. A 2000–2001 "Damascus Spring" blossomed not just among intellectuals, but seemingly in Bashar himself, who permitted cultural and political forums for discussion and debate. Until, that is, he moved against them. Then the US invasion of Iraq in 2003 emboldened Syria's long disenfranchised Kurdish population in the northeast of the country. Tensions escalated and in 2004 an unorganized Kurdish uprising emerged; just as quickly, armed agents of the state lethally repressed it and arrested thousands (Lowe 2006). Another outbreak of political opposition, known as the "Damascus Declaration," emerged in 2005 when the regime's standing was undermined by its purported involvement in the assassination of a former Lebanese prime minister. Syria faced international pressure to withdraw its decades-long military presence from the neighboring country, but the episode ultimately concluded with the delegitimation of an opposition that was distant from the ground and close to Western politicians (Pace and Landis 2009).[2] Through 2010, Asad's grip on power remained firm.

Syria's Uprising

"Nobody thought the revolution would happen, until it happened in Tunisia and Egypt and Libya," a young woman from Aleppo recalled. She continued: "My parents said it would be bloody, because they know the regime."[3] The lethal reaction to Hama's 1982 insurrection pervaded unspoken memories (Ismail 2018) and many feared Asad's response would be fierce. Yet in 2011, in the wake of popular movements across the Middle East known as the "Arab Spring," Syrians rose up.

Their activism during the uprising included protest and a variety of additional actions. Existing accounts of this period (Abdelwahid 2013; Khalaf et al. 2014; Pearlman 2019) emphasize what social movement theorists would call tactical adaptation: activists adapted their actions to events and needs on the ground. My interviewees' narratives likewise flowed freely from mass collective action like protest, to filming and documenting events, to preparing housing for internally displaced people and providing goods and services to substitute for the absence of state services. Nevertheless, an external source of change—namely international humanitarianism—was responsible for driving distinct developments that tactical adaptation cannot alone or completely explain.

Small-scale contentious actions began in February 2011, attracting few people whom security agents quickly dispersed. In March, protest action grew, spanning the country from Qamishli in the northeast to Darʻa in the south. The southern governorate of Darʻa was an unexpected center for the uprising's onset. Before 2011, the rural region—across from Jordan's northern border—was characterized by a relative absence of opposition to the central government. Organized Islamist opposition had long been associated with the MB's presence in cities like Hama and Aleppo. Secular political opposition groups like those connected to the Damascus Spring operated from the capital. Darʻa, in contrast, was considered a government stronghold, from the Ottoman Empire to the Baʻth Party. Prominent Darawi clans were represented in the Baʻth Party (Batatu 1999, 24–26) and according to the 2004 general census, public goods provision was extensive and more than a quarter of residents were government employees (Central Bureau of Statistics 2004).

Yet it was in Darʿa where a cycle of challenger action and repression unwound. One Darawi recounted that after sending videos of demonstrations to satellite channels and posting them online, he was arrested and imprisoned for three months, "during which time I experienced the worst kinds of torture." He continued: "The day after I was released, I rested. The next day, I continued my activity in the revolution. The experience pushed me to participate rather than scaring me away."[4] Such resilience did not go unpunished. Darʿa suffered over one-quarter of Syria's protest-related deaths through June 2011, despite comprising less than 5 percent of the country's preconflict population (Leenders and Heydemann 2012). The southern region would remain rebellious: armed groups initially associated with the nonviolent movement controlled the large majority of Darʿa Governorate from 2014 until mid-2018.

Protests would spread beyond Darʿa and around the country, peaking in the summer of 2011 (Mazur 2019). They were frequent—almost always, but not only, occurring on Fridays. Masses took to the streets in Homs, Idlib, and Deir ez-Zor, or Syria's fourth, seventh, and ninth most populated governorates, respectively. Reinoud Leenders and Steven Heydemann use reported protest-related deaths as a proxy for the intensity of early mobilization, finding that these four governorates took 70 percent of casualties through June 2011, despite comprising just over a fifth of the country's population (2012). Early on, marginalized parts of the capital city, Damascus, and more so its surrounding exurban governorate, Rural Damascus, would also participate in the uprising. Later, parts of Syria's second city, Aleppo, would connect with the insurrection in rural Aleppo Governorate. Overall, Syria's marginalized, peripheral, and border areas would be the strongholds of both the nonviolent movement and the violent rebellion that followed—dynamics that would later help shape the international aid response.[5]

Syrians undertook a variety of nonviolent actions, beyond protest, to contribute to the overall movement. Initially, one of the most prominent nonprotest forms of action was journalism. One activist stated simply, "everyone became a journalist."[6] A Darawi activist, who was a trained journalist prior to 2011, explained the proliferation of the undertaking: "The role of civilians as social activists began with the coordination of demonstrations and then in media, citizen journalism."[7] He continued: "Any civilian person began to transform into something else, into one of these two fields [coordination and media]. The primary reason for the citizen journalism was, first of all, to establish that local media was fabricating events and, second, trying to get the message to the international community about what was happening." As he described, most lacked any prior experience in the field, but they took this route both to document events and repression and to broadcast their mobilization and messages to wider Syrian and global audiences. Foreign journalists had very limited access to Syria and the government censored local coverage and used its own media outlets to push a counternarrative of extremism and foreign meddling.

Relatedly, groups began to publish newsletters and periodicals. From a state of censorship before 2011, at least three hundred publications were released after 2011, though most eventually died out (Syrian Prints Archive 2016). Syrian Prints Archive attributes their decline to technical, printing, and marketing issues. Publications existed on too many platforms for subscribers to follow, and quality and means of distribution were poor. In other words, extensive local mobilization was difficult to sustain without greater capacity.

Syrians also engaged in a range of civil resistance efforts. For example, in Damascus a campaign called Days of Freedom enacted initiatives that included covertly hanging revolutionary flags around the city, dying the water in public fountains, and planting revolutionary messages inside loaves of bread.[8] Activists organized an ambitious Dignity Strike in late 2011. While businesses shuttered in Rural Damascus and in small cities and towns across the country, actions in the major cities of Damascus and Aleppo were less successful (Syria Untold 2013). Still, to its organizers, the Dignity Strike was an assertion of the nonviolent nature of the uprising, which they believed would be more effective than violence against government repression.[9] Campaigns such as these rested on informal organizational structures and were transgressive in their orientation.

Divisions of uprising labor took the shape of coordination committees. As one interviewee noted, "We had someone in charge of filming, someone to monitor the security situation, someone to write the poster language, etc."[10] These spontaneous local coordinating committees, or *tansiqqiyyat*, emerged at neighborhood and city levels and at institutions such as in universities, and their members were "initially unconnected to actors outside their locality" (Mazur 2021, 125). Before long, activists created umbrella groups to coordinate clusters of committees. At the national level, veteran human rights activists created the Local Coordination Committees in Syria in May 2011 to raise awareness, unify and channel messaging, and oversee the coordination of demonstrations. There were as many as seven hundred LCCs across the country under their aegis, though they exerted very little formal control over them (Sawah and Kawakibi 2014).[11] Other national-level umbrella groups emerged too, including the MB-organized Syrian Revolution General Commission, which was formed in August 2011 to represent Islamist activists, and groups representing Kurdish, minority, and secular interests (Sawah and Kawakibi 2014). These coalitions sought to cohere what was often a fractured movement.

At least nineteen of my interviewees were detained for their activism.[12] Their detentions varied in length but often lasted somewhere between a week and a couple of months. LCC leaders, however, were exposed to more severe risks. As one activist described it, "In the beginning they used to release people detained in demonstrations after just eight days. Unless they were coordinators—nobody sees them; the wind doesn't even see them."[13] Among those LCC leaders I spoke to, an LCC founder in a Rural Damascus suburb was detained for three long years.[14] Nahla, whose story opened this chapter, served six months—an unusually long detention for a woman.[15] And a founder of the national-level LCC barely escaped attempts on his life—even from his refuge in a neighboring country.[16] All civil actors, but especially organizers, incurred risks in Syria.

As everyday needs grew, activists participated in new areas, like humanitarianism: "I think we who participated in the revolution, in a way we feel responsible for the suffering of the people," said a young woman from Aleppo whose civil action transformed from protest to underground education.[17] She described her involvement on this front as "humanitarian work that was also revolutionary." These initiatives included medical efforts, such as roving medical teams and pharmaceutical smugglers, as protesting neighborhoods were blockaded or cordoned off by checkpoints, which inhibited access to hospitals and clinics (Abdelwahid 2013). A young man from Rural Damascus explained his role as a driver in one such pharmaceutical smuggling operation. Physicians in training outside of his besieged town would gather medical goods; he packed and prepared the suitcases and drove them to their destinations. This undertaking was extremely risky and some were caught. "But what can we do?" he asked rhetorically—"we had to sacrifice."[18]

For some, these relief-based actions were grounded in a commitment to nonviolence: "When it became armed, I was against that . . . that's when I took the humanitarian direction," said a man from Dar'a who became involved in distributing relief sent across the Jordanian border by diaspora networks.[19] For others, adherence to nonviolence was a strategic imperative; the regime had far greater military might and violent opposition would provide pretext for using it. An Aleppan activist who disagreed with the arming of the opposition explained: "If I go to shoot a soldier, first of all, it's not his fault—he's forced to serve.[20] I know many soldiers who were our friends, who were opposition, and they were killed. And, it gives the justification for the regime to put everyone down with force."

Though opinions on the use of arms diverged, emerging forms of nonviolent action were usually still grounded in commitment to the cause. Some humanitarian initiatives grew out of preexisting charitable associations, but they were not merely a continuation of the status quo; rather, they adapted to the uprising. Ruiz de Elvira, studying Syrian activists in Lebanon, found that "while in the years 2000 Syrian social actors resorted to the frames of 'religion,' 'religious duty' and 'piety' in order to explain their involvement in charitable and social activities, in the post-2011 context they rather frame their commitment in terms of 'patriotism,' 'resistance,' 'responsibility' and 'national duty'" (Ruiz de Elvira 2019, 45). Many service-oriented organizations were newly established to provide relief on behalf of the revolutionary cause. For example, a group that formed from the combined efforts of diaspora Syrians in the Gulf, refugees in Jordan, and their kin in southern Syria, began to coordinate around everyday needs in Darʿa. An activist quoted above, who was against arming, was working with them to oversee humanitarian distribution. He was still very much *with* the uprising: "I consider myself a resister, a fighter; there's more than one way to fight the regime," he said.[21]

Syrians who provisioned relief to people associated with, impacted by, or living in rebel-held areas and in refuge effectively linked themselves, in the view of pro-government forces, to opposition forces. Accordingly, they faced serious risks. As one activist wrote, providing humanitarian relief was a "dangerous [task], as the regime especially targeted relief workers" (Dunia 2014). International aid organizations were aware of this violent targeting of local aid actors. Doctors Without Borders, also known as Médecins Sans Frontières (MSF), noted in 2015 that "almost all of the field hospitals supported by MSF in Homs and elsewhere in Syria have sustained damage from airstrikes and barrel bombs" (MSF 2015).[22] During the war, Syria became one of the "deadliest places for aid workers in the world" according to a humanitarian INGO (CARE 2018). Civil actors were detained, violently targeted, or forcibly displaced throughout the war (Becker and Stolleis 2016; El-Helou and Antara 2018; Martínez and Eng 2018). In peacetime or democratic contexts, action to meet basic needs may appear to be a routine activity. But in a context of insurrection, Syria's wartime activists were engaged in risky contentious action.

The map in figure 3, which plots the observable locations of organizations with operations inside Syria represented on public Facebook pages, makes it possible to visualize the development of nonviolent action in Syria over the course of the uprising and war. It shows 838 Facebook pages that represent Syrian civil organizations with apparent activities inside Syria. These undertakings are concentrated in rebel-held areas: in Syria's northwest, home to Idlib and Aleppo Provinces, as well as Rural Damascus surrounding the country's capital, the Kurdish-held northeastern Al-Hasakah Province, and in Darʿa in Syria's south.

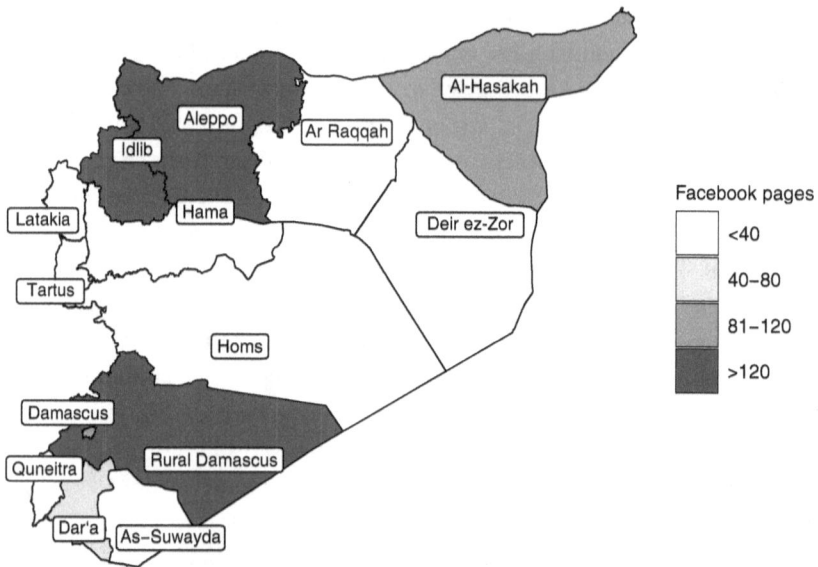

FIGURE 3. Map of Syrian organizations active inside Syria, 2011–2018. Based on observable location information on organizations' Facebook pages. Source: Author's original data.

Syria's Civil War

Violence, Charles Tilly has claimed, "takes shape from the character of power struggles spanning violent and nonviolent action" (2015). Facing uprising in 2011, the Syrian regime undertook political reforms insufficient to the moment. Indeed, the regime could be said to have squandered its many "assets": its popular foreign policy posture, Asad's personal standing as a "benevolent dictator," and the absence of "abject poverty" of the kind that existed in other Arab countries where uprisings occurred, like Egypt (ICG 2011).[23] Instead, the government aimed to squelch unrest through negotiations with local notables where possible and through violence where necessary (Mazur 2021). When these tactics failed and regime challengers enjoyed dense social networks—often in peripheral sections of cities and in rural areas—they responded to violence with violence (Mazur 2021).

The geographic bounds of the nonviolent contentious movement described above hardened—in southern and northwest Syria, in marginalized governorates like Rural Damascus in the geographic center of the country, and in the northeastern provinces that would come under the control of Kurdish-led parties and rebels. A "politics of region" buttressed this spatial character of violent dynamics:

whereas the regime traditionally repressed Kurds, who largely inhabited the country's northeast, after 2011 it deployed tactics to separate the Kurdish struggle from that of the Arab opposition (Mazur and Khaddour 2013). The alliance that both Asads had cultivated between their regime, economic elites, and the Sunni religious establishment also contributed to the government's hold over Syria's two largest cities, Damascus and Aleppo, at least for the first year, after which their stance mattered less than the "brute military force" that upheld the government (Pierret 2014).

As insurgent armed groups formed, violent and nonviolent actors assumed distinct roles. They sometimes collaborated. In the early stages of the conflict, their intersections were linked to activist efforts like demonstrations. As Nahla explained in the chapter opening, those who took up arms initially emerged from among their peers in the demonstrations. Roles were split: "We are the ideas, you defend," she recalled of their discussions.[24] And indeed, members of a burgeoning Free Syrian Army (FSA) began to use their arms protect people against the regime. "We used to protect the civilians," a Darawi rebel on reprieve in Jordan recounted. "We didn't have much in terms of weapons, so we would wait out the regime's raids until it was safe to bring the civilians back in."[25]

By early 2012, armed groups were acquiring territory, often under the banner of the FSA, a loosely organized formation of local battalions. They sometimes took territory through battles, and other times following the strategic withdrawal of the Syrian government. In turn, towns and villages across the country were left with a dearth of functioning institutions—no small loss in a country where the state had a pervasive presence in daily life and the public sector employed nearly a third of the labor force (Central Bureau of Statistics 2004). For instance, concern over welfare provision, in which the Syrian state had excelled—like subsidized bread and free health care—was a critical domain in which authorities in rebel-held territory sought to replace the role of the state (Martínez and Eng 2018). "In every place that was liberated," an activist explained, "there was a need to extend the apparatus that was in place."[26]

Becoming "counter-state sovereigns" (Mampilly 2011) was a domain of concern and exertion among civil actors collaborating with and operating in territory under the control of FSA-affiliated armed groups. Their ideas and efforts would coalesce into what came to be known as *majalis mahaliyya*, or local councils (LCs).[27] LCs often grew directly out of revolutionary councils and LCCs, the armed and unarmed committees working at the local level prior to territorial control. Their basic structure was widely replicated; for example, they had similar "bureaus," including those for demonstrations, displacement, detainees, humanitarian relief, and mills and bread production. By 2013 there were hundreds of LCs—in name, at least. For instance, at its height the Free Aleppo

Governorate Council oversaw 130 LCs in the countryside and 67 in the city (Khaddour 2017).

There was substantial variation in LC effectiveness across localities (Menapolis 2013), but in the early stages of the conflict there was a clear connection between contentious activity prior to territorial control and cooperation between armed and unarmed actors after it. This connection was easily identifiable in LCs. To many involved, there was no contradiction in the alliance of civilian and military elements of the councils. "People working in security and relief, it's the same," contended an Aleppan man who served at many administrative levels of opposition governance over the years.[28]

The convergence of nonviolent and violent action waned over time, however, not least because the FSA did not remain the only nonstate armed group battling state forces. By 2015, at least 150,000 insurgents had joined as many as 1,500 operationally distinct armed groups (Lister 2015). These groups had never been unified under a single organizational structure nor even under multiple exclusive organizational structures. Instead, alliances and rivalries had emerged, shifted, and dissolved. Samer Abboud offers a schema that explains the broad armed networks that characterized the conflict. Abboud argues that "networks of violence" are decentralized forms within which there are independent nodes that operate "in relative cooperation" (2015). Arguably, the most prominent networks of violence were:

1. The Syrian government and local, regional, and international partnered forces
2. The Islamic State (initially the Islamic State of Iraq, then the Islamic State of Iraq and al-Sham, then the Islamic State)
3. Kurdish forces affiliated with the Democratic Union Party and its armed counterpart, the People's Protection Units (later the Syrian Democratic Forces in alliance with a variety of local militias in northeast Syria and with the support of the United States)
4. The rebels, including the Free Syrian Army, Jabhat al-Nusra, and other Salafi-jihadist groups (Jabhat al-Nusra later became Hay'at Tahrir al-Sham)

Syrians and observers often refer to the fourth network as "the opposition" as this was the armed network that most closely relates to the 2011 protest movement.

Observers have attributed the growth and strength of Salafi-jihadist armed groups within the fourth network to international and nonstate support, including from private donors (Pierret 2013) and governments. Aron Lund notes that "Qatar, Turkey, and Saudi Arabia delivered thousands of tons of military equipment to Syria from 2012 onward," amounting to billions of dollars in lethal aid

(2017a), and this often flowed through the Turkish border (Phillips 2015). Military aid recipients were not limited to Salafi-jihadist groups. In 2013, the US government reportedly initiated one of the costliest covert action programs in its history in support of the FSA (Ignatius 2017). Although US president Barack Obama ultimately decided not to lead an international military intervention against the Syrian government, the efforts of international supporters seemed to be buttressing the rebels and their push toward Damascus appeared plausible by mid-2015. However, the Russian military intervened on the government's side in September 2015, tipping the balance in Asad's favor.

The Syrian regime embraced the geopolitical facets of the conflict. From the start, Bashar al-Asad's public speeches attributed unrest to "traitors" and "infiltrators." As the armed insurgency grew with material support from Syria's "enemies," the government invited military intervention from Iraqi militias and Lebanon's Hezbollah, beginning in 2013 if not earlier, as well as from Iran and—perhaps most consequentially—Russia in 2015. This violent escalation forced millions out of their homes, took hundreds of thousands of lives, and wounded countless more.

More than 5.5 million Syrians ultimately fled to neighboring countries, namely Turkey, Lebanon, and Jordan (UNHCR 2019). Turkey alone hosted 3.6 million, while Syrians constituted around a quarter of Lebanon's population and Jordan estimated the actual number of Syrians in the country to be twice the registered refugee population of 650,000. Hundreds of thousands also fled to Iraq and Egypt.

The pace of Syrian displacement was relatively slow at first. Although the first camps opened in Turkey as early as May 2011, in December 2012 there were just about half a million Syrian refugees sheltering in five nearby countries. One and a half million Syrians, however, fled in 2013 alone. By mid-2015, the war had produced over four million refugees (UNHCR 2018). As displacement grew, the conflict raged on, and integration proved difficult in neighboring host states, some sought asylum further afield. Europe was often reluctant to accommodate, with the notable exception of Germany, which eventually granted asylum to nearly one million Syrians. Within Syria's borders, as many as six million people were internally displaced.

Patterns of displacement reinforced spatial dynamics in areas of insurgency in Syria's south and northwest. Forced displacement in Syria followed, to some extent, a strategic logic of "guilt by location," or what Adam Lichtenheld theorizes as a "tendency for combatants to treat fleeing and staying in wartime as indicators of collaboration or defection" (2020). The Syrian regime attributed disloyalty to IDPs in rebel-held areas and loyalty to those who fled to government-held ones (Lichtenheld 2017), regardless of the legitimacy of these determinations. The regime's decision in this regard could be deadly: scholars have found that "clustering of IDP flows is associated with increases in killings by pro-government forces" (Lichtenheld and Schon 2021).

Figure 4 captures the division of territorial control in mid-2016, showing the areas held by opposition rebels, the Islamic State, the government, and Kurdish forces. It is just one snapshot in time in an evolving warscape, but it serves to show these general spatial distributions (particularly rebels in south and northwest Syria, across from the Jordanian and Turkish borders, respectively) that characterized contention and conflict in Syria.

Through 2024, some nodes of the rebel network that initially corresponded to the 2011 nonviolent movement remained relevant. The successor organization to Jabhat al-Nusra, Hay'at Tahrir al-Sham (HTS), was in control of much of Idlib Governorate in northwest Syria. Within that same network, armed groups allied with Turkish military forces—deployed to rural Aleppo Governorate since 2016—controlled other areas of the northwest, and until 2018 when the government reconquered it, armed groups in the same broad network controlled much of Dar'a Governorate in the south, as well. Kurdish-led forces, under the banner of the People's Protection Unit and then the US-backed Syrian Democratic Forces, controlled swaths of Syria's northeast. The Islamic State, for its part, held large amounts of territory beginning in 2014, which contracted until its final defeat in 2017. In late 2024, HTS made a surprising push against frozen conflict

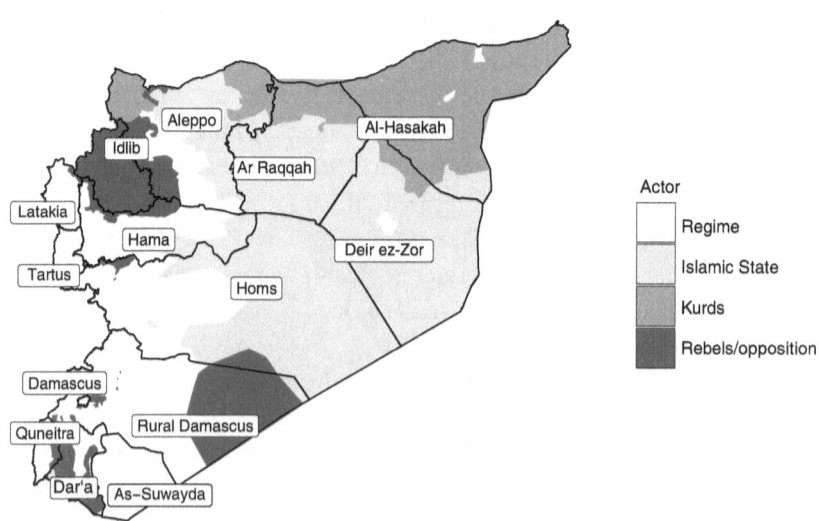

FIGURE 4. Map of territorial control in Syria, May 2016. Source: Data provided to the author by the Carter Center and compiled and visualized by the author.

lines that in a mere eleven days decisively collapsed the Syrian regime, which had been weakened by war, sanctions, and corruption from within and, from 2023, the defeats and distractions of its allies Russia, Iran, and Lebanon's Hezbollah, as Israel's military assaults reshaped the order of the Middle East region.

International Crisis Response

A variety of international aid actors sought to address the evolving crisis inside Syria and in the neighboring countries to which millions of Syrians fled. They included humanitarian organizations that provided emergency relief and engaged in other efforts to promote well-being; nonhumanitarian organizations focused on development, political processes, and stabilization; and governmental, intergovernmental, and nongovernmental organizations, as well as diasporas and nontraditional private and government donors. The international aid response largely conformed to the dynamics of the war: it included cross-border operations from, and refugee responses in, neighboring countries, in addition to the response from within government-held Syria.

The aid responses across these locations differed. For a significant stretch of time, the Turkish government allowed relative autonomy of action to Syria's civil activists and international humanitarian and nonhumanitarian aid actors responding to the crisis in rebel-held (mostly northern) Syria. In contrast, both Syrian activists and international aid actors engaging in cross-border response in southern Syria were relatively more constrained by the Jordanian government. Aid autonomy was blocked in government-held Syria, and it follows that there was no cross-border response from Lebanon given that the Syrian government controlled much of the territory across from the Lebanese border. This variation helps to structure an understanding of aid's effects on wartime activism in rebel-held areas and in refuge.

Prior to 2011, UN agencies and a handful of INGOs carried out some operations in Syria; their purview was limited to government-sanctioned development projects and humanitarian assistance for Iraqi and Palestinian refugees (Howe 2016). Yet the character of the early 2011 crisis demanded attention to civil society, politics, and human rights—domains in which international aid actors were all but blocked by the government. Throughout the war, the regime would continuously obstruct nonhumanitarian aid actors from accessing targets of their aid such as civil, political, and independent oppositional networks, from within government-held territory.

Ironically, government obstruction of nonhumanitarian aid may have heightened donors' embrace of it. This aid included "resilience," "stabilization," and "development-oriented transitional" aid directed toward opposition structures in border regions perceived as "moderate and democratic alternatives to the Assad regime" (Wieland 2021).[29] The United States, especially, imported these existing nonhumanitarian approaches to the Syrian context. The US Agency for International Development, USAID, described their early efforts in terms that explicitly referred to a "political transition." A 2013 US government survey of USAID's "Syria-related activities" described some of their programs in this way: "[The Office of Transition Initiatives] award is designed to support efforts to build governance structures that reflect the will and needs of the Syrian people. Through targeted small grants and technical assistance, the award supports governing bodies, civil society, and citizens to identify and respond to local needs and participate in the political transition" (Trujillo 2013). In other words, in the early years of the Syrian crisis, donors like the United States, as well as several Arab governments, supported political assistance to Syrian activists engaging in various post-protest actions. They primarily did so through cross-border operations from Turkey, as such intervention was relatively more limited from Jordan, and a nonstarter for the Syrian regime from Damascus.

Yet most international aid to the Syria crisis was ultimately directed toward humanitarianism. The UN, donor governments, and INGOs began treating the crisis as a humanitarian emergency in 2012 (Sida et al. 2016). When they did so, they also encountered obstacles erected by the regime. The Syrian government hampered humanitarianism by obstructing access to areas outside its control or areas under siege (Parker 2013). Moreover, the government heavily constrained the autonomy of aid actors even within the territory that it did control (Wieland 2021). As a result, "the quandary of access" became the "overarching problem of humanitarian operations in Syria" (Wieland 2021, 5). As Carsten Wieland describes it, humanitarian assisters faced a dilemma: do the best they can under government-imposed constraints, or find ways to work without the government's consent.

In the first few years of the conflict, organizations diverged in their choices. Some, like the Red Cross (ICRC), acknowledged government obstruction but, noting that their presence in the country depended on the government's consent, maintained that conceding to it was their only channel to access millions in need in government-held territory (Tisdall 2013). And indeed much of the United Nations humanitarian aid to the Syria crisis would be channeled through Damascus to government-held territory despite the severe control, manipulation, and constraints that the regime imposed (Leenders and Mansour 2018). These humanitarian organizations did not collaborate freely with local organizations, but rather worked only with those sanctioned by the regime, namely the Syrian Arab Red Crescent. International humanitarian organizations, in other words, did not establish autonomous relations with nonviolent actors in government-held territory where the state was strong and imposing.

Many nongovernmental organizations, however, were of the view that bending to the Syrian regime's demands was too severe a compromise of principles like impartiality and humanity. INGOs like Doctors Without Borders (MSF) bypassed government-held Damascus and moved to cross-border delivery of assistance from neighboring countries (Whittall 2015), arguing that it was "the only realistic way to increase aid in the rebel zones" (Weissman 2013). These INGOs initially worked through informal cross-border operations together with Syrian activists in order to implement their projects in rebel-held regions, including in Syria's north and south.

Eventually, the UN came to the borders, too. International lobbying by the leadership of the UN's humanitarian coordination agency, OCHA, culminated in July 2014 with the passage of UN Security Council Resolution 2165, which allowed for cross-border operations from Turkey and Jordan with only notification to, rather than permission from, the government of Syria. Resolution 2165 enabled the "Whole of Syria" approach—coordination across "hubs" in Jordan, Turkey, and Syria—and cleared the way for the formal delivery of assistance to rebel-held territory from border countries. Whole of Syria was highly imperfect, but it was a monumental institutional innovation for a system often constrained by sovereignty in the nation-state order. Through the UN cross-border mechanism, international aid actors forged a formal path for reaching Syria's areas of limited statehood.

Humanitarian and nonhumanitarian cross-border operations developed in a manner that corresponded with the territory primarily held by that "network of violence" associated with the 2011 contentious movement and which was largely based in southern and northwest Syria, across the borders from Jordan and Turkey. By 2014, "two parallel systems of aid" had "adapted to the conduct of hostilities and the geopolitics of the region" (Whittall 2015), one in Damascus and another from across borders. A UN staffer in Turkey described the landscape this way: "In other situations, we never accepted that part of the operation is run by one set of actors, and another set in another part. . . . The rift between different sides brought along the humanitarians."[30]

It was not only the responses from government-held Damascus and from across borders that diverged, however. Those across different borders diverged as well: international aid actors in Turkey and Jordan enjoyed differing levels of autonomy vis-à-vis Syrian refugees, civilians, and the nonviolent activists among them. Figure 5 represents beneficiary items in cross-border aid delivered from the Whole of Syria hubs in Turkey and Jordan from 2014 to 2017. It shows that the UN cross-border mechanism delivered far more beneficiary items to Syria's

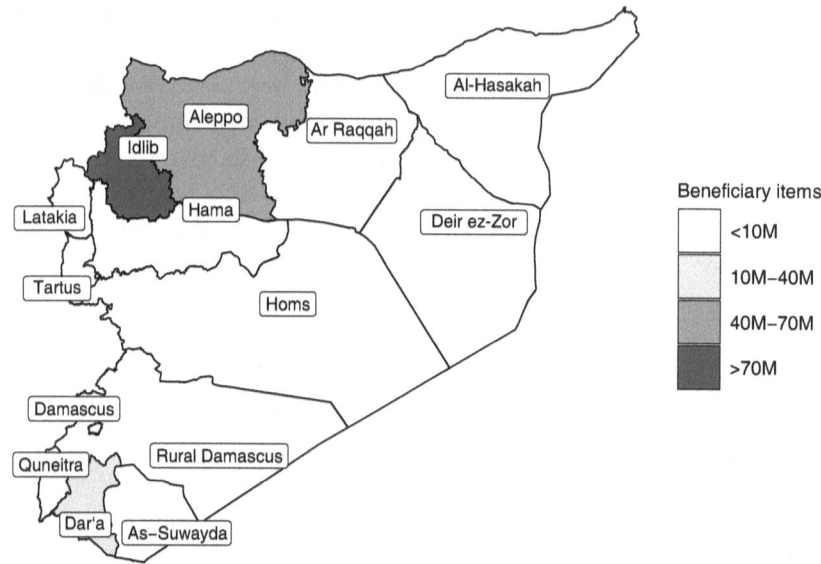

FIGURE 5. Map of OCHA cross-border beneficiary items, 2014–2018. Source: Public reports from OCHA, data extracted and compiled by author from https://www.humanitarianresponse.info/en/operations/stima.

northwest than to the south of the country. To an important extent, this variation reflects diverging population sizes in the country's regions. However, the potential for humanitarian governance in Syria's northwest was strengthened by the allowances made by the Turkish government for international autonomy, at least in the crucial early and middle years of the war.

Turkey, Northwest Syria, and Relative International Autonomy

Turkey, offering geopolitical support to Syria's opposition (Moss 2021) and projecting its power onto the Syrian conflict, allowed relative autonomy to international aid actors within its areas of influence during much of the conflict. It gave activists a "hub from which to mobilize and cross into liberated Syria" and "move supplies through Syria's northern border and distribute resources on the front lines" (Moss 2021, 212). Before long, Turkey was also hosting several foreign-backed military operations rooms and had become the "main route" for its own and others' arms, money, and nonlethal aid to a variety of Syrian rebels (Phillips 2016, 137). These military-based efforts have parallels in their approach to humanitarian and nonhumanitarian aid.

Turkey led and heavily funded its own humanitarian response to the influx of refugees, but it also worked alongside UNHCR (the UN High Commissioner for Refugees) and its partners to enact it. Leveraging the fact that it hosted a significant number of displaced persons, the government at times threatened to "flood" Europe with refugees to encourage international assistance from the European Union (Tsourapas 2019). At the same time, Turkey created space for Syrians to participate in their own refugee response, for instance by allowing Syrian medical professionals to serve the health needs of displaced communities. In other words, Turkey was simultaneously structuring and empowering aid actors' response to Syrian displacement. Political as its purposes may have been, Turkey allowed for a fair amount of autonomy for humanitarian, nonhumanitarian, INGO, UN, and diaspora aid actors in the refugee response.

Likewise, for much of the conflict Turkey enabled the international cross-border response into rebel-held areas of limited statehood. In the early years, Turkey permitted border crossings of nonviolent actors between Turkey and Syria to implement the growing international projects in humanitarian aid and political process or to receive trainings. For example, US government programs in the southern Turkish city of Gaziantep were offering so many trainings for democracy activists that an official referred to them as "endless," "duplicative," and "triplicative."[31]

INGOs were autonomous enough to coordinate aid efforts among themselves and with the Syrians with whom they were growing connections. The Turkish government did sometimes push international and Syrian organizations into partnerships with Turkish organizations (Carpi and Senoguz 2018), yet the international staff of humanitarian, development, and political organizations that I interviewed confirmed the ease of setting up their Syrian operations in southern Turkey during the first few years of the conflict. An international contractor promoting good governance in local councils captures this shared experience: "At the very beginning, 2013 to 2014, Turkey was very easy to work in. It was difficult to get registered and get work permits, and the taxes are high, but *in terms of working in Syria and with Syria, Turkey had no conditions*. They allowed us to do what we needed to do, and the border was open the first year so people could easily come in and out, meaning we could get people out [of Syria] whenever we needed. We were able to work where we wanted to [inside Syria]. It was fluid, the border was porous."[32]

This autonomy was enjoyed by Syria's displaced activists as well, who converged in Turkey to collaborate with international aid actors. The head of a Syrian organization described that ease in a way that was highly representative of the descriptions given by many other Syrian interviewees in Gaziantep, a southern Turkish city that became a hub for aid and activism: "We set up our office [in

Gaziantep] in 2015. It was very easy. We didn't get officially registered here until just two months ago [early 2017]. It was comfortable, much more so than Jordan or Lebanon. Until mid-2016, it was even more comfortable: the borders were open, we could go in and out, bring cadres from inside to here. They [Turkey] had their laws with regards to work permits, but they knew our capacity and it wasn't enforced."[33] The UN's OCHA officially established its cross-border operation in 2014 following Security Council authorization of resolution 2165, though it had already engaged informally before then.

The relative autonomy granted international aid actors in Turkey and those with operations in northwest Syria did, eventually, decrease. Around 2016, divisions of control shifted as the Syrian state retook territory in parts of the south and northwest, Kurdish-led armed groups retook territory from a retreating Islamic State, and Turkish armed forces deployed in reaction to those developments. In August 2016, Turkey began construction of a 435-mile-long wall along the Syrian border and launched a military operation in northwest Syria, Operation Euphrates Shield, that captured swaths of northern Aleppo from the Islamic State. After the military operation was declared complete, Euphrates Shield territory, extending across about a thousand square miles, was overseen by Turkey's Interior Ministry and provincial Turkish governments bordering the territory. Excluding INGOs and intergovernmental agencies from this territory, Turkey proceeded to implement humanitarian, developmental, political, and religious programming through its own agencies and national organizations. Syrian activists in that territory had to shift away from other international aid actors and turn toward Turkish ones.

Inside Turkey itself, international and Syrian organizations were pushed to formally register, acquire work permits for their employees, and abide by other labor regulations. In the first four months of 2017, an Italian NGO was banned, staff of a Danish organization were detained, one of the largest distributors of cross-border aid—Mercy Corps—was expelled, and employees of a US NGO were detained and deported (Cupolo 2017). Following a constitutional referendum in 2017, which received a majority "yes" vote that converted the country to a presidential system, a crackdown on NGOs in Gaziantep began: organizations' offices were systematically targeted and searched to ensure compliance with regulations the government had hardly ever enforced. For months, foreigners and Syrians alike retreated to their homes rather than work in their offices. Ultimately, the autonomy and access that Turkey afforded to international aid actors shrank. Still, Syrian displaced civil actors were relatively less affected by the changes than international staff and organizations. As the Syrian NGO-leader quoted above explained in 2017: "Up until now, despite the challenges, it's still the best place for NGOs compared to any other neighboring country."[34]

Jordan, Southern Syria, and Limited International Autonomy

In political and military matters, Jordan offered limited channels for opposition activity, though these included a multinational military operations room to support rebels in Syria's south. Yet the Jordanian government was generally wary of nonhumanitarian aid. The Jordanians, opined one American development contractor, had "about a 5 percent tolerance for political activity."[35] For example, while Jordan initially allowed the organization of an opposition governance council for Darʿa Governorate in southern Syria by diaspora and refugee Syrians, it quickly became concerned with the group's Gulf sponsors due to their association with the Muslim Brothers. Jordan decided to prevent the international meeting to elect the Darʿa Governorate Council leadership in 2013, which was then held in Egypt instead.

The Jordanian government allowed some nonhumanitarian international governance and civil society projects for southern Syria, but undertook intensive vetting and selection of Syrian field officers, recipient communities, and organizational partners. As one Syrian activist explained: "Darʿa, in a way, is an extension of Jordan's influence. They decide who can work there or not."[36] This control was effective enough that a program backed by a cohort of Western donors to train and fund "Free Syria Police" that supported about eighty stations in northern Syria (from Turkey) supported just one station in the south by late 2016 according to another American contractor in Jordan.[37]

Yet Jordan did encourage a robust humanitarian response to the refugee crisis, enabling the access of dozens if not hundreds of intergovernmental and nongovernmental organizations as well as national and community-based organizations (Dhingra 2022). A "global hub" of humanitarian aid operations (Ward 2020), Jordan made refugees as legible as possible to UNHCR, the UN refugee agency, and negotiated deals with the West that recompensed the country's hosting by providing development aid for Jordanian communities (Tsourapas 2019; Arar 2017).

With its focus on refugees and host communities, Jordan was the origin point of circumscribed cross-border operations. Although the Jordanian government supported OCHA in lobbying for a UN cross-border resolution, the border crossing it hosted was open to only a handful of organizations. International humanitarian operations were permitted to engage in cross-border operations, but their collaborations with Syrian organizations were far more limited. The government limited Syrians engaged in humanitarianism, and the autonomy of international organizations to collaborate with them, by essentially prohibiting the founding of Syrian-led NGOs and Syrians' formal employment.

All that said, displaced Syrian civil actors were not blocked from operating in Jordan and engaging in cross-border response altogether. Many Syrian activists in Jordan participated in formal and informal ways in refugee relief, some cross-border emergency relief, journalism, cultural activities, and education and psychosocial support for children, among other activities. The difference between Turkey and Jordan was one of magnitude. A Syrian humanitarian who engaged in cross-border operations from Jordan explained it this way: In the north of Syria, from Turkey, "the borders are so open, anything goes. In the south [of Syria] and the borders here [in Jordan], it's humanitarian and civil."[38]

Rebel-held territory in southern Syria, as elsewhere including Rural Damascus, was shrinking by 2018. In the summer of 2018, Dar'a's rebels lost control of territory to Syrian and Russian forces; cross-border operations effectively ended immediately, followed by the formal closure of operations by the end of the year. Though it had previously coordinated with the United States and others in supporting rebel forces in the south, the Jordanian government took steps toward normalizing relations with the Syrian government shortly thereafter. This shift in the refugee host state's political strategy meant that the international autonomy of Syria's nonviolent actors, which it had limited for years, was subsequently all but blocked.

Contention and conflict in Syria before, during, and shortly after the 2011 uprising set the stage for the entry of international aid actors onto the scene of the crisis. Those aid responses unfolded differently, in line with the conflict developments that preceded them. In certain spaces, international aid actors enjoyed more autonomy to pursue their objectives than in others, and they did so with and through civil actors on the ground in Syria and in refuge with consequential effects on their wartime activism. By necessity, this chapter is not a comprehensive history of the Syrian uprising or war. I cannot hope to give proper attention to many topics. These include analysis of armed actors and battlefield developments, conflict resolution processes attempted by the Arab League and the United Nations, and the relatively more successful local ceasefire processes overseen by Turkey, Russia, and Iran that froze conflict lines from 2020 to 2024. I am also giving little attention to the everyday experiences of refugees and internally displaced people, or the harrowing journeys some took to reach safety in Europe. Many books can and should be written about Syria's war. My modest contribution aims to shed some light on the extraordinary actions of its nonviolent participants and the manner in which outside actors affected their trajectories.

3
THE FACILITATING PROCESS

Sana joined her first demonstration in August 2011 at Aleppo University.[1] She was a first-year student at a private college outside the city, but the eponymous university of Syria's second city had become a protest hot spot. Sana's parents warned her that a revolution in Syria would be bloody, but their intrepid daughter not only participated, she also joined local coordination committees to organize dissent actions—which were often repressed in the manner her parents had predicted.

As areas around her came under the control of competing regime and rebel armed actors in 2012, Sana adapted. She passed through multiple checkpoints to attend college classes and pivoted to humanitarianism to address the repercussions of violence. As she saw it, humanitarian work was "also revolutionary. . . . We who participated in the revolution, in a way we feel responsible for the suffering of the people." Local schools in government-held western Aleppo, where Sana resided, had been repurposed to house internally displaced people from the rebel-held east of the city; schools in the east had been repurposed to support Free Syrian Army operations. The activists opened secret schools and Sana offered psychosocial support to children through play and reading.

Her crossings to the east were complicated by the pressure Islamist rebels put on Sana to wear a hijab. Soon the risky crossing from west to east was closed. Still motivated, Sana began working with a local organization that predated the uprising, but that had developed significantly to assist IDPs thanks to a partnership with a UN agency. Based as it was in government-held territory, the administration was managed by regime supporters, which eventually drove Sana away. In

2014, she found a position as a health volunteer for another UN agency. Sana joined a team carrying out home visits and documenting health conditions. The position came with a significant stipend: It became "a known fact that the pay from international organizations was better than anything else," she said.

But armed checkpoints, water stoppages, electricity cuts, fear of kidnapping, and continuous arrests of activists were all taking their toll. When her family's apartment building was struck by the FSA in 2015, they fled to Turkey. Sana's friends in Gaziantep, in southern Turkey, were "all working for organizations." They taught her how to apply online ("in Aleppo, applications were still paper") and she accepted a position as a hygiene promotion officer for a large INGO serving Syrian refugees in Turkey.

It was the first time Sana's activism was not directed toward Aleppo. When the project ended, she began working for another INGO, this time "remotely"—tasked with promoting nutrition and hygiene in rebel-held territory through a team of field-workers. Yet Sana began to worry that, in the security of refuge, she'd grown "distant from the revolution." Revolutionary Aleppo, moreover, was held by extreme Islamist rebels before it was ultimately reclaimed by regime forces, backed by Russian airpower, at the end of 2016. By then Sana had received an award from a US organization that would fund a scholarship for her to pursue a master's degree abroad. But she vowed she'd return. Revolutionaries like her "haven't given up," Sana contended. "We are just in a hard period right now."

How could nonviolent actors like Sana persist in the face of so many challenges? War zones are violent and uncertain places, yet activists' sheer conviction and resilience might animate their engagements even when violence is rife. But wars drag on. Since 1945 the average civil war has lasted ten years (Walter 2013). With the passage of time and the associated compounding of needs, deepening of political divisions, physical and security threats, and quotidian demands on civilians to make a living, participation in civil action becomes harder to explain. Individual activists may disengage due to exhaustion, disillusionment, or simply from concern with their professional and familial needs. If individual disengagements pile up, whole movements can demobilize (Fillieule 2015). In times of war and repression, few would be surprised to observe nonviolent actors gradually give up their activism to pursue other life projects—or merely to survive.

Nevertheless, persistent participation in civil action during war often occurs. For example, in Yemen, domestic and international armed actors battled for years after the country's 2011 uprising. Needs became overwhelming in what was already a poor country. By 2017, more than three-quarters of Yemen's population needed humanitarian assistance; more than one-third were in "acute need" (OCHA Yemen 2017). Yet years later, Yemeni women were still engaged in nonviolent action, which was far from routine in a highly gender-segregated and violence-afflicted society. They participated in advocacy for conflict resolution, community-based activism, informal education, and humanitarian relief (Gawfi et al. 2020).

International aid can facilitate participation in such nonviolent action during war. International aid organizations fashion complex conflict responses to contemporary crises. Reflecting their logistical and operational needs, and sometimes their "localization" and "participatory" objectives, they often engage local actors in international undertakings (Mohan and Stokke 2000; Fiddian-Qasmiyeh 2018). Some scholars promote such international-local engagement as a normatively and practically desirable approach to intervention (Autesserre 2014; Konyndyk and Worden 2019).[2] They contend that local actors can be key to the success of international actors seeking to resolve conflict and build peace (Autesserre 2021; Campbell 2018; Mac Ginty 2014).

But how are those potentially productive relations established in the first place? Those Yemeni women referenced above, who are engaging in "quotidian practices of peace-building" against the odds of insecurity and patriarchy, were seen by international aid actors as "providers of data" for needs assessments, *not* as peacebuilders (Yadav 2020). The connections forged between international aid actors and local activists are not a given: International aid actors do not simply arrive and proceed to build on and enhance activists' action.

The development of relations between international and local actors is a process that requires explanation. The theory of civilizing contention makes it possible to understand how nonviolent action can persist years into a crisis. International aid organizations facilitate local participation in crisis response in those times and places in which they enjoy autonomy and access to ground-level civil actors. In those cases, international aid organizations activate processes of change among those local actors first by establishing social, material, and infrastructural relations with them. International aid actors cultivate social linkages with locals to gain information about needs in the conflict, material linkages to enable locals to carry out international objectives, and infrastructural linkages to direct organized action through international channels. These relations help international aid actors achieve their objectives. At the same time, they facilitate the participation of activists in nonviolent action even amid violence and years into a crisis. They do so through mechanisms that constitute local actors as crisis responders and allocate them the capacity and channels through which to act as such.

Through process tracing, this theory seeks to understand how aid facilitates nonviolent action in war through a relationship-building process in the Syrian case. International humanitarians established relations during the Syrian war through a set of social, infrastructural, and material linkages. Local organizations grew and persisted in those spaces where humanitarians enjoyed relatively high levels of autonomy: in rebel-held northwest Syria and across the border in Turkey. Still, international-local relationships are not inevitable: Syrian activist organizations connected with international actors in some conflict-affected spaces but not in others. In turn, participation in nonviolent action was higher in certain spaces than in others. While relations built between international and local organizations are not the only explanation for Syrians' participation in civil action throughout the war, those relations were a critical driver of that participation. The lengths to which international aid organizations will go to gain access and build relations with activists is apparent in the case of a besieged region of Rural Damascus. A local case study shows that international aid organizations should be taken seriously in the study of civilian agency during war.

Participation in Civil Action in the Syrian War

To make the case that international aid facilitates activist participation during war, it is necessary to show that Syrians participated in nonviolent action throughout their country's conflict. There are numerous challenges to a proper auditing of Syrian organizations both in rebel-held territory and in refuge. In rebel-held territory, many local organizations were not formally or legally registered. Those that worked with or received support from international actors often retained anonymity to protect themselves from armed actors or attacks. In neighboring countries, Syrian organizations were similarly not formally registered, or they were registered by host country nationals—complicating a view of them as "Syrian" organizations. Indeed, the situation of Syrian aid workers and organizations in refugee host countries is characterized by legal precarity and shifting political landscapes. Syrians in Jordan, for example, were rarely granted work permits and were often engaged by INGOs on a "voluntary" (but paid) basis. Turkey, however, was permissive in the early years of the conflict: The government did not consistently require foreign organizations to acquire work permits, legally register, or abide by other, often demanding, labor regulations. When Turkey did begin to enforce regulations, it scrutinized international organizations more than Syrian ones, although eventually the uncertainty affected everyone (Badran 2020).

An additional obstacle to a proper audit of the population of Syrian organizations lies in the financial reporting practices of humanitarian assistance agencies that aim to protect local organizations' security. OCHA's Financial Tracking Service provides information on funding flows associated with the two major UN response plans for the Syria crisis. Typical of the publicly available reports is the lack of detail with regard to the funding of local organizations, often due to protective anonymizing practices. Tens and sometimes hundreds of millions of dollars are directed at destination organizations categorized in the public record as "NGOs," which may be international or local. Likewise, reports of country-based pooled funds, namely the Syria Cross-Border Humanitarian Fund, dedicated explicitly to localization efforts, provide no public detail beyond broad organizational types such as "national NGO," and do not record all recipients.

Despite the lack of this pertinent data, there are clear indicators of growth in the population of Syrian organizations over the years of the conflict. Citizens for Syria, a Syrian NGO that emerged after 2011, observes that in the six years between 2011 and 2017, the number of newly founded Syrian civil society organizations (CSOs) exceeded the total registered in Syria in the five decades from 1959 to 2011. That is, it took Syrians just six years of war to create as many civil organizations as they had during half a century of authoritarian rule. Their audit identified about a thousand CSOs and surveyed 748 of them, excluding the many local governance institutions that also emerged during the war. According to their count, a plurality of these Syrian organizations were based in rebel-held territory; among those based outside Syria or with a separate managerial office, a plurality was based in Turkey (Alzouabi and Iyad 2017). Killian Clarke and Gözde Guran have estimated that thousands of Syrian organizations and informal initiatives emerged across Turkey. In the southern Turkish town of Reyhanli, population sixty thousand, forty-seven Syrian initiatives were counted; in another village of just six thousand inhabitants, as many as sixteen independent Syrian organizations were founded (2016). In other words, Syria's activists did not just disappear or take up arms when the conflict militarized. Of course, they did not sustain mass collective action either: Protest events did subside as early as late 2011 (Mazur 2019). But in line with the above counting exercises, Facebook data suggests that participation in nonviolent action persisted and the number of organizations grew.[3]

Figure 6 charts the cumulative establishment of public Facebook pages associated with groups engaging in nonviolent action that ranges from advocacy for detainees to underground clinics. The pages in the dataset were not only or even primarily established around the 2011 uprising. In fact, 60 percent of pages were created between 2012 and 2014—a period characterized by "savagery of ghoulish proportions," during which armed groups were proliferating (Baker 2013). The curve did not flatten until 2017.[4] During this time the nature of mobilization shifted away from protests and toward other engagements. Contention has phases, "differing rhythms" in its course (Beissinger 2002). What is the rhythm of nonviolent action when international aid actors come onto the stage?

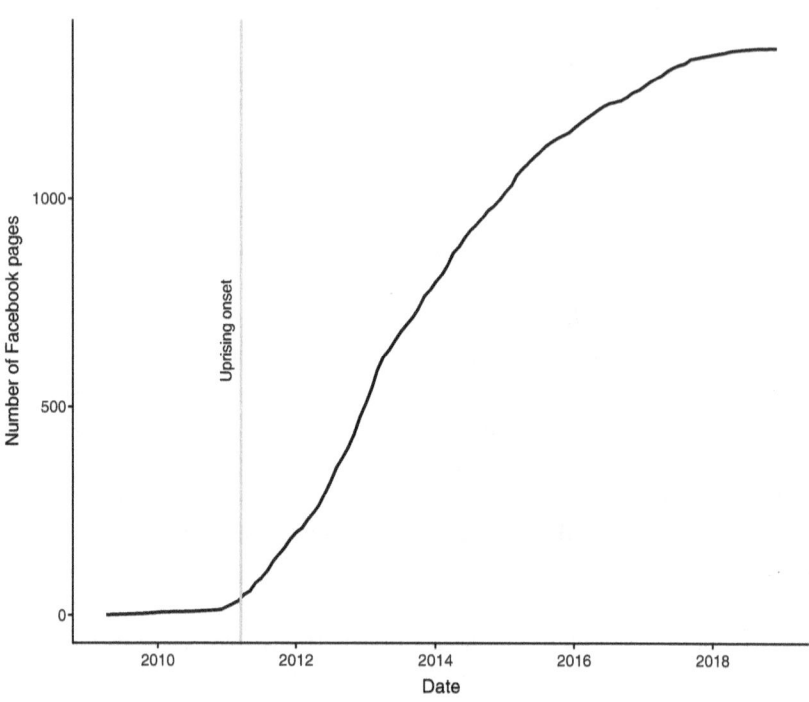

FIGURE 6. Cumulative Facebook page creations. Vertical line at March 2011 uprising onset. Source: Author's original data.

Facilitating Relations

International aid responses to the crisis reflected the ways that nonviolence and violence unfolded from 2011, especially the division of territorial control. Multiple governing authorities shaped the autonomy of aid actors in different territories. The Syrian regime blocked the provision of aid to rebel-held territory, leading many aid organizations to erect cross-border responses for these areas from Turkey and Jordan. Syrian refugees also fled to these neighboring countries, prompting refugee-specific humanitarian responses, as well. Where international aid organizations were least constrained by governing authorities, namely in Turkey and in the areas of limited statehood across the border in northwest Syria, they enjoyed the greatest autonomy in working with and through local actors to carry out their objectives. In the process, international aid organizations built social, infrastructural, and material relations with local activists that helped sustain participation in civil action throughout the war.

Social Relations

Humanitarians knew there was a crisis of needs in Syria but they struggled to assess them with precision from the start. "In mid-2012, eighteen months into the crisis in Syria, most actors agreed that the picture of the humanitarian situation was incoherent and fragmented" (Parham et al. 2013, 29) due to issues of access, insecurity, and a lack of coordination (SNAP 2013). In this context, evaluators of the UN-led response reported that "the UN did not know what much of the need was or where it was" (Sida et al. 2016, 21). Syrians, however, with their local contacts, language, information, and access, were well-placed to know and assess needs (SNAP 2013). To get a handle on the crisis, international aid actors, therefore, forged social relations with Syrians.

As international actors arrived in neighboring countries to access refugees and rebel-held territory, they connected with activist networks in the border regions. This was "the only realistic way to increase aid in the rebel zones," Médecins Sans Frontières explained (Weissman 2013). For example, a Syrian activist in Jordan described his smuggling of medical supplies into southern Syria: His operation grew when a Western government's embassy reached out to him. "They wanted to help us with our work," he said.[5] In Turkey, diasporic Syrian medical organizations merged in 2012 to provide wartime relief in northern Syria. They developed their local contacts inside Syria and created a "referral system for international NGOs seeking to establish a presence inside opposition-held territory" (Hammodeh and Cheung 2013).

Political aid actors also pursued social linkages with opposition actors to help achieve their objectives, be those toppling the regime or pursuing a political process (Phillips 2016). However, governments like the United States initially had almost no ties to local activists inside Syria, so they headed to Turkey, where they connected with diaspora Syrians who established a political opposition body that became the National Coalition for Syrian Revolutionary and Opposition Forces (the Opposition Coalition).[6] A large bloc of countries calling themselves the "friends of Syria" deemed the Opposition Coalition to be the "legitimate representative" of the Syrian people. Donors went on to channel hundreds of millions of dollars in humanitarian, economic, and military aid into it or indirectly to related efforts (Sayigh 2013), but factionalism over representation of competing donor interests, together with the Opposition Coalition's distance from the ground in Syria, left the exiled opposition with a "major problem of legitimacy" (Alsarraj and Hoffman 2020). Although Western governments and diaspora organizations established social linkages with each other, those linkages were more distant than the connections being forged at the local level.

While high-level connections floundered, social connections on the ground were growing. In particular, international aid organizations perceived that local activists with ground-level connections could be crisis responders. International actors recognized that "simply being Syrian," as the more distant members of the diaspora were, was "not enough to gain access in the absence of a solid local network and the provision of effective, reliable, timely, and relevant assistance that brings tangible results" (Haddad and Svoboda 2017). But how could international organizations connect with those in rebel-held Syria, and how could they turn them into crisis responders?

International aid organizations could not and would not establish social relations with every individual activist. Instead, those local actors who presented themselves as organized aid responders were those with whom international organizations could connect. A medical doctor who described traveling from rebel-held territory in northwest Syria to Turkey to secure funding reveals how activists were constituted as aid organizations through these relations:

> The hospital used to provide services free of cost, and the funds were coming from donations. But the director of the hospital knew it would not last long like this. So as individuals we began trying to reach out to funders, to organizations that were present in Turkey at the time. That's why I had come to Turkey. We, a group of doctors [in Syria], were in need so I came out here. Here I felt that organizations don't want to work with me as an individual. I am just one person, but if we are a group with a structure and organization, then it's easier.[7]

As a representative of a medical organization, rather than an individual doctor, he was better able to relate to international organizations who could help fund their efforts inside Syria.

Even while Syrians were being constituted as aid responders, the conflict posed major challenges. Cross-border relations with Syrians inside rebel-held territory were particularly hard to build—but all the more important given humanitarian needs. As security conditions worsened, remote management came to characterize the cross-border response: Syrians "in the field" carried out the activities of organizations that remained at a distance, often in Turkey. Somewhat ironically, this situation deepened the importance of social relations: Internationals' "lack of direct access brought to the fore the role of local organizations" (Haddad and Svoboda 2017). Members of war-afflicted communities could better cultivate "community acceptance" of the aid products that international actors could provision (Haddad and Svoboda 2017).

In this context, Syrian refugees became brokers between international remote managers and Syrians "in the field," that is, inside Syria. An international staffer from a UN agency noted the acquisition of soft skills among Syrians in Gaziantep in southern Turkey. The "first challenge that by now they have overcome," he explained, "was understanding the jargon of donors, of the UN, and of INGOs. Now you have Syrian staff living abroad that can speak the language."[8] The point here is not just that shared languages and jargon were useful for meeting the demands of international aid organizations and securing resources, but that these direct connections were a critical component of constitutive social relations.

Despite the social connections between international actors and Syrians unfolding in Gaziantep, relations with civil actors inside the country developed somewhat uneasily. International actors often wondered if they could trust locals who were at a distance. For example, an international staff member of an INGO reflected that in those facilities where the INGO implemented programs indirectly through local organizations, "They don't understand donor regulations and they are a huge financial risk for us. . . . We could lose millions of dollars, so it's better to implement directly."[9] Some of these social trust obstacles would be overcome through the rules of international aid organizations.

While international aid actors sought to build social relations with locals to achieve their objectives, these nascent relations were bidirectional and coconstitutive. Syrians, for their part, often sought to serve their own interests through international actors. Ali Hamdan found that among Syrians in Turkey, those who were part of the uprising became engaged in practices like conducting needs assessments that made the conflict more legible to international interveners; these same practices served the communities these Syrian activists sought to uplift (2020). The social relations of international and local actors each had meaning in relationship to the other: International actors needed access, information, and implementation, while activists needed support for their efforts to engender change amid violence. Underlying this social relation, however, was a power imbalance. In the words of the medical doctor above, who later became a coordinator of Syrian NGOs in Turkey: For international actors, "It's business, a job. For us, it's life."[10]

Infrastructural Relations

Constituted as potential crisis responders, Syrian activists would be ushered into the infrastructural channels of crisis response through an allocation mechanism that gave Syrians spaces to behave as crisis responders. Beginning in 2012, INGOs established coordination mechanisms, working with nascent Syrian organizations engaged in aid delivery in the border regions. These cross-border responses became UN-sanctioned and formalized in 2014 through Security Council Resolution 2165, which allowed for cross-border operations from Turkey and Jordan with only notification to, rather than permission from, the government of Syria. Security Council Resolution 2165 enabled the "Whole of Syria" approach, consisting of coordination across "hubs" in Jordan, Turkey, and Syria, and would clear the way for the delivery of assistance to areas in rebel-held territory from border countries. Following 2165, OCHA assumed the work of coordination previously done by INGOs, establishing their cluster system to organize multiple forms of humanitarian aid. The OCHA "cluster" approach refers to groups of UN and non-UN humanitarian organizations that coordinate sectors such as food security, health, camps, and nutrition. From within these formal clusters, Syrian organizations participated in the many sectors of humanitarianism.

Telling evidence of the effect of these infrastructural channels on local participation comes from monthly reports of cross-border operations coordinated by OCHA. Partner organizations from Turkey, which included organizations across the border in northern Syria, increased from forty-nine in April 2014 when formal operations began, to more than four hundred in December 2017. The top panel of figure 7 demonstrates this organizational growth in Turkey, where partners increased dramatically, versus in Jordan, where only a handful of partners were engaged over the entire period.

The bottom panel of figure 7 shows that beneficiary items delivered into southern Syria through cross-border operations from Jordan are clearly lower in number than those sent into the north from Turkey. However, two points are worth noting about these differences. First, increases in cross-border deliveries from Jordan do not lead to corresponding increases in partners. That is, even when more items are sent in, there are no more partner organizations delivering or implementing them. Second, variabilities in cross-border deliveries from Turkey also do not translate to variabilities in partners. That is, local organizational partners in northern Syria increase rather consistently even when aid items decline, plateau, or increase. In other words, the number of partner organizations for the cross-border response is not a direct reflection of the quantity of aid, but rather of the fact that it was channeled more easily into international infrastructure for the response from Turkey.

The identity of these hundreds of organizations is anonymous in formal reports. Can we know for sure that these are Syrian organizations, not international ones? An OCHA representative in Turkey, asked about the increase, confirmed that they are "primarily Syrian organizations."[11] He explained: "Literally all humanitarian work between nonstate armed territory is run by Syrians. In the northwest, there are only Syrians on the ground providing assistance." That is, the hundreds of humanitarian organizations engaging through the institutional channels of the OCHA-led response from Turkey were local, Syrian groups, which demonstrates that international infrastructure can powerfully channel

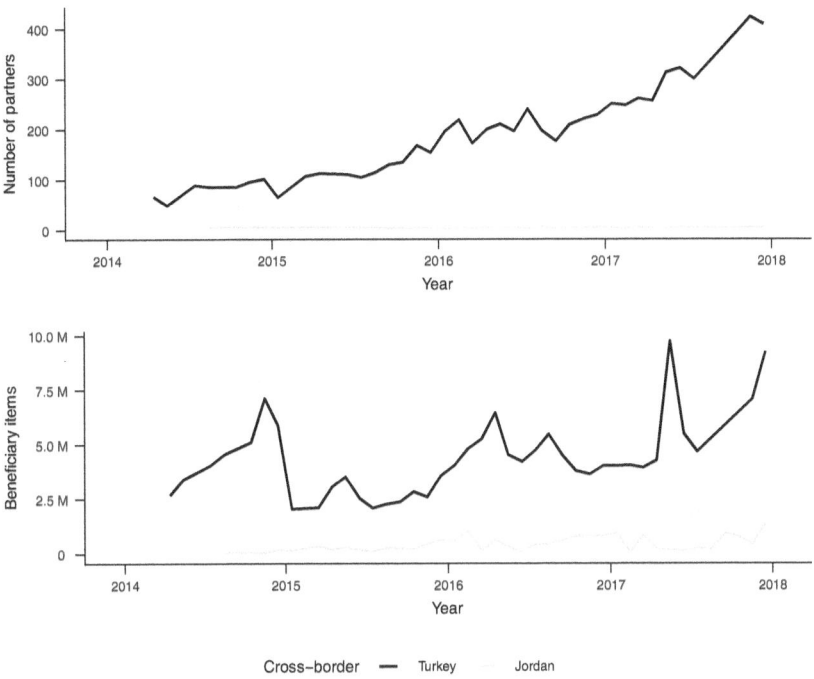

FIGURE 7. OCHA cross-border operations from Turkey and Jordan, 2014–2018. Source: Public reports from OCHA, data extracted and compiled by author from https://www.humanitarianresponse.info/en/operations/stima.

nonviolent action—where those internationals enjoy autonomy and can build relations.

Additional international infrastructure was erected explicitly targeting local organizations for incorporation into the formal response. According to the UN, the multi-donor Syria Cross-Border Pooled Fund was established in 2014 to "enable humanitarian partners, particularly Syrian organizations, to expand and support the delivery of humanitarian assistance across border and conflict lines" (OCHA 2018). Among those projects allocated to Syrian NGOs, more than three hundred was granted to Aleppo and more than four hundred to Idlib, both in Syria's northwest, an area across the border from international actors congregated in Turkey and a place where Syria's nonviolent and violent movements coincided. The next largest recipient of projects, Rural Damascus, received fewer than fifty.

Within the more political and nonhumanitarian international response, institutional channels were created to organize the development of hundreds of local councils across rebel-held territory, including through the donor-backed and diaspora-led Opposition Coalition. As one analysis explained, in order "to synchronize" local council initiatives, "improve their efficacy, and tie their work more directly to external political opposition structures," an organization that became known as the Local Administrative Council Unit, which had "links to the Syrian Opposition Council," was created in March 2013 (Menapolis 2013). One of the original members of a local council in Deir ez-Zor explained: "The Coalition created something called the representatives of the local councils . . . and those members started contacting the provinces to create local councils. We didn't even hear about local councils, we didn't know what they were. . . . They would get in touch and they caused the creation of these local councils."[12] Excluded from the channels of the Syrian government, Syrian activists were channeled into infrastructural frameworks backed by international actors.

Material Relations

Material relations were an additional linkage forged between international and local actors in the Syrian context. New Syrian organizations often emerged in response to the availability of funds and to the general zeitgeist of international aid. Like infrastructural relations, material linkages established between international and local actors operated through an allocation mechanism that gave Syrians the capacity to participate. Arguably, there was a conspicuous boom in Syrian civil society organizations during the war. While activists initially received support from businesspeople and diaspora networks, as an international democracy promotion contractor in Turkey explained, "It wasn't in the amounts they wanted, it was too small." Beginning in 2013, however, "You saw the emergence of civil society organizations. Whoever had time, would open one. . . . And frankly, a lot of international organizations played a role in this, by way of the support that they gave. . . . They would say: 'Write a project proposal.' [And CSOs] would write a proposal."[13]

Shifts from informal or diasporic support to formal or international support also transpired at the individual level. Across sectors, the introduction of salaries by international actors was a significant departure from the "phase of voluntarism" that colored the uprising and the early period of the conflict, as one governance activist described it.[14] In 2013 when his town in Idlib came under rebel control, civilians established a local council, on which he sat. He explained that they received monetary support from their townsmen in Saudi Arabia to provide goods and services, but the council members themselves were volunteers. Regular remuneration would have exceeded the ability of those nontraditional donors, especially as time passed. Eventually, diasporic supporters of the local council "became exhausted": "They didn't anticipate this length of time.

You know, their salaries are limited. They were trying to offer and support their people in the hope that the thing would end quickly. They can't keep raising these large amounts."[15]

Though voluntarism persisted, individual-level remuneration eventually became standard within most Syrian organizations when more traditional aid actors, especially international humanitarian and development organizations, entered the scene (Alzouabi and Iyad 2017; Building Markets 2018). An activist in Dar'a described his reaction the first time he received payment for his work for a development organization: "When that came, I was surprised! I felt I was selling the country. That's how we all were back then."[16] Of course, remuneration was highly warranted compensation for the critical and risky work carried out almost exclusively by Syrians.

From 2013 to 2017, annual funding appeals for the UN response plans for the Syria crisis, one for inside the country and the other for refugees and the countries hosting them, were among the largest ever made by UN humanitarian agencies; donor commitments, though they fell short of the appeals, were also among the largest on record (Urquhart 2019). Within these plans, donor funds were contracted and subcontracted to numerous agencies and implementing partners. By 2019, funds were reaching hundreds of known destination organizations and unknown numbers of unspecified NGOs whose identities were concealed for security reasons.[17] The data cannot tell us which partner organizations were funded through the cross-border responses and which through the Damascus "hub" in government-held territory. Survey research and audits, however, provide some clues as to the extent of resource transfers to Syrian organizations engaged in rebel-held territory and in refuge. For instance, among nearly three hundred surveyed Syrian organizations in Turkey, 40 percent reported receiving support from INGOs, 20 percent from UN agencies, 16 percent from Turkish NGOs, and 15 percent from donor governments (Building Markets 2018).

Additionally, mechanisms were established to transfer resources directly to local organizations. Allocations made to Syrian organizations through the Syria Cross-Border Pooled Fund increased over the conflict years, as shown in figure 8. This data does not indicate whether the number of recipient organizations was increasing, whether the funds were increasing while the number of recipient organizations remained stable, or both. It is clear, however, that material relations between international and local organizations were growing.

The process by which resource transfers fed into organizational growth also colored the creation of oppositional governance bodies. A development worker noted that local councils—initially targeted by his American development agency to support anti-regime activism—were emerging precisely because Syrians understood them to be targets of international aid. "You had all these local

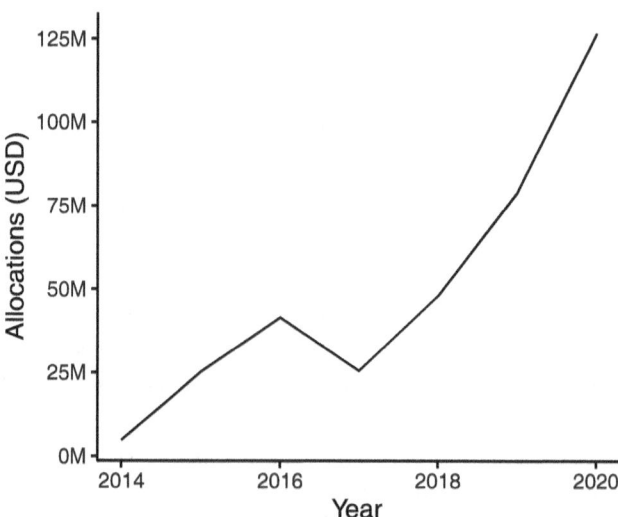

FIGURE 8. Annual allocations to "national NGOs" from OCHA's Syria Cross-Border Pooled Fund. Source: Public data compiled by author from the UN's Country Based Pooled Funds Data Hub, https://cbpf.data.unocha.org/dataexplorer.html.

councils popping up," he explained. "They'd see [that] and think, 'oh, if I want assistance, I need to create a local council.'"[18] Figure 9 shows large spikes in Facebook pages representing governance institutions following the establishment of the Opposition Coalition. Donors had urged the coalition to support the establishment of local councils inside the country.

To be clear, material relations facilitated participation in nonviolent action, but the associated resource transfers were not equitable. Syrians implemented most aid projects but received little direct funding (Els et al. 2016). They assumed risk while internationals remained protected abroad (Scott 2022). Ultimately, Syrian organizations would exert significant energy and time navigating an "NGO scramble" (Cooley and Ron 2002) that they were largely brought into by international aid organizations.

Civil Action Under Siege

Theory-building process tracing demonstrates that institutional processes activated by international aid facilitate local participation in wartime activism. A skeptic might point to an endogeneity problem: International aid might facilitate activism where conditions for nonviolent action are already favorable. But

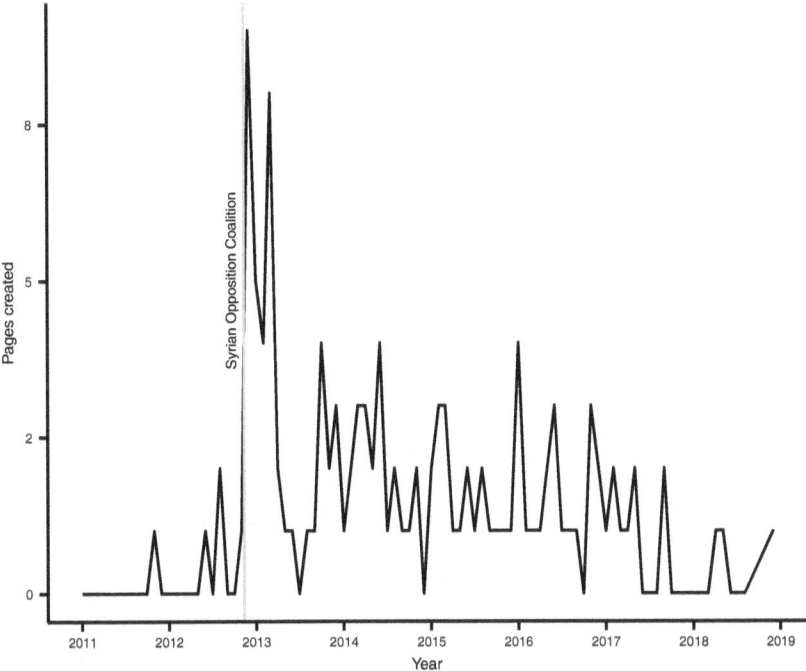

FIGURE 9. Governance (mostly local council) Facebook page creations by month. The vertical line represents November 2012, when the diasporic opposition was restructured as the Syrian Opposition Coalition. Source: Author's original data.

where armed groups are hegemonic, repression and violence are overwhelming, or conflict processes render the original political impetus for activism irrelevant, civilian engagement will remain limited. Activism developed in areas from where the authoritarian regime withdrew—a logic reflected by Syrians dubbing these "liberated" territories. Accordingly, the establishment of civil society groups "coincides in many cases with the ending of government control in the respective region . . . a context that afforded them greater freedom to do so" (Khalaf et al. 2014). The inverse is also asserted: Civil groups were subsequently constrained where extremist groups assumed territorial control and under the general constraints of armed conflict (Elhamoui and al-Hawat 2015; Khalaf et al. 2014).

It is true that international aid is targeted based on the ease of getting local actors involved, hence the role of autonomy and access in creating the conditions that facilitate local participation. Nevertheless, this potential endogeneity problem presents a chance to explore the boundaries of these conditions. Do international actors only establish relations when activists are particularly easy to reach and ready to connect with them? Or do aid organizations try to establish connections with local actors even when doing so is difficult and activists are hard to reach?

The case of besiegement, in this instance in the Eastern Ghouta region of Rural Damascus Governorate, demonstrates that aid organizations can facilitate activism even in the face of severe structural threats and thus, even where we may not expect it. Eastern Ghouta was characterized by significant internal and external structural threats during the war. First, external threats were severe. Syrian pro-government forces imposed a siege on the area for more than five years, which the UN described as "barbaric and medieval," characterized by "near daily bombardments and extreme deprivations" (OHCHR 2018). Second, Eastern Ghouta was "among the most militarized rebel strongholds in the country," presided over by Zahran Alloush, the Salafi leader of the Jaish al-Islam armed group, a "firebrand preacher" who "hoped to build an Islamist mini-state ruled by sharia law" (Lund 2016, 2017b). Threats in this context were stacked against nonviolent actors—a point made clear by the late 2013 disappearance and presumed deaths of the "Douma Four." The Douma Four were activists whose secularism and contacts with Western governments is believed to have cost them their lives, allegedly at the direction of Alloush.

And yet, civilians in Ghouta participated in nonviolent action. In part, their action was an extension of rebel governance, such as the judiciary institutions that were manned by civilians. Critically, they also acted separately from armed groups and with support from the international response. UN agencies generally lacked the flexibility and appetite for risk needed to bypass the siege, but more supple INGOs and nonhumanitarian aid actors assisted activists throughout the siege years. With the support of the donor-backed Opposition Coalition, activists in Ghouta selected a governorate and local councils (Turkmani et al. 2015). USAID's Office of Transition Initiatives managed to transfer nearly $1 million USD to local councils in Eastern Ghouta in the siege years for which data is available (Carnegie et al. 2022). A separate project promoting good governance, run by a UK-contracted development company, was cautiously implemented thanks to social relations with local actors. A Syrian activist involved from Jordan explained that the donor was initially reluctant to work in such a challenging context, but was convinced by Syrian staff to set an example of good governance close to the capital city.[19]

One of the Douma Four founded an organization that remained active in the years after her kidnapping. It received international resources to pay the salaries of local council members and fund their projects, to support women's participation and leadership, to train and coach other local organizations, to increase participation in and inclusiveness of local decision-making processes, and even to support projects in another rebel-held governorate (IATI 2019). Another organization—administratively managed by Syrian activists in Turkey—received support from Western donors to run agricultural projects and a medical project that employed seven hundred people (Turkmani et al. 2015). More than twenty hospitals and health centers in Ghouta received monetary support from MSF throughout the siege, including one featured in an Oscar-nominated documentary film, *The Cave*. Under bombardment, treating patients subjected to apparent chemical attacks and navigating the underground tunnels of the hospital, the brave physician at the heart of the film received support for her hospital's monthly expenses from INGOs (MSF 2020).

Structural constraints did impede aid and its associated mechanisms in important ways. Given the UN's absence, the aid infrastructure was not formally institutionalized. INGOs and nonhumanitarian aid actors behaved rather flexibly rather than through the formal infrastructure erected elsewhere in the warscape. One activist involved with a governance project explained that donors "got around the siege," as others did, through underground tunnels and by proffering US dollars at checkpoints.[20] Another, involved with a relief organization in the area, explained that support from INGOs reached her group and others once they paid informal "transfer fees" imposed by war profiteers on both sides of the siege.[21] This suggests that infrastructural relations with local actors were necessarily tenuous because of the siege and thus generated less change than they might have otherwise.

These limits on formal international infrastructure may well be related to the reputation of Ghouta activists as particularly creative and resilient (Angelova 2014; Hallaj 2017). Such a reputation is also associated with the humanitarian wings of the Eritrean and Tigrayan rebel groups opposed to the Ethiopian government, with whom INGOs, but *not* the United Nations, connected with through cross-border operations from Sudan (Prendergast and Duffield 1994). Those decentralized aid operations to rebel-held areas in Eritrea and Tigray were characterized by relative informality in the UN's absence and apparently did not alter the fundamentally political motives of local nonviolent actors (Prendergast and Duffield 1994).

The siege of Eastern Ghouta was deadly and devastating, but the case suggests that aid organizations put significant effort toward intervening even in highly threatening structural environments. As Peter Andreas has dramatically illustrated in the case of besieged Sarajevo, even these spaces can be arenas of interaction between international and local actors (Andreas 2008). Relations between international and local actors do not simply manifest naturally or automatically. Accordingly, the development of these relations should not be taken for granted. Instead, the theory of civilizing contention explains this development.

When contention turns violent, nonviolent action does not necessarily disappear. Nor do international aid actors mechanically build on and enhance the efforts of nonviolent activists to respond to crises. International and local actors meet, as organizations, in the dynamic transnational spaces of contemporary war zones, and the former forge social, infrastructural, and material linkages with the latter in order to achieve their objectives. Through the everyday routines of crisis response, international aid organizations transform wartime activism—constituting crisis responders and facilitating their ability to remain active despite the unforgiving contexts in which they operate. A close analysis of a local case probed the boundaries of a key scope condition—international aid autonomy—and showed that international aid actors engage in deliberate efforts to reach and forge relations with local nonviolent actors. Syrians were also agents of change in these interactive relationship-building processes.

The empirical analysis in this chapter identified sources of variation in the strength of international-local linkages, including those related to host-state strategies and the embeddedness of local actors in conflict communities. In the Syrian case, these factors produced strong relationships in and across from the host state that allowed greater international aid autonomy, Turkey. Syrian activists in Turkey and in Syria's rebel-held northwest founded a large number of civil organizations as they were channeled into the international crisis response.

The facilitating process is the first of three processes in generating *civilized contention*. It explains the formation of civil organizations, facilitated by international aid actors attempting to get a handle on the conflict and ways to engage in it. These emergent civil organizations ultimately constitute something like a civil society, although civil society, by definition, requires protection from a state. When something like a civil society is built during war to serve humanitarian ends, not only do civil organizations lack state protection—they may become subject to targeting and repression by the state and other armed actors. After all, they are operating in violently divided contexts from which claims of neutrality are insufficient shields. There are reasons that aid rules insist on those shields anyway.

4

THE FORMALIZING PROCESS

Rami and his friends had traversed fraught boundaries to act on behalf of their Damascus community before 2011, in a country where "there was no such thing as civil activism."[1] Their volunteer visits to an orphanage were successful. A street cleaning campaign ended with several arrests. Carrying out even the most quotidian forms of action under the Asad regime could risk crossing red lines and might fail to persuade people to act collectively.

When the uprising began, Rami again experimented with informal, diffuse forms of activism. He joined a local coordination committee that organized demonstrations but struggled to organize sit-ins and boycotts. He pursued a campaign of small-scale actions that could reach wide audiences, like dying the water of public fountains and hanging revolutionary flags around town, but his LCC's efforts to coordinate across communities was challenging: "Maybe our approach wasn't successful, and maybe people's awareness was not well developed," he reflects. Eventually, several LCCs did manage to coordinate a strike that saw businesses shutter in small cities and towns across the country. Yet as Rami persisted in civil resistance, the risks of punishment grew. In 2013, he was arrested.

Rami suffered a year-long detention in the regime's prisons. Upon his release, he escaped to Lebanon and began to grasp that "the phase of the revolution had ended; it had turned to organizational work." Rami got involved in an organization that his friends had founded to provide psychosocial support to children after shelling began in Rural Damascus. Rami participated remotely from Lebanon and saw the group's remit expand to include education and child protection, a shift motivated by revolutionary visions: "The goal of the organization was to create a Syrian society in which children enjoyed their rights," Rami said. "If we can create this among children, this will change the whole society in the future."

Lebanon, however, limited international autonomy and did not permit Syrians to register organizations. The group wanted to register "for the sake of relations with donors, INGOs, and accepting money through a formal bank." The board decided that their external office should be in Gaziantep, so Rami set off for the southern Turkish city and launched "a significant organizational phase in the life" of the once informal and underground group. In the past, "We could pass by each other and not know who we are in Damascus." Now Rami was overseeing the development of administrative offices like human resources and finance.

He was also deepening relations with INGOs that were enjoying autonomy in Turkey. He explained: "Our relationships developed in 2015 and after. We were trying to look for INGOs that specialize in child protection, to learn from them and try to build strategic relationships with them that will last a long period." These relationships were "very formal," he said, and there was something "shared among all the donors that, for the most part, they are unable to be close to the context." Skepticism among donors toward the local actors they now worked with led to seemingly unreasonable demands on people working in conflict zones, like insisting on original paper receipts for transactions in rebel-held areas rather than photographs of those receipts.

Yet Rami, who code-switched to English when using organizational terms, effectively navigated the UN's coordination structure, which brought together this burgeoning population of hundreds of Syrian civil organizations to coordinate humanitarian efforts inside Syria. In his view, many of these new organizations needed greater capacity-building than international aid organizations could offer, but under his own capable leadership, Rami's organization secured projects that allowed him to make not just operational decisions, but long-term strategic plans. He did this even as the organization faced the persistent challenge of shelling, in addition to siege, and "tightening from armed groups."

The staff in Syria grew to over three hundred and the organization's work expanded to additional rebel-held areas as well. Adhering to humanitarian principles, he avows they would have impartially served children in government-held areas too if the regime had allowed it. Projects had to stop periodically due to regime shelling. "This happened so many times that I can't remember the number," he said. The team in Gaziantep, meanwhile, was part of a crisis milieu, an "organizational situation." For the Syrian activists in those networks, "It's like a state of war when it comes to business," a "twenty-four hours per day" commitment, Rami says. When friends met socially, they'd talk about work. He would stay up late into the night, sometimes conducting meetings with his field-workers inside Syria at 11:00 p.m. "because the internet is strong in Syria at that time." It's stressful, he concludes, but he does it on behalf of Syria. "We'll die fighting for a cause.... We won't surrender. I will persist."

How do activists in situations of war grapple with their political commitments and organizational missions while also navigating physical insecurity, shifts in territorial control, displacement, and other violent processes? In what ways do their undertakings shift as they adapt to war, and what role do international aid organizations play in inducing these shifts? Rami's story demonstrates that when contention is militarized, activists may continue to participate in conflict processes without the use of violence. Their relations with international aid organizations can facilitate this participation and those organizations' rules can affect what that participation looks like. All the while, they face multiple risks from state and nonstate armed actors—for whom their adherence to nonviolence does not entitle them to protection.

Wartime activism is dangerous. After the military takeover of Myanmar in 2021, for instance, health care workers in opposition-held territories came under attack. In just one and a half years, at least 750 health care workers were arrested and dozens were killed (Root and Nu Nu 2023). These arrests and deaths suggest that it was not only civilian infrastructure that was under attack, but individual activists themselves. Civil actors operating in territory controlled by Myanmar's opposition reported such selective targeting as having their homes burned, their families displaced, and their movements tracked by the junta's forces (Root and Nu Nu 2023). International aid organizations enter into such highly contentious spaces and impose rules that activate a formalizing process that contains the politics of civil action in war.

International aid organizations, when they enjoy autonomy, work with and through local actors to carry out their crisis responses. They actively and deliberately forge relations with local actors to achieve their objectives; in the process, they facilitate the participation of these local actors in civil action during war. Through repeated interactions, international actors generate further change in that civil action. As an institutional regime, international aid is characterized by rules. "Impersonal rules are the building blocks of a bureaucracy," according to Michael Barnett and Martha Finnemore; rules can be applied to actors inside and outside a given organization, they can shape how bureaucrats see the world, and they can be used to make that world "amenable to intervention by bureaucrats themselves" (2004, 18). In complex conflict contexts, international aid organizations lean on, reproduce, and impose their rules on themselves and on those with whom they interact. These rules contain the politics of wartime activists, even in highly politicized contexts.

Process tracing through the Syrian case makes it possible to build a theory of how international aid organizations impose rules on local nonviolent actors with whom they have developed relations to carry out their objectives. These rules are based on sources of international organizational authority: rationalism, moralism, and professionalism. They operate through coercive and normative mechanisms to produce change in the politics of wartime activism. Rational rules occupy the time and energy of local actors in the production and provision of knowledge, which is used as information and data that furthers the objectives of international actors. Moralistic rules push local actors to present themselves as neutral crisis responders, which reduces perception of risk for internationals working with actors embedded in the conflict context. Professional rules elevate those activists who enjoy technical qualifications and expertise, which often have to be forged through "capacity-building" measures meant to build those capacities that serve international priorities. Together, the imposition of these rules activates a formalizing process that generates change in nonviolent action in war, specifically the containment of its politics.

This analysis explores how international rules operated, through coercive and normative pressures, and how they affected local nonviolent actors in the Syrian war. Theoretically and empirically, space for internal drivers of change is maintained: Rami's story demonstrates that Syrians' own preferences and objectives can sometimes lead them to willingly adopt the normative templates of international actors—especially those related to moralism and professionalism. However, temporal and spatial evidence exists that internal drivers cannot alone explain. When nonviolent action it is not subjected to the rules of international aid it is largely informal and diffuse—resembling efforts like those undertaken by Rami in the first year of the uprising but reflecting novel challenges in the conflict state.

By unpacking specific mechanisms, this theory-building empirical analysis illustrates that formalization is not merely an endogenous process. For as much effort as it consumed, rationalism served to make local organizations more rule-abiding, not more efficient. Moralism could not protect Syrians from political reprisals and targeting; implementing international relief made them targets anyway. These pathologies underscore the added value of a process-based analysis. It is not a given that international organizations that come "to help" would cause harm; specificity about organizational pathology (Barnett and Finnemore 1999) can explain how unintended outcomes are generated, if indeed they are.

The Politics of Nonviolent Action in the Syrian War

To make the case that international aid contains the politics of nonviolent action during war, a first step is to show this outcome in the Syrian case. There are numerous challenges to identifying this outcome with precision. One indicator could be the formalization of grassroots or community-based organizations into NGOs; as Rami described it, the Syrian movement had changed from revolutionary to organizational work during the period of his detention. Arguably, NGOs became a ubiquitous associational form among Syrians during the war despite their lack of historical experience in independent organizing, but often these were what Estella Carpi and Elena Fiddian-Qasmiyeh refer to as "de facto NGOs" that were not legally registered (2020). Displaced Syrians usually lacked legal employment and organizational registration rights in refugee host states. Even in Turkey, Syrian organizations were operating in a "completely foreign regulatory environment and unstable political context" (Badran 2020). Those in rebel-held territory, meanwhile, navigated fluctuating nonstate armed group control and unstable security conditions. Operating as they were in nonstate territory, those organizations were also not formally registered with the central government in Damascus. Finally, it is not possible to draw on lists of organizational recipients of international aid because those lists have been deliberately anonymized by donor and contracting agencies.

Despite these data challenges, there are other ways to gain a view into the adoption of the NGO organizational form. For instance, even in places where there was no sovereign entity, the trappings of organization were manifest among Syrian activists. Governance bodies associated with the Syrian opposition commonly "registered" NGOs in rebel-held territory. Figure 10 is a document image posted on the Facebook page of the Rural Damascus Governorate council, an opposition governance institution. It shows the registration certificate of a local NGO in February of 2016 as an official "legal entity," though of course only insofar as legal goes in nonstate territory. The background images in the document display the "Free Syria" flag adopted by supporters of the 2011 uprising.

NGO registration efforts were common in opposition governance institutions, including at the town level. Local councils in rebel-held territory kept lists of the local organizations operating in their areas. These lists were valuable to international actors who relied on those organizations to implement and deliver relief. The more legible the organization, the better it could serve international interests. As a relief activist reported to MSF: "We were told by donors and some foreign organizations that they could not support us unless there is an official status of the organization" (quoted in Whittall 2014). It is no surprise then that a registration certificate such as the one in figure 10 was printed in English, side by side with Arabic.

Another way to show the outcome is to focus on at least one of its specific observable implications. The theory of civilizing contention argues that the formalizing process has three of these, which, in the aggregate, contain the politics of nonviolent action: activists become consumed by knowledge production

FIGURE 10. Registration certificate for NGO in rebel-held area. NGO name redacted by author. Source: Facebook page of the Governorate Council of Rural Damascus.

procedures, they present themselves as neutral, and they are elevated on the basis of technical qualifications and expertise. Process tracing identifies how international aid rules of rationalism, moralism, and professionalism, respectively, generate these outcomes through coercive and normative mechanisms. Population-level evidence of one of these observable implications demonstrates temporal and spatial increases in more neutral claims-making among Syrian organizations. I have coded pages in the Facebook dataset of Syrian civil organizations according to their "political orientation." This coding is based on observable markers on groups' public pages in their cover photos, profile pictures, the content of recent posts, their group names, and descriptions on "about" pages and linked websites. This information can demonstrate whether groups make visible political claims and affiliations or not. Political orientation on Facebook is an imperfect proxy for actions or internal beliefs, but it is a reasonable one for capturing outward claims-making.[2]

"Anti-government" organizations, as represented by their public Facebook pages, constitute a majority of all pages (867 pages; 64 percent of the total). They were coded as such based on at least two markers of political orientation such as images of the "Free Syria" flag and language referencing the *thawra* (revolution), regime repression, political detainees, torture, and regime violence including sieges, use of barrel bombs and chemical weapons, and so forth. Other codes included Islamist (as a political orientation, not a cultural one), pro-government, Palestinian nationalist, the Kurdistan Democratic Party (KDP), and, separately, Rojava (the political project associated with the Kurdish Democratic Union Party), each of which accounted for less than 3 percent of page totals.[3]

These other conspicuous political orientations did not constitute a large proportion of pages. Instead, nearly one-third of all pages are coded as "not visible." These are pages that were clearly engaged in civil action but were doing so without betraying obvious political claims or positions. Humanitarian groups were especially likely to be "not visible" in their politics; there were nearly twice as many humanitarian groups (215 pages) that were "not visible" as those that were anti-government (118 pages). Groups engaged in development (long-term social and economic processes) also had "not visible" (69 pages) more often than anti-government orientations (42 pages). In almost all other areas, including advocacy, media, arts and culture, coordination, and governance, pages were primarily anti-government.

These anti-government and not visible–oriented pages, representing Syrians' civil organizations, can serve as proxies for political versus neutral public-facing orientations. An observable implication of the formalizing process, and especially of humanitarianism's moralistic rules, would be a shift from political/anti-government to neutral/not visible orientations over time as the interactions between international and local actors deepened. To look for this temporal change, I look at cross-page trends in page creation dates.

Figure 11 shows the average number of anti-government and not visible pages created per month in each year. Pages created in 2011 and 2012 were likely to be anti-government. New pages created each month in 2013 began to converge in their orientations, though anti-government pages remained very dominant. From 2014 to 2018 new anti-government and not visible pages were created at close and sometimes indistinguishable rates.[4] In sum, figure 11 shows a temporal shift in the outward political orientations of Syrian groups, and in particular a rise in neutrality.

Spatial evidence provides further insights into the public-facing politics of civil actors. International aid actors enjoyed greater autonomy in Turkey and northwest Syria than they did in Jordan and southern Syria. Assuming that international aid's relations were greater and deeper in the former, and therefore nonviolent action was facilitated more easily in those spaces, it should follow that

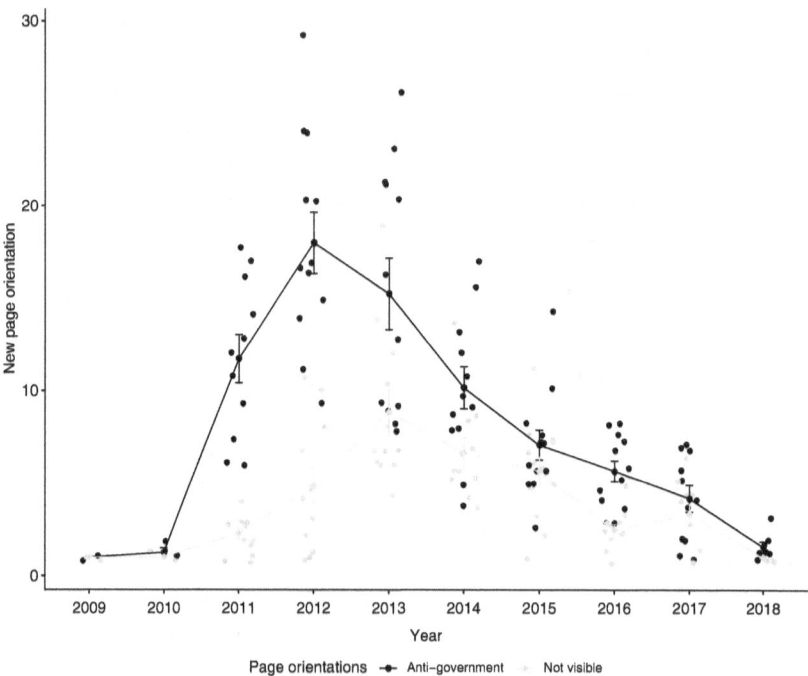

FIGURE 11. Facebook page creations by political orientation. Average monthly foundings, per year, of anti-government and not visible Facebook pages. Source: Author's original data.

international aid's rules produced substantively different outcomes across these spaces as well. In particular, we should expect more indicators of outward neutrality in the north of Syria and in Turkey. As table 2 shows, this is the finding in the Facebook pages. Groups in Idlib and Aleppo in Syria's northwest as well as those in Turkey, respectively, were less likely to present an anti-government orientation than those in Darʿa in the south and in Jordan.

This evidence is more striking when we recall that the Turkish government outwardly encouraged Syria's anti-government political opposition, while the Jordanian government was far more circumspect. Yet of these four locations of Syrian organizations, it is those with greatest proximity to international aid—in Turkey—that were most likely to present outward neutrality. Still, these descriptive snapshots cannot establish a causal relationship between the political orientations of Syrian groups on Facebook and international aid organizations. Rather, it is process tracing analysis that provides the fine-grained detail that establishes the sequences and mechanisms of change.

TABLE 2. Political orientations of Facebook pages with apparent activities or offices inside Syria or in neighboring states

	ANTI-GOVERNMENT ORIENTATION	NOT VISIBLE ORIENTATION
Northwest Syria	69%	27%
Turkey	59%	37%
Southern Syria	73%	23%
Jordan	67%	33%

Formalizing Rules

The relations established between international aid actors and local nonviolent actors in Syria facilitated the latter's continued participation during the war even as it wreaked havoc on their country. Their individual and organizational concerns shifted along with the conflict itself, and sometimes aligned with those of international actors. Ali Hamdan has analyzed the practices of Syrians in Turkey, who coordinated between international actors and locals inside the country (2020, 6). He argues that those Syrians in Turkey deployed a practice of "rendering technical the problems of governance." Syrians who were part of the uprising became engaged in organizational practices like conducting needs assessments of Syrian communities that made the conflict more legible to international interveners. These efforts were not initially the stuff of revolution, but they served the communities these Syrian activists sought to uplift (Hamdan 2020).

The implication is that Syrians adapted their behavior toward technical or formal means of action—not in abdication of their contentious objectives, but rather as adjusted means of realizing their principles to the extent that was possible under adverse conditions. Yet to say that Syrian organizations adapted to technical tasks does not tell us how they acquired the skills and capacity to do so, why certain tasks were prioritized over others, who benefited from the fact that they did so, whether such moves were sustainable, how they were pursued in administrative and substantive terms, and at what costs. An account of international aid rules can address these multiple questions, while still allowing that Syrian organizations often also had their own internal reasons for partaking in this process of change.

Rational Rules

International humanitarians want data and information to respond to needs in crisis contexts. Understanding that Syrians enjoyed local knowledge and access, they established relations with them on that basis, although they then had to push

Syrians to produce and provision that knowledge according to the mechanisms, protocols, and standards on which international actors rested their rational authority. In late 2011, the international aid regime began growing its response to the spiraling Syrian crisis. Knowledge of needs was difficult to glean, even while it was critical to the delivery of relief. Scholars note that "in mid-2012, eighteen months into the crisis in Syria, most actors agreed that the picture of the humanitarian situation was incoherent and fragmented" (Parham et al. 2013, 29).

Inside Syria, this lack of knowledge of needs was the result of issues of access, fears over informational security, the absence of coordination structures, the dynamism of events, and hesitancy and sensitivity among local populations (SNAP 2013). In neighboring countries to which Syrians were fleeing, obstacles to information included the urban contexts refugees were inhabiting and uncertainty regarding the responsibilities of various agencies and host governments. Humanitarian organizations were better at gathering needed knowledge about refugees in camps, where assessment was "relatively 'easy'" and the crisis was "more visible and easier to manage" (Healy and Tiller 2013, 24–25). The problem with this approach, however, was that most Syrian refugees did not reside in camps.

Aid agencies and organizations activated practices for knowledge production. The INGOs that gave up on waiting for the Syrian government to allow access and moved to border countries, especially Turkey, established a coordination forum among themselves with a secretariat that "included an information capability" (Sida et al. 2016, 31). When OCHA gained access to rebel-held territory through cross-border operations in mid-2014 via UN Security Council Resolution 2165, the accumulation of information across "hubs" in Damascus, Jordan, and Turkey became possible. Interviewees within humanitarian agencies seemed to sigh with relief whenever we discussed 2165. "Data is the crux of the political issue in the crisis," one UN staffer explained, and 2165 made the response much more transparent.[5] The staffer of another UN agency showed off a map of outcomes of needs assessments gathered by two dozen organizations, a feat made possible by coordination across the three Whole of Syria hubs, he explained.[6]

Local actors were a critical channel through which to gain such information. International organizations established projects specifically geared toward building knowledge, including the Syria Needs Analysis Project (SNAP) and later the Humanitarian Needs Assessment Programme (HNAP). SNAP noted in 2013 that "civil society actors in Syria have the capacity to undertake assessments and should be involved because they are aware of the context and they have access to different areas" (SNAP 2013). Their role was critical in refugee host states, as well. In urban refugee contexts, "networks of refugee outreach workers" enhanced UNHCR's knowledge and reach (Voon 2013).

To develop the needs assessment capabilities of these local actors, international actors had to train Syrians and ensure they followed the rules. Like other organizations, OCHA made specific efforts to build the capacity of Syrian NGOs in needs assessment for the cross-border response, a move deemed by evaluators a "wise investment" and "good practice for future contexts" (Sida et al. 2016, 32). International aid organizations trained hundreds of local enumerators, many remotely, in principles and tools for assessment, best practices for selecting and questioning interviewees, and methods for triangulating and ranking the confidence of collected data.

Reflecting on the information gathering they were trained to do, a Syrian working for an INGO described the "infinite number of papers, reports, and bills," and connects such documentation to the knowledge acquisition that buttresses the rational authority of international aid: "Each donor has a preapproved report template that defines the type of information needed, which strips the employee working close to actual people in the field of the ability to express themselves freely and paint a more holistic picture, and makes the template-maker the authority on information-selection and narrative steering" (Al-Oballi 2020). The "types of information needed," in other words, were the types of information that international aid actors cared about, and included those variables that fit under designated system sectors like education; shelter; and water, sanitation, and hygiene.

Though they learned tools and techniques, conflict conditions did not make knowledge provision easy for Syrians. Some sympathetic international staff recognized that the activists they relied on for information could not always fulfill formal protocols. An American development contractor recalled that she was "easy" on her field officers, including one whose work of directing underground hospitals precluded timely reports about the armed groups governing his northern Syria neighborhoods. She would tell him not to worry—she would fill out the paperwork as long as they had a quick Skype meeting so she could find out what was going on.

Yet in general, Syrians were expected to fulfill formal protocols that aligned with the rules-based rationalism of international aid organizations for needs assessment, and were also used for monitoring, evaluation, accountability, and learning, or in shorthand, monitoring and evaluation (M&E). Many Syrian organizations took up M&E as best they could under coercive pressures. These practices "consumed more time and resources" than local actors had, were occasionally "prohibitive," and posed security risks (Howe et al. 2015). Kimberly Howe and her colleagues relay stories of organizations and activists in rebel-held territory bending over backward to meet international requirements: communicating daily despite risks, costs, and lack of internet; providing the names of individual beneficiaries despite security risks; hand-delivering invoices despite checkpoints set up by armed groups; quoting local vendor estimates with official stamps despite the informality of their business models; and so forth (Howe et al. 2015).

Both international aid actors and local civil ones were cognizant of these rule-based demands and the time and energy they consumed. Aware of, if not overly sympathetic to this pressure, one US development contractor remarked: "We have a really high accounting standard, a 100 percent receipt requirement, which drives [Syrians] all crazy."[7] At the same time, several Syrian interviewees noted that ideologically driven supporters (generally from the Gulf and with Islamist leanings) did not impose such accountability standards; other Syria researchers have made similar observations about nontraditional aid donors (Howe 2016). But while diaspora and other informal funding decreased as the conflict deepened, international aid commitments only increased. Syrians complied, even if it "drove them crazy," because international actors were gatekeepers to their continued participation in the crisis response.

A Syrian woman penned a devastating reflection on the informational requirements and standards of international organizations. Nayla Mansour wrote "My Name is Kafrnabel, and I Do Not Need Training in Needs Assessment" from the perspective of a town in rebel-held Idlib famous for its revolutionary spirit and activity: "Organization calls for working and monitoring mechanisms and *non-stop data collection*. But what is the meaning of such mechanisms in the face of explosive barrels and Scud missiles? . . . This literally means regulating one's death, making it subject to a regulatory mechanism; deep down it means *rationalizing*, and thus normalizing, the current situation" (Mansour 2013, emphasis added). Mansour invokes the rules-based mechanisms that consumed nonviolent actors' time and energy ("non-stop") even as the politics, rights violations, and destruction of the conflict raged on.

Those politics were not coincidental to these regulatory processes; indeed, politics threatened the very data collectors carrying out the objectives of international actors. The Syrian government was irate about the data collection taking place through cross-border humanitarian operations. In a letter to the UN, reporters explain, the Syrian government declared that it "wanted to control data on conditions throughout the country. . . . It will 'not recognize any illegitimate programs or the numbers to be presented' by those programs. . . . The work of the data collectors, the letter continued, constitutes 'illegitimate collection of information and espionage'" (Lynch and Worley 2023). For following the rules and assessing needs according to rational standards, Syria's nonviolent actors faced accusations of espionage from a vengeful regime.

While civil organizations were oriented toward compliance, they understood the value—and the politics—of their knowledge. In 2016, more than seventy Syrian NGOs protested the UN's cooperation with the Syrian government in Damascus by temporarily suspending information-sharing with the Whole of Syria system (Beals and Hopkins 2016). That is, they struck at international aid by withholding their knowledge. A coordinator of Syrian humanitarian NGOs in Turkey explained the move: "For us, Syria is not just one of many missions around the world. They [international organizations] have other missions; [if] it doesn't work they say they'll learn for the next one. But for us, we can't afford to fail and then write a paper about lessons learned. . . . Yes they are our partners, but we have to pressure them. And we believe their basic structure is wrong. Syria is a conflict, and the main party is the regime—which they consider the official government. There's something wrong here."[8] Ayah Al-Oballi, Nayla Mansour, and this coordinator were condemning not just the rationalism of the system, but its erasure of politics.

Moralistic Rules

From 2011 through mid-2021, at least 479 Syrian aid workers were killed, kidnapped, or wounded in the country.[9] Medical care workers in rebel-held territory were "effectively criminalized" as "enemies of the state," as hundreds of hospitals and clinics were violently targeted by government and Russian forces (Koteiche et al. 2019). Yet, for international actors, humanitarianism was supposed to be separate from politics. In one of the "deadliest places for aid workers in the world" (CARE 2018), the system for humanitarian governance sought neutral local responders.

In this context, international actors voiced general concerns about the political preferences of Syrians engaged in emergency response. One group warned of expressing "any solidarity with doctors supporting the opposition movement . . . because of the political position such a stance entails," concluding gravely: "the neutrality of hospitals and other medical sites is brought into question in such an environment" (HPG 2012). A leader of OCHA in Turkey described the "arguments" his agency had with Syrian actors about their political commitments. In so doing, he also decoupled civil society (that is, advocacy and activism) from humanitarianism: "Activism in one sense of the word is the last thing we want to happen, because we want all humanitarian actors to be impartial, neutral, not taking sides. So the arguments we had with Syrian NGOs has been to accept that either you are a civil society organization that promotes a particular course, or if you want to be a humanitarian, you have to follow certain principles."[10]

Despite framing these interactions as debates, OCHA, as the primary coordinator of cross-border operations, held the literal purse strings over Syrian organizations. The moralism of international bureaucracies operates through coercive pressures.

Some expressed specific reservations about working with local faith groups. They were concerned that those groups' religious commitments would be at cross-purposes with neutrality and impartiality—a sentiment unironically shared with researchers in Jordan by a representative of a Christian INGO (El Nakib and Ager 2015). Syrians observed such international distrust. In a sardonic social media campaign that trended with the hashtag That's_What_The_Donor_Wants (Hayk bidhu al-donor), a Syrian quipped: "There's a donor at the door. Hurry up, remove this prayer rug . . . and if they ask you, you tell them this is a prayer room for all different religions" (Syria Untold 2015).

Tensions over moralistic rules also played out over the opposition's local governance institutions: local councils. Some sought ways to work with LCs by containing their political character. Cognizant of local councils' knowledge advantage, one UN staff member noted that "local councils are good for information. . . . They're crucial because they know numbers."[11] The "main issue and challenge," however, in the opinion of the Centre for Humanitarian Dialogue, "is to depoliticize the councils, in order to facilitate the return of technical capacities. . . . This would allow local civil society groups to maintain a space for political activism in opposition held areas, but it would also restrict local administration to service provision and civil administration" (2014).

Others preferred to sidestep LCs altogether. Despite their informational advantages (which would have elevated rationalism), certain humanitarian organizations came to view nongovernmental organizations and technocrats as more appropriate and less political partners than LCs. A Syrian charged with distributing food baskets in the northwest described the inefficiencies created by the humanitarian INGO for whom he worked because they would not use the population lists of the LCs. The INGO took their stance based on a moralistic authority, claiming that not all LCs enjoy "legitimacy," so, as a rule, it was better to work with relief organizations. The Syrian activist asked, rhetorically: "But does the relief organization have legitimacy? The relief organization could just be a group of four or five people who decided to start an organization."[12] He was not the only one to wonder about this. International humanitarian agencies struggled to decide what to do about LCs. An international staffer of a UN agency, operating from Turkey, described the indeterminate thinking around LCs in the industry: "It has never been made clear who is supposed to support the first level of governance, in this case the local councils. Who is engaging with them? Nobody and everybody. . . . If there were a political decision taken, we could say that all of them have their salaries paid, without standards or preconditions, and then judge their performance later. But in the absence of this decision, there's a lot of confusion."[13] For humanitarians, working with nonstate political actors was a moralistic conundrum due to their potential conflict with humanitarian principles.

Nonhumanitarian interveners, who advance development, stabilization, peacebuilding, and other interventions, are not bound by core humanitarian principles. They nonetheless associate their authority with the technocratic impartiality of their approaches. For example, one of the leaders of US government programming in Syria described the "three pillars" of the US response in a manner that united them under a shared framework of apolitical impartiality: first, humanitarianism, which should "follow the need and resist any efforts to politicize it"; second, nonlethal assistance to armed groups, who would ideally "stay back and protect a place" rather than do as the rebels preferred and "chase the ball, fight the regime"; and third, support to civil society, which he strongly felt should go to technocrats that could "keep communities running," like teachers and police.[14] Under the banner of these three pillars, (1) neutral humanitarianism, (2) constrained rebel groups, and (3) support to technocrats, one might conclude that US policy toward Syria's opposition activists was based on fixed morals.

In practice, justifications for the nonhumanitarian aid response shifted with the conflict. The US government's response was initially concerned with representation, civil society, and transition. These priorities later gave way to stabilization and countering violent extremism. The shift reflected an effort to align with facts on the ground, including al-Asad's strength following Russia's 2015 military intervention; the predominance of "proscribed" Salafi-jihadi groups in the armed insurgency (rather than the "moderate" Free Syria Army); and the divided control of Syrian territory by the Islamic State, Turkey, and Kurdish armed groups.

Rather than pull away, the United States promoted less political and more technocratic approaches over time. For instance, it disinvested from opposition governance institutions even while it invested in "stabilization committees" linked to those same institutions. Through stabilization, the United States was perpetuating service provision in shrinking noncontiguous opposition-held or Kurdish-held areas with nontransformative objectives and a maintenance of "moderate" actors (Brown 2018). The Syrians involved in stabilization efforts were often the same ones the United States had previously supported based on its promotion of representation and transition. One contractor supporting the stabilization committees noted of a Syrian they worked with: "In the early days he was a fiery activist. The donors asked us to do a lot of coaching. . . . Now he has become much more restrained, at least in official settings."[15]

Syrians could certainly judge the dimming prospects for their revolutionary objectives based on the same ground-level assessments of the conflict, but they were being asked to adjust—and contain—their politics from within the international framework into which they were incorporated. A Western development contractor supporting governance projects explained: "We moved very much away from thinking about a political transition, to how do we counter the expansion of extremist groups in opposition areas. Which is very difficult for our Syrian staff because: how do you do that in a context of a war? Essentially, you're saying to them that the revolution failed and now you're dealing with the negative outputs that are within the revolution, not even the regime."[16]

Among the Syrian organizations shifting toward "countering violent extremism" (CVE) were those who shared the objective of countering extremism because it was consistent with their own values. That is, there were elements of a normative "pull" toward the same "moderate" transcript. Many Syrian humanitarians also strongly affirmed their adherence to humanitarian principles. The leader of a diaspora medical organization with operations in rebel-held territory declared: "We are completely neutral to what's going on. . . . As a humanitarian organization, we should just recognize that there are people in need" (Hammodeh and Cheung 2013, 14). He and several other interviewees insisted they would provide relief in government-held territory, given access, but they were relegated to refuge and rebel-held territory by the decidedly unneutral Syrian government.

In other words, neutrality was not necessarily imposed on Syrians against their will, but their presence in a highly contentious and risky conflict context was fundamentally political. Researching this dilemma, Rania Sweis identifies the near impossibility for local humanitarians like those in Syria to be neutral even if they wish to be. While Syrian doctors are "guided by a professional impulse to save human life impartially, it is action that is grounded in real-world conditions that require doctors act in politically constituted ways," as they assume extreme risks on behalf of the country to which they feel emotionally and physically bound (Sweis 2019, 598).

Despite this dilemma, international aid actors did impose coercive pressures on Syrians to contain their politics. For instance, a 2017 call for grants from a US State Department bureau read, "New grants must meet the [same] 'Defeat Daesh [Islamic State] and CVE' requirements as all new grants" (confidential correspondence 2017). That is, money would not go toward projects that did not explicitly adhere to CVE objectives. These impositions had costs. These included reputational costs: as one interviewee noted: "you can get branded as selling out."[17] They also included existential costs. "Currently, the support is for programming that is anti-Daesh [Islamic State]," a Syrian journalist in Gaziantep, Turkey said about donor preferences and demands. "But that puts our people in danger, and is not our priority anyway. Three people in this very building were assassinated because they were writing against Daesh," he concluded.[18] Even in the relative security of refuge, Syria's nonviolent actors were not protected from the politics and risks posed by armed actors like the Islamic State. Those risks could be exacerbated by donor efforts to "counter" those very armed actors with and through the locals engaged in the crisis response.

To maintain financial support for the undertakings they cared about, Syrians understood they had to comply with the coercive pressures of international organization rules and regulations. Indeed, they could spell out those rules themselves. Marcel Shehwaro, the well-known leader of a Syrian civil society organization based in Aleppo and Turkey, reflected powerfully in 2019 on the "unwritten rules" of international organizations, including in matters of language: "State violence shouldn't be referenced; statements should use the passive, nonpolitical voice. 'The schools got bombed, the activists got killed,' etc. Naming the perpetrators is considered political if the perpetrator is the state, of course. However, if the perpetrator is an Islamist extremist, naming is encouraged. We must act 'neutral' toward the state and overly apologetic regarding our linkages to extremism. The 'revolution' should be termed the 'conflict' and the 'regime' should be the 'government'" (Shehwaro 2019).

Professionalism Rules

Research participants routinely referenced their pre-2011 roles in government bureaucracies, retail, or industry, or as students in high school or college. The uprising and conflict opened a new space for people to engage in activism in ways few of them had ever experienced. The vast majority, about 80 percent, of those surveyed in Jordan had not taken part in any form of social, economic, or political activism prior to 2011 (Khoury 2020). Individuals with smartphones became citizen journalists, those with cars became smugglers of supplies to besieged areas, those with college degrees opened educational spaces for internally displaced children, those in medical school manned clinics to treat the war wounded, and so forth. Syrians were compelled to apply their skills and competitive advantages as activists, even if they lacked the experiences and professionalization enjoyed by practiced dissidents or civil society actors elsewhere.

When international aid actors began to respond to the crisis they bemoaned the struggle of operating the system in partnership with such amateurs and in the absence of more professional activists. As evaluators of the humanitarian response noted, "Many well-educated activists who could have been professional and bicultural counterparts had fled or been detained by 2013. This made it difficult for NGOs and community partners to fulfill the complex requirements of anxious donors" (Slim and Trombetta 2014, 47–48). That is, death, detention, and displacement of potential local partners was an obstacle to international interveners.

Nevertheless, those aid organizations that sought access through cross-border operations recognized the necessity of working with nascent Syrian organizations that enjoyed extensive networks, even if they lacked capacity. Researchers for Refugees International explained in 2013 that Syrians understood the principles and rules that donors prioritized and only needed support and capacity-building to reach their potential: "[Refugees International] discovered that nascent Syrian aid groups recognize the importance of humanitarian principles . . . and donor requirements for effectiveness and efficiency. This mindset . . . complements the more experienced international humanitarian NGOs. These organizations will need training, funding, and ongoing mentoring, so traditional donors . . . should immediately support programs that will enhance the capacity of these emergent NGOs" (Grisgraber and Hanson 2013).

Through a plethora of capacity-building efforts and trainings, many Syrian activists gained the skills international aid actors sought. INGO reports boast that they have trained hundreds or even thousands of Syrians and offered dozens of courses and certifications (see, for example, Mercy Corps n.d.). When OCHA established the cross-border pooled fund to support local organizations, the agency noted that the "number one strategic priority" for the "newly established" Syrian organizations was strengthening capacity and training staff. Potential recipients of funding would undergo capacity assessments that measure the potential "risk" they may pose in terms of timeliness, documentation, financial management, and implementation. After receiving grades of A, B, or C, applicants that did not qualify received feedback and the opportunity to try again (OCHA 2015). Syrian organizations were incentivized, trained, and refined into more capable and professional organizations.

Professionalization occurred in the realm of political and civil society aid, as well. A media outlet for online reporting on the Syrian conflict, based in a neighboring country, illustrates international efforts to train and professionalize Syrians. While operating as a news agency, the organization also ran a donor-funded training program for aspiring journalists. A cofounder of the organization noted that Syrians who were younger in age were a better fit for this effort: "The Syrians who started working there were old and political. We needed young people so that we could train them."[19] One of the organization's international staffers understood that young Syrians also were political, but training could address that issue: "We recognize that these are activists we are working with and try hard to make it clear to them the difference between activism and journalism," he said.[20] Professionalism, in other words, could close the gap between the "objectives" of international assisters and the subjectivities of local actors.

Those in refuge were especially likely to adopt the desired qualifications. Some such skills were technical. One activist who came to Turkey late, having been in detention inside Syria for a long three years, described becoming acquainted with computer programs like Microsoft Word and Excel. "[My friend] gave me a laptop. I didn't know how to do anything on it, or on the smartphones. It took time to learn how to use these things," he recounted.[21] A striking characteristic of successful Syrian NGO managers in refuge was their English competency—an asset that led to the most successful grant applications as well as an ability to navigate and participate in IGO, INGO, and donor networks in the border countries. My interview with Rami, whose story opened this chapter and who was one of the founders of a reputable humanitarian NGO in Gaziantep, was almost entirely conducted in Arabic. However, whenever he described organizational topics, such as "business model," "case management," "donors," and "organizational structure," he code-switched to English.[22] When I pointed out the same tendency with a Syrian employee of a US development company in Turkey, he countered: "I'm having this memory in English because I wrote the proposal in English."[23]

My method of snowball sampling for interview research may have sometimes led to well-connected and successful Syrians in Turkey and Jordan who may have been more prone to these tendencies, and although my interview research was not limited to them, this class of individuals and organizations is of critical importance. Like elsewhere in the developing world where NGOs have been studied in peacetime contexts, the stratum of internationally connected local NGOs tends to receive the most external funding (Henderson 2002; Barr et al. 2005).

Professionalization was not always a smooth process, however. A third-party monitor reflected that Syrian organizations are on a "learning curve" and though many wish to perform well, they are often beset by their "*inshallah* orientation" (meaning their "God willing orientation") when it comes to meeting deadlines.[24] This statement is both matter-of-fact (international expectations *were* an adjustment for local actors) and patronizing in its invocation of a cultural trope. As international access from Turkey to rebel-held territory was limited beginning in 2016, in-person trainings for activists who could cross through the borders from northwest Syria became fewer and farther between, exacerbating the challenge of professionalizing those "in the field."

Professionalization also worked through a normative mechanism; that is, local actors were drawn to it—it was not only imposed from above. Local activists' pursuit of professional qualifications could be instrumental to advancing their interests. In their ethnographic study of a Syrian news agency headquartered in Gaziantep, Yazan Badran and Kevin Smets observe the outlet's trainings and workshops. While these programs had the obvious advantages of training Syrians in journalistic practices and of enhancing the quality of their media output, it also gave the organization a means to maintain staff despite offering relatively low salaries. Staff development served as reputational currency and a dedicated in-house program that trained a cohort of aspiring journalists every two months "turns the newsroom into a 'self-repairing' place where there were constantly new journalists being trained on the job, according to one editor" (Badran and Smets 2021, 11).

These cohorts of aspiring journalists signal the pull that Syrians felt toward professionalization. Syrians were able and often eager to acquire new skills and qualifications and to advance their careers while serving the Syrian cause. Nearly 95 percent of Syrian activists surveyed in Amman, Jordan had completed at least a secondary education and nearly half had completed tertiary education. Moreover, about 70 percent were between the ages of eighteen and thirty (Khoury 2017). They had room to grow professionally. On an individual level, professional development has served and may continue to serve many activists well in the long run. On a population-wide level, professionalism also arguably functioned as a stopgap that mitigated tensions between international and local actors. While rationalism and moralism operated through coercive pressures and were fraught, professional skills could ensure that tasks would be completed anyway.

Informal Activism Without Rules

The formalizing process has three observable implications that, in the aggregate, contain the politics of nonviolent action: activists become consumed by knowledge production procedures, they present themselves as neutral, and they are elevated on the basis of technical qualifications and expertise. International aid rules of rationalism, moralism, and professionalism, respectively, generated these outcomes through coercive and normative mechanisms. Given that this is true, what does nonviolent action look like when it is not subjected to the rules of international aid? While many Syrian civil activists that interacted with international aid became part of a formal organizational population, some did not. The informal and sometimes diffuse nature of their trajectories makes it challenging to present their experiences in a straightforward manner as one might do in the case of an organization, population of organizations, or a locality. Instead, I rely on the narratives of research participants who engaged in informal action throughout the war—and not just at its start—including political activists in the Turkey-Syria borderlands and humanitarian activists in Jordan.

Civil Resistance Without Rules in the Turkey-Syria Borderlands

Rami's first uprising year was characterized by his involvement in local coordination committees organizing demonstrations, boycotts, symbolic public campaigns, and so forth. This kind of civil resistance did not cease to exist when international aid organizations entered the Syrian crisis and forged relations with local civil actors on whom they began to impose their rules, but those who continued to undertake it often navigated long and winding roads to develop approaches to resistance under the circumstances of a deadly and complicated war. Like Rami, many began as members of LCCs, and like Rami, they also entered into the "organizational phase of the revolution," trying their hand at new forms of wartime activism in local councils or organizations, including those that forged relations with international aid actors. But some in the Turkey-Syria borderlands evaded the rules of international aid, even while others like Rami found success in remaining in that new formal environment.

The experience of people like Marwan from Aleppo is representative of those who persisted in civil activism without aid's rules in the Turkey-Syria borderlands.[25] In 2012 Marwan watched as oppositional local councils were forming, and competing, in Aleppo City after it came under rebel control. He became disquieted by the turn toward service provision unaccompanied by the revolutionary visions that had initially inspired regime opponents. "During the days of the regime, what we were lacking was not services, it was awareness," he explained. So he and a group of activists reverted to the idea of the local coordination committees and founded a new informal group. The group did not turn away from governance institutions—instead, they became advocates for the role of the local council as a political and democratic institution. Despite its flaws, he said, "The local council was a form of democracy in one sense or another." To support it, they asserted its rightful place in Aleppo's new complex environment, where extremist armed groups were asserting greater control even as the regime continued shelling.

Marwan recounted demonstrations and pressure campaigns the group coordinated, such as preventing a non-FSA armed group from taking street cleaning equipment used by the local council and condemning the Islamic State's harsh punishment of a boy who misbehaved. Their actions came with severe risk and sometimes the best they could do was spray graffiti, but their gains were sometimes quite tangible. When people in the community complained about unmarked cars associated with kidnappings, Marwan's group led a campaign urging the Aleppo Governorate Council to take charge of numbering vehicles; the council established an Office of Transportation within a week, according to

Marwan. His group's efforts extended to education, media, and a range of grievances behind which they threw their activism.

Such actions were based on people's time and volunteer labor, not financial or technical support or capacity-building trainings. That is, their energy was explicitly geared toward civil resistance campaigns, not the nonstop demands for data collection and evaluation. Marwan explained the deliberateness of this position: "We had no support at all. It all came from us. We were offered funding at one point and we refused because we knew it would destroy what we were doing."

Eventually, though, other risks threatened to destroy what he was doing. In 2014 militants associated with the Islamic State pursued Marwan at home and in the area his group gathered, but did not find him. When he learned of their visits, he fled to Turkey. In Gaziantep, he began working on a Western-backed project to support local councils in northwest Syria. It was internationally supported, but still political enough for his preferences. Indeed, his political commitments served him well in this capacity. For example, the project aimed to support a local council that was relatively isolated in Idlib and under the eye of Islamist armed groups. The local council members were "fearful of unknown organizations," he says, but "by way of my relationships in the revolution I wasn't known as an organization person—I was a revolution person . . . so we could relate to them as the revolution, and they were really trying to develop themselves." This work persisted for some time and Marwan was content with it. In the local councils it strengthened, "in addition to transparency, participatory democracy. It was very important work." The international staff also followed the Syrian team's ideas, but eventually the program stopped and funding from the US government was cut.

Then, Marwan reverted to his past activism, working with a small group in Turkey to support an informal and secretive network in northwestern Syria opposing extremism. For a time, this was based in relationship-building more than action, which was enhanced by his border crossings from Turkey to Aleppo and Idlib. Among other campaigns, they secretly distributed awareness-raising pamphlets in rebel-held towns and they conducted campaigns on specific issues such as one that opposed the routinization of carrying arms among civilians.

Their efforts gained financial support from international organizations concerned with countering violent extremism. Marwan's normative pull toward CVE allowed him to meet international actors where they were, but by virtue of their work, which entailed no goods, cash, heavy equipment, or relief distribution, such support was inherently limited, and it did not depend on or require them to formally register or make public appeals. To the contrary, as Marwan describes: "We're a network, we rejected registration. If we register, we come under the eye of the Turkish government. This way is better, they don't know who we are. And anyway, most of the people are inside. Our team here in Istanbul is just four or five people working online. We have eight groups inside, independent from each other, but we all work together when there is a campaign. There are risks in this kind of work. We do our best to stay under the radar." Marwan reflects on the state of activism late into the conflict. He understands why service provision was necessary, but he does not accept that all the revolutionaries had to take that path. He's at peace with the pursuit of civil resistance, without rules, in the Turkey-Syria borderlands. "We have principles, and we'll keep fighting until we attain them."

Refugee Response Without Rules in Jordan

In Jordan, where autonomy was more limited, informal activism among Syrians was even more discreet. My interviews with political activists in Jordan were so hushed and guarded that I cannot infer they enacted much of any civil resistance beyond 2012 or 2013. Instead, informal action in Jordan was often geared at providing relief for those refugees who were not served by formal organizations, including by people like Bassel, a Syrian born and raised in Jordan.[26] Bassel was ambivalent toward Syria until the uprising; his heart lifted in that moment: "Once the revolution started, my view of Syria changed altogether." So in 2012 when Dar'a had come under rebel control and needs emerged, he partnered with a Syrian in northern Jordan to send in medical supplies. He managed to cross the borders in that time when it was still possible to do so and it was a revelatory experience. "When I went inside [Syria], I saw how much the aid helped people—I felt like I had to keep doing it. I sold my own possessions to be able to continue helping."

So Bassel continued crossing in and out of Syria, delivering goods. He did so about a dozen times, until the border began to harden and Jabhat al-Nusra had established a presence in southern Syria. Bassel redirected his action toward the growing population of Syrian refugees in camps in Jordan. Zaatari, which had emerged spontaneously in the north of Jordan, would become the largest and most well-known of the Syrian refugee camps in the country. Its location was isolated and movement in and out was quickly brought under the control of the Jordanian authorities, but Bassel managed to sneak in, "undercover," and he conducted his own informal assessment of growing needs. He also realized that he would need to work with others.

From then on Bassel began to straddle the boundaries of formality and informality. Humanitarian work, unlike resistance campaigns, requires significant resources, but he found a way to balance his political commitments and humanitarian energies by working with academics, for whom he became a field researcher and interlocutor. For example, he brought their attention to child marriage in the camp: he documented and collected data on dozens of cases. Then he turned to education, helping with a program to train teenagers to teach younger children.

Eventually, Zaatari would be fully serviced by international aid organizations and these small-scale but important efforts would fall away. Jordan was also planning and building new camps to hold some of the continuously growing refugee population. These new camps were securitized from the outset—the government wanted to ensure refugee camps were structured and controlled. In response, Bassel set his eyes on informal camps. These small, sporadic camps, also aided by other Syrians who were informally volunteering in refugee response, were in remote locations and barely serviced by international organizations. Volunteers, including Bassel, collected community donations to deliver to the camps' inhabitants and organized some youth programming for the children who were generally not enrolled in school. He also conducted interviews and surveys with refugees for his continued research with academics.

All the while, Bassel was studying at a private college. He graduated in 2014, at which point he "wanted to find work related to Syria, like for an organization. I had done so many studies—I had a lot of experience. But because I am Syrian, they refused." Bassel resented being treated like a refugee and subjected to the employment restrictions that were placed on them, but he did not stop volunteering on their behalf. "I feel I have to keep on this path, doing this work, because eventually Syrians—we're going to go back. And when we do, we have to be prepared."

International aid directed at the Syrian conflict facilitated activist participation in crisis response. Buttressed by multiple sources of authority, these international institutions and organizations proceeded to impose rules on these local nonviolent actors. Operating through coercive and normative pressures, these rules contain the politics of wartime activism: they position local actors as producers and provisioners of knowledge, limit their public expressions within the bounds of neutrality, and professionalize and train them in technical skills.

Process tracing through evidence from the Syrian war supported this theory-building exercise. Syria's nonviolent actors began their contentious journey on the streets in collective protests. Their nonviolent action looked very different years later. It became common for them to adopt formal organizational structures, to acquire skills and qualifications that international organizations valued, and to use language and engage in practices that obfuscated the politics of their actions, all the while putting themselves at risk. The mechanisms that contained the politics of Syrians and their organizations were activated in and around the conflict state, but they were most pronounced where aid actors enjoyed the most autonomy—especially in Turkey. Probing a counterfactual condition within the case demonstrated that there are alternative pathways for civil resistance during war that are diffuse and informal and not reliant on resource-intensive undertakings. Resources present another arena in which these civil actors are enabled and constrained by those who come to help. International resources filter local actors, rewarding those who meet their demands, and letting go of those who do not. Organizational survival becomes a key struggle for local actors, who are already struggling for physical survival in a war zone.

5
THE FILTERING PROCESS

Mustafa was specializing in neurosurgery in Damascus in 2011, quietly excited by the uprising unfolding elsewhere in the country.[1] During rounds, a desperate mother asked him to covertly discharge her son—a wounded dissident—fearing that security agents likely awaited his release. Mustafa obliged, only to find security agents in his department the next day. He fled to his family's village in northwest Syria, telling himself he would complete his specialization eventually. Needs in the underdeveloped area focused him on the present, and Mustafa became a practitioner of general medicine. He served in a private clinic where locals, lacking financial means and physical access to government-held territory, received free care.

Yet the clinic could not continuously dole out treatment. "There is no funding to be had on the inside," Mustafa explained, except for donations from a few businessmen. Over the next two years, Mustafa learned to respond to needs in a shifting warscape. In 2012 he organized a group of doctors, understanding that the international organizations assembling in Turkey "did not want to work with me, as an individual. . . . If we are a group with a structure and organization, then it's different, it's easier." They created a medical body for their Idlib region and following the advice of activists in Turkey, gave it a formal governance structure. By 2013 they had assembled a directorate of health for Idlib, a rebellious substitute for absent government institutions.

Nevertheless, the directorate would not receive much support: "Funding was going to organizations," he said, which humanitarian INGOs preferred over political institutions. One such organization in an Idlib town, particularly clever in its publicity, received significant attention—and funding—from Western donors. Mustafa echoes many others when he speculates that this very favoritism led an extremist Islamist armed group to target the town and to assassinate the head of that organization, a poster child for donors. Meanwhile, Mustafa's village, a few kilometers away from the town, received very little support despite the extreme vulnerability of the IDPs it sheltered. Antagonisms continued to grow between members of the medical body. "We didn't have a sense of unity—and I think this is what destroyed the revolution," he reflects. Other towns would get funding and "we'd say hey, remember us? In the beginning, we used to think on the national level. But it didn't stay that way."

Mustafa finally left Syria. In Gaziantep, Turkey, he found that the number of Syrian organizations had increased in "an astonishing way." Yet he noticed too that many felt that their organizational voices were unheard. They sensed that international organizations applied templates used elsewhere, without concern for the specifics of the Syrian context. In response, a dozen or so Syrian humanitarian organizations initiated an alliance, which Mustafa would help build. He navigated international networks, came to understand their (limited) appetites for risk, and respected their breadth of experience. At the same time, he understood it was Syrians who excelled in access, knowledge, and connections; he was determined that Syrians should not compete with one another for international support. Meanwhile, Syrian organizations also faced an external threat: Rebel-held territory was shrinking. In each case of government reclamation, civil organizations disappeared. International organizations would move on when the war ended, while Syrians would be left behind. Mustafa wondered what would become of the Syrians. "For [internationals]," he said, "it's business, a job. For us, it's life."

How do nonviolent actors survive war? What role does international aid play in their survival? The answers are partly literal: Activists can physically survive by fleeing, by operating underground, by gaining the protection of armed actors, or by getting lucky. International humanitarians can contribute to their survival by providing them with food and shelter and by advocating for the protection of civilians from harm. We can also approach these questions from an organizational frame of reference. Activists like Mustafa can survive in a resource environment structured by international aid by selecting strategies that secure project contracts, such as formalizing their organizational governance and procedures. They can enhance their organizational legitimacy, in the eyes of funders, by becoming non-governmental relief providers.

Local actors in other conflict arenas have also experienced the contract-based and ideational resources of international aid that filter some organizations for survival. The Kurdish administration in northern Iraq in the 1990s, for instance, was brushed aside as a political body by international aid organizations concerned about their relations with the central government in Baghdad. Instead, they worked with local Kurdish NGOs through subcontracted projects to bring relief to people suffering food insecurity. The NGOs were so favored that some enjoyed larger budgets than that of the Kurdistan Regional Government and government ministers even had "to approach the NGOs for funds before starting a project" of their own (Ofteringer and Backer 1994). International aid resources activate a filtering process that favors some local organizations over others.

International actors, when they enjoy autonomy, work with and through local actors to carry out their crisis responses. The relations international aid organizations establish with local actors facilitate the latter's participation in crisis response while helping achieve international objectives, while the rules of international aid organizations place constraints on the politics of civil action despite the contradictions and inadequate protections of international organizations' authority. The third institutional quality of international aid is its resources. Aid organizations disburse resources down an "aid chain" (Watkins et al. 2012), at the bottom of which sit local civil organizations. Those local organizations that can meet the contracting demands and ideational preferences of international actors are filtered into the response; others are filtered out. Ultimately, the collectivity of civil actors is undermined by the clamor for organizational survival. In conflict contexts, physical survival is often at stake too. Being filtered into international networks can promote organizational survival but it can also place a target on those organizations' backs in the view of other conflict actors. Or, at the least, contracted and ideational resources directed at some groups can reduce the lifesaving support that reaches other groups and beneficiaries in a war zone. That is, a focus on contract and idea-based resources implies that international aid filters recipients for reasons other than, or in addition to, efficiently reaching those in greatest need. While needs matter, so too do everyday ways of doling out projects and international notions of which locals are legitimate.

Process tracing through the Syrian case allows us to build a theory of how international aid organizations distribute resources to local nonviolent actors with whom they have built relationships and on whom they have imposed rules. These resources take the form of contracts and of ideas. Contracted resources induce insecurity and competition among nonviolent actors, many of whom learn to focus on their organizational survival even in a context where their physical survival is at stake. Ideational resources— observable through the "money talk" of local actors—create novel hierarchies and sources of cleavage among local actors and make some vulnerable to the attacks of rivals. The analysis reveals that international aid resources activate selection and legitimation mechanisms by which local actors strategically deploy their agency and learn through competition, even as international actors structure templates that dictate what makes a local partner good and fitting for crisis response. Together, the distribution of contract- and idea-based resources activates a filtering process that generates change in civil action in war; specifically, it limits collective action. Varying levels of international aid autonomy demonstrate that some local actors were filtered into the international response while others—even those most committed on the front lines—were not.

International aid resources were not the only source of fragmentation among Syria's activists—far from it. Still, the analysis should demonstrate that those resources were a constraint on collectivity among the population of nonviolent actors who were facilitated into the crisis response. The case of an organization heavily favored by donors and on the receiving end of a very high value of international aid illustrates how contracted project and ideational resources generated novel sources of cleavage among Syria's nonviolent actors. The contracted and ideational resources this organization received filtered it to the top of a hierarchy of local organizations—a height that brought upon its field-workers antagonisms, kidnappings, and ultimately a dramatic descent.

Nonviolent Survival in the Syrian War

In order to make the case that international aid resources filter civil action—promoting the survival of some and not others—the first step is to show this outcome in the Syrian case. Doing so entails identifying specific observable implications of the theory. It is not possible to explain any and all fissures or fragmentations in the opposition to the Syrian regime, which by all accounts were rife (Gani 2015; Mazur 2019; Phillips 2015, 2016; Sayigh 2013); international aid was not singularly nor primarily responsible for fragmenting local actors. International aid did, however, structure a resource context for those local organizations whose participation was facilitated by international humanitarian relations and on whom aid's rules were imposed. From this standpoint, there should be least two observable implications among the population of organizations: declining growth rates and survival among some organizational forms.

First, the findings so far have pointed toward growth in the population of civil organizations as a response to international aid's relations. And, due to international aid's rules, there has been particular growth in formal organizational forms. Formal organizations can enjoy resources and legitimacy, which spur further growth (Hannan and Carroll 1992), yet organization theories of "population ecology" do not anticipate nonstop growth. Rather, they expect that when a population of organizations becomes dense, competition over resources leads to declining growth rates (Hannan and Freeman 1977). Michael Hannan and John Carroll's empirical implication is curvilinear: "Initial increases in the number of organizations can increase the institutional legitimacy of a population, enhancing the capacity of its members to acquire resources. However, as a population continues to grow, competition with others for scarce common intensifies. Combined, the mutualistic and competitive effects suggest a ∩-shaped relationship between density and founding" (Baum and Amburgey 2017, 312). These insights from population ecology have been useful to the study of international relations, where scholars have found that the rates of growth of populations of international intergovernmental and nongovernmental organizations enjoyed expansion and then slowed over time (Abbott et al. 2016; Bush and Hadden 2019).[2] It is likely that this trajectory would unfold quickly in crisis contexts, where the influx of international resources, actors, and infrastructure is relatively rapid.

The data show that the density of Syrian organizations grew, their growth rates peaked, and foundings subsequently diminished. My dataset of public Facebook pages of Syrian groups shows a trend line in page foundings that follows the expectation of an inverted U curve when a population of organizations becomes dense, as per figure 12. Growth rates rose rapidly through early 2013; the number of pages continued to grow thereafter, but at a slower pace.

Syrians observed this trend in organizational growth rates, including declines. One human rights activist who had been involved with both Syrian and international organizations in Turkey opined: "There was inflation, and now it is going back to a normal level. It was never normal that there were eight hundred organizations. So now it might be survival of the fittest."[3]

A key question then arises, who were the fittest? The Facebook dataset does not reveal which of these organizations were recipients of international aid. But an analysis of page foundings based on the represented organizations' specialties offers some suggestive evidence. I coded nine broad specialties based on self-descriptions, photographs, and recent posts among the public Facebook pages representing Syrian organizations.[4] While activists were engaged in a diversity of sectors, beginning in mid-2013 humanitarian engagements ultimately took precedence over all others, including advocacy, politics, and justice; coordination; and media.

Arguably, humanitarianism took precedence because *needs* took precedence, yet this growth is in Syrian humanitarian organizations in particular, not international ones, and Syrians could not respond to the enormity of needs alone. Other processes were likely also at play. Kendra Dupuy and her colleagues draw on population ecology to examine NGO survival and selection processes. Following organization theory, they find that generalist (rather than niche) organizations working in relatively safe issue areas like service delivery are more likely

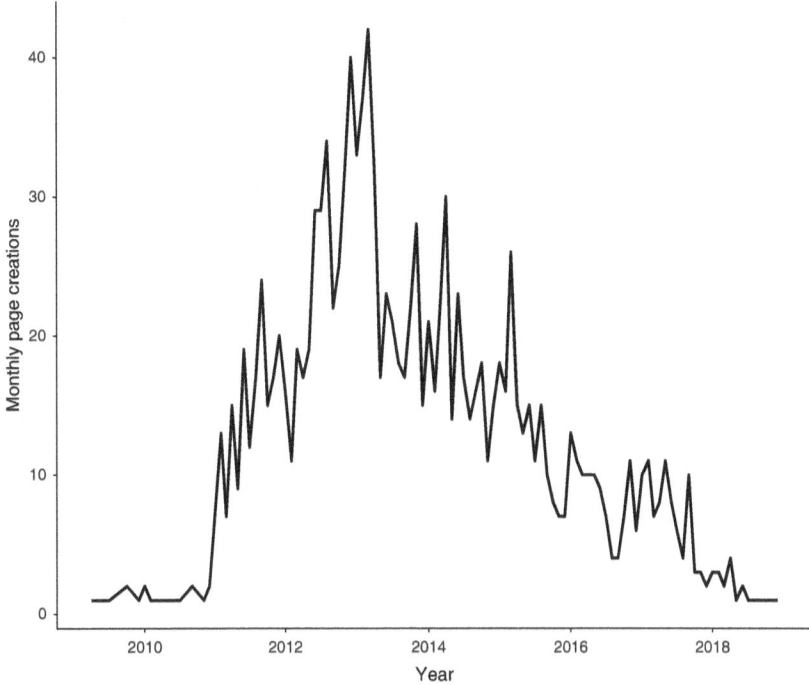

FIGURE 12. Facebook page creations by month. Source: Author's original data.

to survive in an inconducive context (Dupuy et al. 2015).[5] The Syrian context was certainly inconducive. It follows that those generalist organizations delivering services—especially humanitarians—were poised to survive.

To be sure, Syrians were agents of change, sharply unequal in power though their relationships with international actors may have been, and they wanted to help people in need, including by providing them with humanitarian relief. While international aid structured their resource environment and legitimized certain forms of engagement over others, local activists exhibited strategies to better their organizational circumstances despite competition and cleavages that reflected international contracting practices and ideational preferences.

Filtering Resources

International aid responses to the crisis that unfolded in Syria from 2011 reflected conflict developments, especially the division of territorial control. Multiple governing authorities shaped the autonomy of aid actors in different territories. The

Syrian regime blocked the provision of aid to rebel-held territory, leading many international aid organizations to erect cross-border responses for these areas from Turkey and Jordan.[6] Syrian refugees also fled to these neighboring countries, prompting refugee-specific humanitarian responses. Where international aid organizations were least constrained by governing authorities, namely in Turkey and in the areas of limited statehood across the border in northwest Syria through 2017, they enjoyed the greatest autonomy to work with and through local actors to carry out their objectives. In the process, international aid organizations disbursed contract- and idea-based resources to local activists that favored some civil action during the war.

Contract Resources

The international response to the Syria crisis brought with it the market-based contracting practices that have characterized contemporary aid (Cooley and Ron 2002). In turn, Syrian organizations experienced the insecurity, uncertainty, competition, and, ultimately, focus on survival that the new economics of organizations would lead us to expect. These contracting dynamics often revolved around projects (Krause 2014). The primary funds for channeling aid to Syria were two UN response plans, one for inside the country and one for refugee host states. Each year these funds grew and were contracted to organizations, namely UN agencies and NGOs, the numbers of which reached, in 2019, hundreds of known destination organizations and an unknown number of NGOs whose anonymity was maintained for security reasons. Syrian organizations were downstream recipients of these funds and others via projects contracted to—and subcontracted by—international organizations.

(Sub)contracted projects became fiscal lifelines for Syrian organizations. An international staff member of a Syrian medical care organization described the situation: "It's always a race. Projects last three to six months, at most one year. So by the time you set up the work, you need to *scramble* for funding again."[7] The fates of individuals and organizations alike were tied to the project lifeline. The head of a Syrian organization that supports internally displaced children named the biggest challenges they faced as first, security, and second, the inconsistency of support; projects last six months to a year, and in between they can lose employees who need to make a living.[8] What's more, the renewal of grants was hardly guaranteed at the end of projects; initial influxes of aid do not continuously feed into more projects and organizations. Indirect project funds were vital, and inconsistent.

Unlike many international humanitarian resources, OCHA's Syria Cross-Border Pooled Fund enabled direct (rather than indirect) project contracting to

Syrian organizations. Overall, as shown in table 3, Syrian organizations funded directly through the cross-border pooled fund were on the receiving end of more and more projects over the course of the response.

Publicly available data does not distinguish between individual organizations, however. The pooled fund data does not show whether a few organizations were taking on more projects, or whether projects were going to a greater number of organizations. Either way, projects allocated to Syrian organizations were assigned smaller budgets, on average, than those allocated to UN agencies and INGOs, despite the fact that larger numbers of projects were awarded to local organizations. For example, international NGOs were contracted for less than one-third of the Cross-Border Pooled Fund's projects, yet they consistently had higher budgets, direct costs, and indirect costs than those of national NGOs.

It is not very surprising that novice organizations were allocated smaller project budgets than established international ones, but although they were sometimes barely surviving, Syrian organizations often did not know that they could request core and overhead costs in their grant proposals (Els et al. 2016), or even think that they had the "right" to ask for them (Howe et al. 2015). Many international organizations failed to inform their local implementing "partners" that they could make core cost requests, and even refused to provide them when asked (Els et al. 2016; Howe et al. 2015). Such stances may be suggestive of internationals' patrimonial thinking regarding the risks of feeding into "war economies" or their romanticizing of local "efficiency." They were also in contrast to international organizations' own professional practices. Within the Syria Cross-Border Pooled Fund, Syrian organizations received far less support costs per project, on average, than did UN agencies and INGOs.

TABLE 3. OCHA Syria Cross-Border Pooled Fund allocations to "national NGOs"

YEAR	PROJECT COUNT	MEAN BUDGET (USD)	MEAN PROJECT LENGTH (DAYS)
2014	17	264,443	212
2015	46	404,755	275
2016	71	435,315	251
2017	60	322,517	234
2018	84	500,657	205
2019	127	534,240	253
2020	153	672,709	263

Source: Data compiled by author from United Nations County Based Pooled Fund Data Hub, https://cbpf.data.unocha.org/dataexplorer.html.

Project-based survival is precarious for local organizations, not only because they receive less funding than international ones and lack the same capacity to navigate the NGO scramble. Their precarity also derives from being "in the field," in a war. In interviews, staff of Syrian organizations with operations in rebel-held territory commonly cited security as a primary challenge in their operations. Security problems could threaten not just individuals but whole projects. For example, an INGO supported civil documentation efforts in rebel-held territory from 2017 to 2019, but they withdrew their assistance when the Syrian government retook the territory. It remained unclear what happened to the centers they set up and to the three hundred thousand documents they produced (Lund 2020).

The head of a US-funded development company's Syria response described another one of the administrative pathologies that accompanies projects associated with war—security vetting. Grant funding for his donor-contracted projects lasted up to nine months, but before implementation, he explained, all the members of the granted Syrian organization are vetted, which can take up to six months. That vetting is only good for twelve months, so when they reapply for another grant, the vetting begins again.[9] He went on to describe a case of funding for a medical association in rebel-held territory; the project implementation was repeatedly delayed because nearly half of the doctors were killed during the vetting. Syrians in the field navigated a deadly conflict environment atop a resource environment.

Audits and evaluations also required additional focus from local actors. Because donors and contracting organizations relied on remote management, they were especially wary of shortcomings in implementation, such as fraud or waste, when carried out by Syrian field-workers. To buttress effective implementation, INGOs regularly conducted capacity assessments of Syrian organizations but without sharing the results with one another, straining Syrians' energies (Building Markets 2018). Third-party monitors were also commonly deployed. An American third-party monitor sent to Turkey described the timeline for her evaluations as "tiny" as she reflected that nascent Syrian organizations struggled under these conditions.[10] INGOs enjoyed dedicated staff and years of experience in such modes of doing business and therefore they were poised to excel. But newly established local NGOs, whose members and motives were likely oriented toward affecting change on behalf of the Syrian cause, were not initially structured around these organizational demands.

This wartime NGO scramble exhibits processes that are well understood by scholars of aid. First, the pursuit of strategic and normative objectives was often sidelined by the priority of survival. The head of a Syrian humanitarian NGO described to me his perception of OCHA-led cluster meetings, which were meant to coordinate emergency relief. Organization representatives sat in and learned that there was a fund for projects in Idlib, and subsequently competed for that fund: "Where there is money, that's where they will go. . . . There are very few organizations who are working on the basis of a strategy."[11] However, focusing on strategy was not easy when organizations were contracted to achieve other tasks. As one Syrian explained, the local research organization he worked for tried to carve out space for focusing on their own priorities, but energies were stretched: "We're also trying to do work that we aren't hired for, but there's not enough time."[12]

The sense that strategies were circumscribed by survival tactics was commonly shared. This is not to suggest that Syrians sold their efforts for any price. In his thoughtful account of Syrian media organizations navigating between strategies and tactics, Yazan Badran demonstrates the ways some organizations adapted to the visions of development actors and their funders while maintaining space for their own preferences and priorities in their content (2020). Moreover, the balance between strategies and tactics was not the same for all Syrian organizations. Those organizations "concerned with rights and freedoms" were often more able to remain focused on their objectives from bases outside Syria, including in Turkey, than those "concerned with humanitarian needs" inside the country (Nasser et al. 2020, 116–17). In other words, simply being in the field filtered in favor of humanitarian organizations.

A second, expected implication of international contracting was that Syrian organizations oriented toward their vertical relations with donors, sometimes at the expense of efficiency and horizontal coordination. One Syrian activist working for an INGO recalled his efforts to coordinate Syrian groups within one substantive subfield. He was in direct contact with more than thirty organizations in Gaziantep and had trained dozens of their employees, but found it almost impossible to convince them to coordinate: "In every field, no matter how specialized, there are at least three or four organizations working on it. Every organization has a different supporter, a different donor country, a different funder. . . . And they don't speak to each other."[13] Espen Stokke and Eric Wiebelhaus-Brahm identified a similar challenge of horizontal coordination among a plethora of Syrian transnational justice organizations based outside Syria and placed the blame on the patronage relations they built with donors (2019). Researchers investigating Syrian faith groups in Jordan documented several incidents, including the resistance of local groups to an effort addressing duplication in beneficiaries because the groups "knew their access to beneficiaries was a comparative advantage which they could use to attract donors and international agencies" (El Nakib and Ager 2015, 23).

In the new NGO scramble, Syrian organizations were downstream of the international organizations that were seasoned and fluent in the project and contract hustle. Operating in a war zone, their physical survival was also at stake. Syrians adapted nonetheless. Local activists exhibited strategies to better their organizational circumstances amid the declining growth rates, competition and insecurity, and inequalities and cleavages that resulted from the marketization of aid. In particular, they showed evidence of "competitive learning," which Sarah Bush describes as the process by which some new organizations come to understand and adapt to strategies for success, while those that adhere to older models recede in importance (Bush 2015).

My Syrian interlocutors were cognizant of survival through selection and adaptation. An impressive example of this adaptation is of a Syrian humanitarian organization that grew in size and scale against the odds in Lebanon, where there was very little Syrian participation due to constraints on aid autonomy. "We kept opening center after center, and there was no plan, no vision," one Syrian staffer said. She continued, "I wondered how much we were doing was quality, or whether it was just that we were good at writing proposals."[14] The same pattern also occurred with some governance institutions in rebel-held territory of the northwest (despite the more general uncertainty around LCs). The former president of a reputable and well-organized LC in Idlib explained: "Every project I propose to [donors], they say OK, so long as it's [redacted city]." Why? Because the local council is "being worked well, because it's building institutions," and because "we had no problem meeting donor conditions."[15]

The idea of competitive learning suggests that local actors are not merely *acted on* by international actors. They learn and act, too. Another piece of evidence of competitive learning is the creation of coalitions of organizations. My research identified seven such coalitions, representing dozens of organizations, mostly based in Turkey with operations in northwest Syria. Many were organized around shared organizational missions, such as medical relief, transitional justice, civil society, or humanitarianism. Mustafa, whose story opened this chapter and who helped develop a coalition of humanitarian organizations, described the coalition's efforts to achieve greater representation in international humanitarian decision-making bodies. They based their lobbying on the sources of their competitive advantage as ground-level local organizations: "We want to show we are able to have better access to places the UN can't," he related. "We have access, we know how to work with the parties, how to speak the language."[16] Coalitions also helped pool lessons learned about the processes activated by international aid. A consultant to a coalition of civil society organizations explained: "As the situation here [in Turkey] became tighter and as organizations moved from nascent initiatives of friends to semi-structured organizations, they began to realize they need to become a little more official. . . . They needed to coalesce their institutional knowledge, their access to the donors, their shared programmatic challenges, to make each individual organization stronger."[17] Syrians took up additional strategies, as well, learning the language of communicating with international organizations, undergoing trainings, and adopting less political outward representations of their organizational priorities.

Some signs of competitive learning were less licit, if no less strategic. For example, rumors were common in Amman that Syrians, whose education was often interrupted by their displacement, were forging degrees on resumés they then submitted to international, or internationally funded, organizations. Yazan Badran and Kevin Smets documented one Syrian media organization's strategy of keeping staff salaries artificially low, lest higher salaries suggest to their funders that the organization was no longer in need of support (2021). Empowered to conduct needs assessments on behalf of international organizations, some Syrian activists learned how to create assessments that brought more assistance to their communities. A governance activist in southern Syria explained: "There was a lot of pressure at the borders, and there was a need for flour . . . and the [INGO] determined the proportion of those in need was 20 percent. But the reality is 100 percent! We realized we had to learn how to answer the questionnaire. So we "suggested" to people that we were in need of a mill, and then the questionnaires came back all saying we need a mill."[18] Such strategies demonstrate that local actors have agency even in a structurally imbalanced resource environment.

Ideational Resources

Given the enormity of needs, humanitarian relief in Syria was necessary. At the same time, humanitarianism was often marginal to Syrian civil organizations' original missions. A coordinator for a coalition of Syrian CSOs lamented that groups that "can trace their lineage back to protests . . . now all of a sudden do food baskets, livelihoods, PSS [psychosocial support], waste management. They're just completely lost because they're running after whatever trend exists."[19] This coordinator's impression was duly confirmed by a survey of organizations inside Syria; it found that about one-third of *non*humanitarian groups were engaged in humanitarian efforts (Khalaf et al. 2014). In chasing ideational trends, Syrians expanded beyond their alternative or niche concerns and toward general, humanitarian ones.

Even within the nonhumanitarian international response, political programming was downgraded as the conflict wore on and notions of regime change withered. Over time, civil society was tasked with providing services above all else (Brown 2018). As the US official then at the head of the US government's Syria response explained to me: "These endless trainings on how to run a meeting and the importance of elections and all this stuff, we didn't need to do any more. That money instead was buying garbage trucks, paying stipends."[20] Local councils, once conceptualized by activists and their proponents as revolutionary institutions for participation and governance (Aziz 2013), mostly evolved into (albeit important) coordinators of aid. Mustafa, describing his experience as a member of a council in Idlib, observed, "We had imagined that governance would be the primary role of the local council; but it turned out that it was relief."[21]

Transition and stabilization programs often consisted of similar substantive content, like support for civil administration and the promotion of civil society. The former was an investment in a political vision, while the latter "is intended to be short term" (OIG 2018). As recounted in the previous chapter, the United States, for instance, disinvested from opposition governance institutions even while it invested in "stabilization committees" associated with those same institutions. A Syrian contractor for US political programming explained the hedging involved: "Today they want to work on governance, but somehow without it being long-term, without making promises to Syrians that the support will continue. So rather than working with the [Syrian Interim Government], they're working with this entity called the stabilization committee that is not going to be around long-term, and the committee itself knows that—after the period of liberalization from [the Islamic State] and they do their work in that area, their role ends."[22] Syrians were being asked to adjust the international framework into which they had been incorporated from within.

In order to demonstrate that these international ideas filtered civil action it is necessary to find a way to observe them. One approach is to listen to the way people talk about money, or "money talk." Money talk reveals the meaning and cleavages associated with material resources (Parkinson 2016). It is an observable manifestation of organizations' "enactment" of the resource environment. Enactment refers to how organizations interpret, perceive, and, essentially, construct their resource environment; enacting the resource environment allows organizations to grapple with their position of dependence within it (Pfeffer and Salancik 1978). As numerous contracted and contracting parties intervened in the Syria response, their differing remuneration practices produced real and perceived inequalities between Syrian activists. Cleavages took shape between activists inside rebel-held territory versus those in refuge, in Turkey versus Jordan, between international and local organizations, and between sectors of the response.

Syrians inside Syria perceived those who worked with international organizations as gaining more than those who worked with local organizations. One humanitarian activist explained that when she was working for a Syrian charity providing schooling to displaced people in Aleppo, her wage was so small as to be symbolic. When she began to volunteer for a UN agency, she made a much higher income despite her volunteer status. "It became a known fact," she explained, "that the pay from [international organizations] was better than anything else."[23] Indeed, Aleppo and the broader northwest region of Syria were a focal point for money talk. Activists there acquired a reputation among some for being spoiled for options, because the presence of so many suppliers allowed them to pick and choose which international organizations to work with or even allowed them to work with several at once. In contrast, in the south, namely Darʻa, fewer suppliers working from Jordan (reflecting more limited aid autonomy) meant that activists were perceived as particularly committed to the cause.

This variation in international autonomy and its manifestation through money talk can be explored further through the case of the "White Helmets" or civil defense. One restriction Jordan introduced, earlier and more severely than Turkey, was on the border passage of activists. This limitation prevented international organizations from offering in-person trainings to those based in southern Syria, even when the same organizations did so in Turkey for activists in northern Syria. In turn, Syrian organizations with geographically distributed operations were cleaved by international resources. This variation affected members of the Syrian Civil Defense, popularly known as the White Helmets, who earned little whether they worked in Darʻa in southern Syria or in Aleppo or Idlib in the northwest. But intensive training was almost exclusively available to those working in the northwest, who underwent weeks-long courses in Turkey that equipped them with the skills to undertake rescue operations in response to aerial bombardment.

Those risky operations earned the White Helmets additional funding, worldwide goodwill, yearly nominations for the Nobel Peace Prize, and celebrity, including an Oscar-winning Netflix documentary. It also brought on the wrath of the Syrian and Russian militaries. Persistent Russian-led right-wing disinformation campaigns, which included accusations and intrigue related to the funding sources of the White Helmets, seemed to climax when the group's British founder tumbled to his death from an Istanbul balcony in 2019. The Civil Defense in Darʻa, meanwhile, rarely undertook rescue operations, for which they lacked training. Out of the spotlight, they focused on public services, like the repair of electricity lines. Even nonmaterial support can cleave local organizations—not just in the view of fellow activists, but in the view of warring parties, as well.

Syria's civil actors would generally agree that field-workers inside Syria in both the north and the south, who were living in vulnerable communities and among beneficiaries and armed groups, were dedicated and faced severe risks. Any amount of compensation to them was justified. Those on the outside, however, appeared to enjoy a different sort of privilege. One activist spent three long years detained in Syria for his leadership in a local coordination committee; when he emerged and fled to Turkey, he found that his peers there had "huge salaries" and had, in his view, become "distant from life inside, the situation inside."[24]

Those in Turkey were not above self-reflection They laid the blame on the marketization of their work. One civil actor who fared particularly well in Gaziantep by becoming a source of rich ground-level data described the differences that interveners created between Syrians mobilized into the response and regular Syrian refugees: "They created a parallel society, so disengaged from the Syrian society living here—the gap between us and them, it's so massive, that we're not committed . . . the economic gap, the way of thinking gap, the opportunities gap, it's so fucking massive. And at the end of the day, these other people are living in shitholes. They can survive for one month on what I can pay for two dinners."[25]

To be sure, working from Turkey or for international organizations was understood as rational, even if normatively complicated. In tracing this line of thought, one international humanitarian worker identified the multiple layers of the response hierarchy:

> You've got an international NGO employee you're paying $8,000 a month to do educational programming in Syria. That person is outsourcing their work to a Syrian employee in Gaziantep who they're paying $4,000 to do educational programming in Syria. Those people are basically outsourcing all their work to Syrians in-country that they're paying $1,000 a month to do educational programming. And those people are relying on [local council] members who they're paying $200. And the local councils are training people to do education programs. What happens to those people? They're going to say, I can work for $80 a month here, or $4,000 if I leave the country altogether.[26]

At the same time, Syrians understood that international practices were not based on location alone. Their money talk revealed their experience of donor priorities that distinctly valued different sectors and types of engagement. A representative selection of activists' experiences reveal why they saw the hierarchical valuations of international actors in the way that they did. For instance, a project assistant for an intergovernmental organization described their position as "nice, also humanitarian. But the salary was very low." A development company offered them twice the salary.[27] A local council member said his salary was very low, particularly compared to a civil society organization job "with a salary of two and a half times as much."[28] Another activist explained that she remained committed to working for a Syrian rather than international organization out of a sense of ethical obligation: "I know they are much better than others but can't afford to pay people as much as others can," she explained.[29]

While Syrians interpreted and enacted the international ideas underlying their resource environment, international organizations themselves were also navigating a contracting and idea-based resource environment structured by donors and larger organizations higher up in the aid chain. Many treated remuneration practices as a technical matter. For instance, INGOs may have maintained lower salaries for their field-workers inside Syria than for their staff in border countries based on distinct costs of living. But ideas and hierarchies mattered too. While field salaries were generally higher than those otherwise available in the local economy, not all international actors agreed about best practices. One humanitarian INGO, as a matter of principle, paid its field officers inside Syria an income equivalent to that of its Syrian staff in Turkey: more than $1,000 USD per month.[30] A staffer for a US nonprofit organization in Turkey was frustrated by the relatively high salaries offered by for-profit interveners. "There are organizations that did go in and created the inflation we see here. It's known, [this consulting company] pays salaries inside of $1,600. Whereas we pay ours $600, $100 of which is for transportation."[31] He wondered how his nongovernmental organization with a pro-democracy mandate could keep up with the pay dispensed by other interveners.

While there is clearly validity to existing ideas in the political economy of organizations related to the idea of an "NGO scramble" popularized in the study of INGOs, international resources operate in conflict contexts and with local actors in specific ways. First, the stakes are high and even physically threatening for novice, local, and vulnerable organizations operating amid violence; this NGO scramble is a dangerous one. Second, interpretation of the meaning-making of nonviolent actors, through their money talk, reveals that the resource environment is enacted by local actors in ways that transpose values and prejudices onto international action, whether or not these are intended or genuinely held by international actors.

Filtered Up and Down by Aid

What does civil action look like when it is on the receiving end of an extreme value of aid? At the start of the conflict in Syria international actors lacked access to activists inside Syria, even while they were eager to help them. The accessibility of local activists in an autonomy-allowing host state, Turkey, situated one group in particular on the receiving end of large influxes of international resources and attention in this early period: the Assistance Coordination Unit (ACU). I leverage this situation to closely examine the distribution of contract and idea-based resources on wartime activism.[32] A methodological advantage gained by this case selection technique is in the exploration of pathway variables (Seawright 2016).

The filtering process should be especially influential in a case study in which the explanatory variable—aid—is high.

Prior to being affected by the filtering process, the ACU went through the facilitating and formalizing processes. The seeds for the ACU's facilitation into an international framework were planted in 2011, when the diasporic political opposition coalesced in Turkey, gained the support of external governments, and evolved into the Syrian Opposition Coalition. Despite the coalition's factionalism and weaknesses, donors collaborated with them to achieve their Syria objectives (Phillips 2016). In 2012 these objectives came to include humanitarian response, leading to the creation of the ACU as the relief arm of the coalition. According to one of its former employees, the United States "basically created" the ACU in the hope that it could simultaneously play a primary role in the coordination of relief to Syria and "boost the Syrian opposition."[33] Indeed, the official who shepherded the US government's assistance response informed me that the ACU was his idea. He recalled telling members of the coalition, "You're going to have donor countries around the world throwing money at you," and an entity like the ACU would allow Syrians to set their own priorities for how to use it.[34] With the technical and financial help of the United Kingdom, the United States, and INGOs, and the hospitality of Turkey, the ACU was born.

International humanitarian organizations were wary of a political body charged with relief efforts, but they were also in need of the knowledge that actors with local connections could provide. The ACU, and particularly its Information Management Unit, could deploy hundreds of field-workers to enumerate and assess needs across Syria (especially in rebel-held regions) and underwent the formalizing process largely on this basis. INGOs and donors undertook capacity building, trainings, and staff secondments to develop the ACU's abilities in monitoring, surveillance, and assessment that would feed into INGO analyses (Slim and Trombetta 2014). UN leaders recognized the value of the ACU for its access (IRIN 2013b), and OCHA evaluators conceded it used "professional needs-assessment methods" (Sida et al. 2016). Even those INGOs like MSF that "kept a distance" from the ACU due to its "politicized approach" allowed that "pragmatic interaction has taken place in the exchange of data" (Whittall 2015, 21). Development companies, meanwhile, worked with the ACU to help connect with, evaluate, and select local councils for implementing donors' political projects (Chemonics International 2016). Facilitated and formalized into the crisis response, the filtering process adversely affected collectivity within and around the ACU. To be sure, factionalism in Syria's diasporic opposition was preexisting, yet the mechanisms associated with the filtering process—while not a first-order cause of opposition factionalism—had particular effects on the ACU as a local NGO engaged in the aid-based response.

As the US government official predicted, donors from the global North and Middle Eastern countries threw money at the ACU, promoting their distinct ideas about the conflict through material resources. Money talk ensued. Many perceived the ACU and the coalition more broadly to be on the receiving end of too much money, which corrupted them and increased their distance from events—and suffering—inside Syria (Alsarraj and Hoffman 2020). Condemnations of their meetings in five-star hotels were commonly heard around Gaziantep. But these donors also used their resource power to push distinct priorities and valuations of local efforts. An American staff member described the ACU's donor relations portfolio as "schizophrenic" and the site of a "civil war."[35] Views differed over whether the organization's role was to coordinate or to implement; to meet accountability standards or to send money swiftly with limited conditions; to represent secular activists or to represent a diasporic Islamist opposition. From the US perspective, by the estimation of the same official who thought up the ACU, "Something terrible happened": Qatar dumped millions of dollars into the organization;[36] Gulf interests "ended up winning the fight entirely."[37]

These differing ideational approaches affected collectivity within the ACU by provoking and exacerbating cleavages around normative values. ACU staff fragmented internally between, broadly, secular and Islamist tendencies. In late 2013, the former organized a strike to assert their objection to the practices of the latter which, in their view, were doing more harm than good for Syrians in need. Nearly half of the staffers in the Gaziantep office went on strike for a month. In the end, "The lefties lost entirely and got pushed out one by one" so that within a few months, none remained.[38]

While it lost faith in the ACU as a humanitarian coordinator, the US maintained a vision of propping up local governance institutions, specifically local councils, and countering violent extremism through the ACU. "Once the [regime] transition was moving further away" as a priority, explained a development staffer whose company worked with the ACU, "we rejiggered our strategy to focus on local councils that we thought were in open competition" with an increasingly powerful Salafi-jihadist armed group, Jabhat al-Nusra.[39] This turn to CVE and stabilization substantively took the form of service provision. In the new NGO scramble, the ACU would adapt to these donor priorities in order to survive.

They would need to adapt, even if people involved felt that the donor's focus on service provision might have actually undermined CVE objectives, given that extremist groups were not threatened by the depoliticized local councils that the ACU was "rejiggered" to support. As the development staffer for the ACU portfolio explained: "The local councils are working with humanitarians and underemphasizing their political role and political nature . . . like we're just here to oversee services. . . . But we saw that Jabhat al-Nusra doesn't mind other people filling in the gap, because they're not providing an alternative. Jabhat al-Nusra could say: Sure, fill the gap, who cares, makes it easier for us—we'll open up the *Dawa* [Islamic missionary] school, and we'll do children's competitions, and all these activities to recruit and promote and embed ourselves, while you pick up the bill."[40]

Sometimes dozens of local councils were the end recipients of support that came via the ACU, making them subject to money talk, too. The ACU provoked "criticism within Syrian society" for " 'promoting clientalism' in its development of local councils and the $20,000 grant that comes with such status," evaluators of the humanitarian response noted, adding that activists assign the blame to the coalition and its donors (Slim and Trombetta 2014, 48). But much of the time, only a few local councils were selected to receive assistance, feeding into local cleavages. As a former ACU staff member said, "When you give a ton of money to one council, every council around it is looking at them and saying, 'What did they do?' You're establishing a relationship of bitterness and distrust."[41] For the development companies working with the ACU on these distributions, the selection of local councils might simply be a matter of size or capacity to receive them. But for the Syrian activists engaged in this supply chain, money talk could become dangerous.

In cooperation with the ACU, the US conceived a CVE program to offer special support to local councils that worked in towns where Salafi-jihadist armed groups were weakened. The program included "massive humanitarian deliveries, fast-track stabilization projects, and cash infusion[s]" worth millions of dollars.[42] Only a handful of towns were selected, but the rollout was complicated by filtering dynamics. Armed groups and Islamist factions suspected that such a massive influx of resources was meant to undermine Islam. Understanding this strand of money talk, a member of one of the targeted local councils said that they signed onto the project without disclosing the agreement with the local Islamist battalions, although the battalions found out, incited reprisals against the council's leader, and one of the armed groups kidnapped him.[43] Another activist working with the ACU on the project was kidnapped while crossing through a checkpoint in rebel-held territory; their route, they explained, was known to only one person—a colleague at the ACU opposed to their secular "whiskey clique" faction within the organization.[44] Both were released after brief detainments.

The project hit another obstacle when a Syrian partner in the ACU was in a car accident while driving between Syria and Turkey (by all accounts a random event). The project was downgraded and moved out of the ACU and to the opposition Syrian Interim Government, which grew out of the opposition coalition, but which the United States could not recognize (as a government) and did not formally fund. The ambitious services-for-CVE program was whittled down to small projects in a larger assortment of towns.

Following these high-profile chapters in the ACU's trajectory, the filtering process shaped it into one among many Syrian NGOs in Turkey—one that "struggled to survive, holding on by tooth and nail," according to a close international observer.[45] While political factions fought over the ACU, humanitarians came to rely on the new dense population of local NGOs they had facilitated and formalized into the response. In turn, the ACU's cash and in-kind grants dropped dramatically from $190 million USD in 2014, to $35 million in 2015, and down to just $13 million in 2016 (ACU n.d.-a, n.d.-b, n.d.-c).

A development consultant seconded to the ACU at a later stage of its trajectory explained that some donors remained invested in their early vision of the ACU and continued to support products like the reports of the Information Management Unit—commonly regarded as the most professional part of the organization. ACU staff, for their part, also seemed to maintain an expectation of support thanks to the organization's political identity. But they had not experienced the competitive learning that peer organizations had and their products had limited utility to actors on the ground.[46] Other Syrian organizations, in contrast, which had never enjoyed extreme high values of aid the way the ACU did, were scrambling to become competitive in order to win projects from subcontracting international actors based on their professionalism. The ACU had become a "small NGO" in a dense population, a shadow of its former self.[47]

While the causes of fragmentation of contentious movements are many, a filtering process associated with international aid affects the very population of organizations that aid has facilitated and formalized into a framework of crisis response. International aid actors that engaged in the Syria conflict response brought their market-based practices and legitimating ideas into an unequal resource environment. In turn, they introduced novel sources of cleavage and hierarchy and exacerbated existing ones. This analysis should not understate the central role of armed actors in fundamentally, primarily, and existentially threatening unarmed actors in this war and others. Nonmilitary interventions can have unintended and even dangerous consequences for those they come to help.

Together, the facilitating, formalizing, and filtering processes generate something like a civil society in those areas where international aid actors enjoy autonomy to work with local actors to achieve their objectives. But after contention has been "civilized" in this way, its constituent parts are left to withstand, or not, war's violence and aftermath. International aid actors do not and cannot provide protection to the population of local organizations that they have supported and trained to structure their crisis response. When those international actors exit the scene of the crisis, or when their autonomy decreases, local actors are left exposed or wanting for protection from some other governing authority. They did not find such protection in Syria in those times and spaces where the state reclaimed territory from rebels, where host states reduced international aid autonomy, and where a natural disaster struck and isolated Syria's civil actors. The sudden fall of the regime in December 2024 may, finally, bring something like a civil society to its state.

6

COMPARATIVE CASES

In the preceding chapters, we delved deeply into the Syrian case to understand how international aid generates change in civil action during war. A population of civil organizations engaged in nonviolent action on behalf of Syrian causes and communities against the odds of conflict was spurred by institutional characteristics of aid that enable and constrain wartime activism. Together, processes activated by aid civilize contention: International aid organizations seek to impose some order on war, and are particularly able to do so over those local actors with whom they interact the most and who help achieve international objectives. The something like a civil society that emerges from these interactions exists with humanitarian governance but without a government; it is vulnerable during war and potentially in its aftermath when aid for crises declines or ends.

One might wonder whether this theory of civilized contention, built in the Syrian case, can explain conflict processes elsewhere; that is, whether it is "generalizable." In order to discover the answer, this chapter looks at conflict contexts that broadly fall under the theory's scope condition—that is, situations in which international aid actors enjoyed some autonomy to pursue their objectives with and through local actors. We would expect to find such conditions in areas of limited statehood or in areas where powerful actors do not obstruct aid autonomy. Because central governments often do exert some control over aid actors, aid organizations often establish operations in rebel-held territory or in countries neighboring the one in conflict. Those rebels and neighboring states may be powerful too, but they often allow for international autonomy to further their own interests. As a result, border areas emerge as spaces of convergence for international and local actors—a finding common in studies of conflict.

With autonomy as a starting point, the following case study of Myanmar appears to align with an overall set of processes involved in civilizing contention. Each of these individual theorized processes also appears in brief probes of a wider set of cases, including southern Sudan, Ukraine, Afghanistan, and Western Sahara. In each case, facilitating, formalizing, and filtering processes are plausibly at work, generating change in civil action. The beginning and end points in any given case may differ, but the causal processes unfold in relatively predictable ways regardless. In other words, the exact measurement of the explanatory variables (international aid) and outcome variables (something like a civil society) is less important in a process-based theory than showing that causal mechanisms are operative under a given condition. As a final probe, I explore the Islamic State in Syria—a case wherein armed actors blocked aid autonomy altogether. In this case, ideology and territorial control, rather than the theorized causal mechanisms of civilizing contention, are paramount in shaping civil action, or a lack thereof. These case illustrations will not benefit from the fine-grained knowledge that is crucial to process tracing. Their more modest application is to demonstrate the theory's plausible generalizability.

Civilizing Contention in Myanmar

In February 2021, Myanmar's military staged a coup that undid a decade of democratic opening. Protesters took to the streets, organized strikes and boycotts, and faced violent repression for their dissent. The junta's forces killed, wounded, arrested, and imprisoned thousands of civilians (Matelski et al. 2022). Myanmar's activists adapted to the escalation of contention. Some took up arms, fleeing to border regions and forming people's defense forces or joining with preexisting ethnic armed groups that had long challenged the government (Egreteau 2022). Others stuck to nonviolent means, also fleeing to border areas and undertaking new forms of civil action such as providing first aid and health care or documenting human rights violations (Root and Nu Nu 2023). In so doing, they did not avoid violence: Myanmar's civil activists, including first responders displaying Red Cross symbols, have been directly targeted, beaten, and killed (ICG 2021). This was not the first time that civil actors had found themselves under attack and seeking safety and participation in the borderlands.

A pro-democracy social movement arising in 1988, in what was then called Burma, had also faced violent repression, and the military had asserted itself as the government. Then, too, borderlands had become spaces of risky engagement

(Callahan 2007). Refugees escaping conflict were joined by nonviolent activists and nonstate armed groups in border regions and neighboring countries, namely Thailand. International humanitarian organizations arrived on the scene to help. Between 1990 and 2010, international aid organizations "established administrative bases in neighboring countries, typically in Thailand" (Fumagalli 2022). These organizations, more than fifty of which came to be based in a single Thai border town (Callahan 2007), relied on local actors to help achieve their objectives. To enact cross-border humanitarian operations into Burma, international actors were "de facto working alongside nonstate organizations and alternative governance systems often aligned with armed ethnic organizations," Matteo Fumagalli explains. Funds, supplies, and technical assistance were "channeled to local organizations already operating in the borderlands," and they included community-building and civil society organizations working in education and health care (2022).

In the 1990s, aid organizations on the border with Burma enjoyed autonomy, a condition that allowed them to interact with local actors relatively unimpeded by states or obstructive armed actors. This relative autonomy was not granted by the Burmese government, but by the neighboring Thai government and by conditions of limited statehood inside Burma's border regions where the central government lacked control. The executive director of a coordinating body of INGOs that arrived at the border in the 1980s described Thai government policy as pragmatic and tolerant, allowing aid organizations "to provide essential humanitarian services in a generally unhindered and well-coordinated manner" (TBC 2004, 9). Those INGOs, though initially few in number and responding in an ad hoc manner, would demonstrate qualities of organized international aid that characterize bureaucratic and resource-endowed institutions. These institutional qualities would enable and constrain possibilities for civil action among civilians and refugees in the Thai-Burma border region.

First, international aid actors would forge relationships with local actors that would help the former achieve their objectives and facilitate the participation of the latter in crisis response. When INGOs arrived at the scene of the Karen refugee crisis in the Thai-Burma borderlands, they found Karen activists already acting on behalf of their communities. Resilient and adaptive as they may have been, however, local actors lacked the capacity to meet needs: Their leaders were writing letters "pleading for help" and trying and failing to grow rice to feed the population. International humanitarians began to build relations with these nonviolent actors, "forging the foundations for enduring partnerships" (TBC 2004).

Through these relationships, international actors benefited from the access, knowledge, and connections that locals enjoyed—and from the risks locals were willing to take by crossing through the border to deliver relief to people inside

Burma (Horstmann 2011). Local actors, for their part, grew their capacity and their population of organizations, which included groups for youth and women as well as alternative schools and health care systems. These social, material, and infrastructural relations did not always proceed smoothly. In the Burma borderlands, the INGO coordinating body reports, "The newfound relationships, involving steep learning curves on all sides, weren't without their frustrations" (TBC 2004, 21), yet international humanitarians constituted local activists as crisis responders and allocated them capacities to act as such.

The framework of civilizing contention suggests that as relations are built, international aid organizations impose rules on local actors that constrain their politics despite their eminently political contexts, thus formalizing their ways of engaging. Though they participated in humanitarian efforts, Karen activists were hardly strangers to politics. Local organizations were overwhelmingly affiliated with Christian religious networks and with the dominant rebel group in eastern Burma and its governing arm, the Karen National Liberation Army (KNLA) and the Karen National Union (KNU), respectively. These local relief organizations "support the resistance and insurgency against the Burmese military regime," scholarly observers have acknowledged, and international humanitarians "consciously or unconsciously thus support and keep alive a political and military project and help to legitimize and justify the evangelical imagination of a Karen homeland" (Horstmann 2011, 514).

However, international humanitarian organizations in the Burmese case promoted an order based on rules of rationalism, moralism, and professionalism. They insisted on the "independence of the refugee committees" and decried instances of interference from the rebels, while working closely with local actors who could provide reliable data and information, who were educated and professional, and who could present themselves as unbiased (TBC 2004). Gradually, the rules forged nonviolent actors into formal crisis responders. Ashley South explains: "As the refugee situation along [the] Thailand border was gradually internationalized, with the presence of more international NGOs—and since 1998, the UN High Commissioner for Refugees—the refugee committees have been obliged to become more responsive to their clients, the refugees" (South 2007, 70). Refugee-focused organizations, as well as cross-border assistance groups, began to "develop relatively independent of their 'parent' insurgent organizations" and to "demonstrate transparency and accountability to donors and beneficiaries (their local communities)"—even if they shared the same ethnonationalist goals as the rebels (South 2007, 71).

In the Thai-Burma borderlands, as elsewhere, international aid resources were distributed based on needs, but not exclusively so. When needs are immense and resources are finite, their distribution reflects contracting practices and ideas about appropriate recipients, which together filter some for receipt of aid. When the Thai-Burma Border Consortium established itself in 1984, it was dominated by Christian INGOs for whom Karen Christian Baptist relief networks "emerged as natural partners" in the border areas (Horstmann 2011). Those Karen Christian networks dominated the KNU, and thus international aid organizations were "shoring up the authority" of the rebel group's ethno-nationalist project (Horstmann 2011). Although the Karen population was more diverse than these Christian networks would suggest, the latter were educated, themselves educators, and they successfully selected into international frameworks and met donor expectations and ideational preferences—especially in a Cold War context in which they represented anti-communist ideas (Brenner 2019). The democracy uprising of 1988 brought more international awareness to the plight of Karen refugees, "rising aid budgets," more secular INGOs, and even more favor for the KNU's national project and its associated nonviolent organizations (South 2007).

Ultimately, through repeated interactions, the institutional qualities of international aid—its relations, rules, and resources—facilitated activists' participation in nonviolent action in the Thai-Burma borderlands, formalized its politics, and filtered the population of local organizations involved. The processes of change activated by international aid occurred in concert with Karen activists who brought their own experiences, adaptations, and preferences to the field of action. Altogether, international aid arguably civilized contention among local actors in the Thai-Burma borderlands. As they sought to bring order and routine to the conflict, international aid organizations forged something like a population of civil society organizations among activists; these organizations served the objectives of international interveners but could not enjoy the protection that civil society needs. Why does it matter that something that was close to, but not quite civil society arose in the borderlands? What is at stake for nonviolent actors in civil war contexts?

At the height of the Karen rebellion in the late 1980s the KNU's armed wing, the KNLA, controlled significant swaths of eastern Burma while its civilian wings dominated education and other nonviolent sectors in the borderlands in relationship with, following the rules of, and with resources from, international aid organizations. But as early as the 1990s, the tide began to turn for the Karen rebellion on the military and geopolitical fronts (Brenner 2019). First, the Karen rebellion became the primary target of the Burmese military as armed organizations elsewhere in the country signed ceasefire agreements with the government. The Burmese government, meanwhile, benefited politically, economically, and militarily from the shifting geopolitical landscape of the post–Cold War period (Brenner 2019). In particular, the Thai government, which had previously given leeway to Karen rebels, began to embrace "constructive engagement" with the

Burmese government and was joined in its exploitation of natural gas in Karen territories by Western governments that had previously isolated the Burmese government (Brenner 2018).

As the KNU lost territory and geopolitical assets, internal divisions—once obscured by international aid organizations that filtered KNU affiliates to the top of their preferred hierarchy—became increasingly evident as dissenting factions broke from the KNU and made deals with the central government (Brenner 2019). The almost-civil-society of those facilitated, formalized, and filtered nonviolent organizations was becoming disconnected from shifting realities on the ground. Foreign aid, South contends, had "insulated the KNU and its supporters from the realities of life in Burma, while empowering one among several competing concepts of Karen nationalism" (2007). Eventually, a faction within the KNU's own leadership entered into a ceasefire agreement with the central government and community-based organizations became more disconnected still; the "political demands of the Karen revolution and the grievances of its grassroots ... remained unaddressed" (Brenner 2019, 97). Nonviolent actors in the borderlands were left unprotected as the KNU weakened and the Burmese government reclaimed control. At the time of writing, the civil war that began anew in Myanmar following the 2021 coup has exhibited many of the same processes, and nonviolent actors continue to work in this violent context. International aid organizations are operating alongside and with them in the borderlands. The civilizing contention framework can allow us to grapple with their situation.

The Processes of Civilizing Contention

Additional cases exhibit evidence of the theorized processes associated with civilizing contention—facilitating, formalizing, and filtering—that follow from the relations, rules, and resources that characterize contemporary international aid. The overall process of civilizing contention was apparent in southern Sudan during the 1990s Sudanese civil war, prior to its independence and evolution into the world's newest state, South Sudan. Components of the overall process of civilizing contention are also observable in Ukraine, Afghanistan, and Western Sahara.

During the 1990s Sudanese civil war, international aid agencies established a two-pronged humanitarian response that served both northern government-held areas and southern rebel-held areas. This UN-coordinated aid response, Operation Lifeline Sudan (OLS), enjoyed greater autonomy in the rebel-held south where armed groups were more permissive of the UN's role than was the central government in the north. This arrangement and the associated dynamics are strikingly similar to the "Whole of Syria" response that enabled the coordination of UN aid separately into government-held territory and cross-border from Turkey and Jordan into rebel-held areas. Scholarly analyses and an independent review of Operation Lifeline Sudan by humanitarian evaluators reveal the ways aid organizations created something like a civil society in southern Sudan—one in which local participation was enabled but politics and collectivity were constrained.

Through a Kenya-based cross-border operation into southern Sudan, OLS developed formal mechanisms and "ground rules" to engage with local actors. In so doing, they activated facilitating and formalizing processes: They would constitute local actors as crisis responders and direct their actions toward formal (and less political) ways of engaging. The evaluators of OLS describe a situation in which INGOs agreed to train and build the capacity of Sudanese organizations and the civilian wings of armed groups agreed to respect humanitarian principles (Karim et al. 1996). In turn, there was a "phenomenal increase" in the number of Sudanese indigenous NGOs; "community-based relief committees" became nodes for assessing needs; and in the process, rebel-affiliated humanitarian organizations gained in professionalism and expertise, as well as influence (Karim et al. 1996; also Mampilly 2011). The growth in the population of local organizations was no accident. It was an "intended consequence of the political strategy of humanitarian agencies," according to Volker Riehl, because INGOs needed those local organizations in order to achieve their objectives (2001).

However, some of these groups received more support and legitimation than others, initiating a filtering process while the formalizing process was also underway. In particular, USAID favored the humanitarian arm of the Sudanese People's Liberation Movement/Army, the Sudan Relief and Rehabilitation Association (SRRA). As a major donor, USAID wielded its preferences so that INGOs "would have to go through SRRA structures" (Mampilly 2011, 152). At the same time, and with mixed success, OLS sought to devolve authority from rebel groups toward "more formal structures of civil society administration." International humanitarians aimed to see the SRRA "as capable of acting independently of its political environment, by transposing a construct of neutrality onto the SRRA" (Prendergast and Duffield 1994).[1] Ultimately, OLS contributed to the advancement of international humanitarian objectives in southern Sudan while also giving way to an "emerging civil society" (Karim et al. 1996). At the same time, it deployed a "rules-based framework to temper the manner in which internal wars are fought" (Karim et al. 1996). That is, international aid organizations engaged in institutional practices that aimed to pacify war. In the process, civil action was enabled, and politics and collectivity were constrained.

The Facilitating Process

When Russia invaded Ukraine in February 2022, nonviolent actors in the country resisted by blocking tanks with their bodies and protesting occupation. Within a few weeks civilians had organized smuggling routes into targeted cities. From Dnipro, for instance, a group of friends would transport supplies to men on the front lines in Kharkiv and bring fleeing civilians back out with them (Hauer 2022). Ukraine's civil actors, in other words, were prepared to participate in wartime activism in 2022.

At that time Ukraine was already home to a well-developed civil society and international aid presence. A social movement catalyzed major shifts in the country's politics during the Maidan Uprising of 2013 to 2014 and activists organized civil and other humanitarian responses to the armed conflict in eastern Ukraine that followed. International aid organizations established themselves in the country in response to address the needs of internally displaced and other conflict-affected populations. In other words, Ukraine was home to a bustling population of civil organizations as well as international aid actors in the 2010s. Given this backdrop, international and local actors would presumably have been poised to respond jointly to the immense crisis that shook Europe in 2022. That was not the case.

An early assessment of the humanitarian response to the 2022 Ukraine crisis observed that hundreds of small groups of civilians organized and implemented "virtually all humanitarian aid inside Ukraine" in the weeks following Russia's invasion (Stoddard et al. 2022). Facing grave risks, these upstart volunteers strove to meet Ukrainians' needs. Nevertheless, and despite unprecedented funds directed at INGOs and UN agencies to respond rapidly to the crisis, the international humanitarian sector failed to meet these groups where they were, "uncertain how to incorporate them" into their response structures. International actors worried that "powerful feelings of national unity among Ukrainians . . . pervaded humanitarian action in the country" (Stoddard et al. 2022). That is, the solidarity of Ukrainian activists with the armed resistance conflicted with international humanitarian principles. International aid actors were also concerned about "fiduciary risks" posed by local groups lacking the organizational capacity to meet fiscal compliance standards. Finally, most international aid actors were concentrated in secure western parts of the country and across the Polish border, from where they struggled to connect with local actors (Stoddard et al. 2022). As elsewhere, productive relationships between international and local actors were not a given.

International actors needed to establish relations with Ukraine's wartime activists, including social relations to achieve access and information, infrastructural relations to channel that action into international infrastructure, and material relations to support local capacity and spur organizational growth. As is common elsewhere, international actors operating in Ukraine found that achieving access to frontline areas was as crucial as it was challenging. They understood that local NGOs excelled at delivering "aid to hard-to-reach areas, often close to the front line," from where they could "provide humanitarian assistance and protection to the most vulnerable" (OCHA 2023, 41). Accordingly, the international humanitarian community had brought 342 Ukrainian partner organizations into their official response, about 63 percent of their total partners, by October 2023. Moreover, a country-based pooled fund was established to direct donor contributions to "unearmarked funds to support local humanitarian efforts" (OCHA 2023, 95). This fund contributed to the growth of Ukrainian civil organizations, or "eligible partners," engaging from directly within the international response (OCHA 2023, 42). The population of Ukrainian humanitarian organizations grew "exponentially" from the start of the war (Mercy Corps 2023, 3).

These international aid relations activated mechanisms that constituted local activists as crisis responders and allocated them the capacity to act as such, and yet as is common, the relationships were not without friction, despite the well-developed starting point of Ukrainian organizations. Direct funding to Ukrainian organizations remained limited, and even though "stakeholders found that Ukrainian CSOs' overall capacities are relatively high," international actors remained concerned about their technical capacities while local actors remained wary of international mechanisms, acronyms, and jargon (Mercy Corps 2023, 4). We might expect that the formalizing and filtering processes would follow in the Ukrainian case to bring local actors in line with the rules of international aid and to favor those who best navigate the contracts and ideas associated with international crisis response.

The Formalizing Process

In 1979, the Soviet Union intervened in Afghanistan to back the communist government against an Islamist insurgency. During their decade-long presence, the Soviets' tactics and generalized insecurity led millions of Afghans to seek refuge in Pakistan and Iran. Fighting continued after the Soviet withdrawal in 1989 until the Islamist rebels finally gained control of the central government in 1992.

The civil conflict that followed the Soviet withdrawal coincided with a restructuring of the humanitarian aid response to Afghanistan and Afghan refugees in Pakistan (Donini 1996; Novak 2013). International aid actors agreed on an "Afghanization" drive to involve Afghans more deeply in the crisis response. The first part of Afghanization can be understood in terms that coincide with the facilitating process: International organizations established social, infrastructural, and material relations with Afghans who had access and connections in their own communities and could help achieve humanitarian objectives. International aid organizations "encouraged the establishment of Afghan NGOs by providing funding, training, and registration facilities" (Novak 2013, 879). The intended outcome, "an increased number and relevance of Afghan NGOs," was an "undeniable success" (Novak 2013, 880). Much of this occurred from across the border in Pakistan; even when Afghan organizations moved their operations inside Afghanistan, they maintained managerial offices in Pakistan. But Afghanization did not end there: A formalizing process ensued. International actors would impose rational rules on these new Afghan civil organizations that would orient local actors toward producing and provisioning knowledge; moralistic rules that encouraged "impartial" claims-making and humanitarian principles; and professionalism rules that would favor those who might acquire, or who already possessed, technical qualifications and expertise.

International aid organizations engaged in Afghanization were, from the start, worried about the political connections and commitments of Afghan nationals (Donini 1996). In addition, they were concerned with the capacity of the new Afghan NGOs and their ability to adhere to donor requirements (Novak 2013). Therefore, international aid actors pursued capacity-building and professionalization of local organizations. International agencies' focus on these rules began to make "Afghanization" look something like "Westernization." Paolo Novak explains: "Accurate budgeting, monitoring procedures, a clear project proposal, participatory and accountability mechanisms, etc., became pre-requisites for obtaining donors' funds. Such managerial systems, however, did not originate from the Afghan context" (2013, 881). Those Afghan civil actors who were able to operate in this international aid context were educated and middle-class English speakers, those with Western training, and those who already worked for international organizations or who had been bureaucrats in the former Soviet regime (Novak 2013, 881).

Despite the rules imposed on Afghanistan's civil actors, their existence in the conflict context remained fundamentally political. Afghan aid actors were personally and politically connected to networks inside Afghanistan; their embeddedness in the local context was hard to avoid—indeed it was the very quality that encouraged international actors to work with and through them in the first place. What stands out is not the failure of international actors to depoliticize Afghan civil actors, but the fact that the rules on which their bureaucratic authority is built are imposed through coercive and normative pressures to contain those politics into more rule-abiding, outwardly neutral, and professional forms—all in an effort to achieve international objectives of managing the fallout of war.

The Filtering Process

Spain formally withdrew from the territory of Western Sahara in 1975. The Sahrawi national movement proclaimed independence, which Morocco swiftly rejected. Morocco seized most of Western Sahara, displacing tens of thousands to the Algerian desert. Since that time Sahrawi refugees in Algeria have been dependent on humanitarian aid; they have also gained a reputation as a "good" or "idyllic" community among international observers for their democratic values, gender equality, and participatory practices (Fiddian-Qasmiyeh 2014; J. A. Mundy 2007).

Sahrawi political organization is at the "core of the refugee experience" in the borderlands, specifically in the camps in Tindouf, Algeria, with the Algerian government's support (Khoury 2011, 5). The armed group fighting Moroccan domination of Western Sahara, the Polisario Front, established a civilian administration (the Saharan Arab Democratic Republic) for the camps that "evolved into a kind of state in exile, a space where Western Saharans could practice the kind of citizenship and governance that they hoped to achieve upon independence" (J. A. Mundy 2007, 278). While almost entirely dependent on international aid, Sahrawis (more or less) democratically participate in camp management at multiple levels of administration. Their state-in-exile government has dedicated such attention to education in the camps that Sahrawi refugees have become among the most literate communities in Africa (J. A. Mundy 2007) and their "mass organizations" represent the interests of labor, youth, and women in the refugee community. The last of these—the National Union of Sahrawi Women—has become particularly venerated by the international actors supporting Sahrawi refugees. In Elena Fiddian-Qasmiyeh's estimation, the Sahrawi women's union became an "ideal" partner in the eyes of international aid organizations like the UN Refugee Agency and the Spanish civil society organizations invested in aiding Sahrawi refugees (2010). The women's union was lauded for promoting women's inclusion and participation in all elements of camp life. Fiddian-Qasmiyeh finds that representatives of the union "actively fostered" sentiments of shared sisterhood and women's empowerment with these international agencies: They strategically used the language of "gender equality mainstreaming," projecting themselves in the terms on which they understood international support to be based.

International aid projects, in turn, were repeatedly directed at the same target groups associated with the women's union, even as other—potentially more vulnerable—beneficiaries were passed over (Fiddian-Qasmiyeh 2010). Fiddian-Qasmiyeh's point is not that the women's union and the beneficiaries it represented were undeserving or manipulative; the needs among them, like other Sahrawi refugees, were immense and humanitarian aid was crucial for their survival (Fiddian-Qasmiyeh 2014). Rather, her analysis and that of others, like Clifford Bob (2005), suggests that local nonviolent actors understand and act according to the incentive structures of international aid organizations, which rarely reflect needs alone. This filtering of support to some and not others on the basis of contracts and ideas is evident in the sector of women and gender issues. Its manifestation in the context of a relatively unified national movement is notable and relevant: With US and French backing of the Moroccan government, a political resolution that addresses self-determination for Western Sahara remains a distant prospect. Aid to something like a civil society, which can distribute goods and services to generations of refugees, is a useful stopgap for the international community.

The Total Absence of Aid Autonomy

What does civil action look like in the complete absence of international aid? International interventions in domestic crises and development are nearly ubiquitous, even if many are relatively modest and underfunded and many others suffer from obstacles to access and autonomy. Very few cases lend themselves to examining situations of "no aid" (Phillips 2020). Yet the Syrian war included such a situation in the large swaths of Syria and Iraq controlled by the so-called Islamic State (IS), a zealously extremist armed group that, for a time, seemingly menaced both its domestic victims and the global nation-state system. International aid autonomy in these areas was essentially nonexistent. This dramatic situation makes it possible to examine the politics of civil action where international aid was at an extreme low value.

The Islamic State was largely financially independent. Although it received limited support from individual donors abroad who invested in its transnational ideology, observers agree that most of IS's finances derived from within, including from oil revenues, taxes, extortion, asset seizure, kidnapping, and border crossings (Humud et al. 2015; Robinson et al. 2017). At the same time and despite some early examples to the contrary, international aid was mostly barred from the territory due to donors' counterterror legislation, extreme insecurity, and IS's own restrictions on and violence toward international aid workers (Svoboda 2014; Howe 2016; Parker 2018). Aid, responsive as it is to war dynamics, was thus blocked from IS territory.

While an extremely low value of the explanatory variable of aid offers an opportunity to explore a counterfactual, the situation in IS territory also presents a substantively interesting puzzle. Although IS prohibited nonviolent action by civilians, the group did erect institutions for technocratic and bureaucratic governance. That is, despite the absence of aid, there seems to have been a formalizing process underway that was driven by ideology and territorial control. It differed fundamentally from the organizational mechanisms of international aid institutions.

When what was then the Islamic State of Iraq crossed into Syria in 2013 and became the Islamic State of Iraq and Syria, it was one among many armed groups alternatively competing or collaborating in areas outside of government control (Lister 2015). Like other Salafi-jihadi rebels, IS was fairly pragmatic with regard to civilian activism already at work in these territories. Though IS cracked down on protesters who had grievances against it, it cautiously left space for LCs and other Syrian organizations partaking in the provision of relief and services, which allowed them to focus on their institutions of choice, especially courts (Barber 2013; Khalaf 2015; Lister 2015). This pragmatism, however, gave way to dogmatism where IS assumed full territorial control.

When and where IS achieved exclusive territorial control, as in its Syrian "capital" of Ar Raqqah and in Iraq's Mosul, it established centralized and ambitious institutions for rebel governance. The broad scope of IS's governance interventions was evident in the multiple domains in which it operated: education, public services, proselytization, health, tribal outreach, public security, finances, public morality, taxation, agriculture, and military recruitment, among others (Lister 2015; Al-Tamimi 2015c). Independent organizational and council activity were off limits for civilian activists, many of whom fled or retreated, and a few of whom bravely resisted IS domination from underground (exemplified by Raqqah Is Being Slaughtered Silently, an activist organization).

Yet IS did rely on civilians to advance their governance across these areas. Moreover, it made demands on them that were in some ways aligned with those of international aid organizations. These demands did not rest on bureaucratic authority—instead, they rested on brute force. IS needed professionals to enact its objectives. In the realm of health, for instance, Islamic State suffered such a "brain drain" of medical professionals that it gave them ultimatums to return or else face confiscation of their homes (Al-Tamimi 2015b). IS drew on existing personnel who already worked in government offices, declaring that its employees were appointed for their "technical skills" and their trustworthiness (Revkin 2020). It also held local actors to high accountability standards—again, through brute force. It undertook searches of local businesses to battle hoarding of goods (Al-Tamimi 2015a); created standards for taxation concerned with minute details that would ensure proper filing (Revkin 2016); and supported cadres to monitor and enforce their "microregulations" of women's bodies—an apparent manifestation of governmentality (Salih and Kraidy 2020).

But the underlying drivers of the IS project are distinctly different from those of aid. Islamic State's concern with the provision of goods and services derived from their sense of "divine obligation" (Revkin 2016). In this ideological view, practices like collecting receipts from bakeries were undertaken to ensure financial accountability—not to donors, but to the "Muslim populace" in its realm (Al-Tamimi 2015a). Likewise, acts like restricting access to health care outside its territories reflected an "ideological end-goal of self-sufficiency"—the opposite of efficient or rational solutions for people in need (Al-Tamimi 2015b)—and its obsession with controlling women expressed practices of power steeped in an "intense fear" of the female body and justified by an "ultraconservative religio-political ideology" that can be understood as biopolitics. This same distorted governmentality was also a politics of death, or necropolitics, when applied to non-Muslim Yazidi women enslaved by the group (Salih and Kraidy 2020). In its effort to "profoundly rearrange social and political relations" (Kalyvas 2015a), the Islamic State's revolutionary ideology often generated formal and technocratic behavior among the civilians that manned its rebel governance institutions.

Realizing these ideological goals depended on an antecedent condition—territorial control. Without exclusive territorial control, IS's bureaucratic propensities were immaterial. In cities across Iraq and Syria where IS lacked unilateral control, the group was "unable or unwilling to invest in the governing apparatuses and regulatory regimes seen in Raqqa and Mosul. . . . Instead, the group spent the bulk of its time attempting to consolidate military control and, where unsuccessful, destroyed key infrastructure and wrought violence" (Robinson et al. 2017). The same pattern extends to IS projects further afield, like in North Africa, where its inability to hold territory corresponded with the "collapse of the state project" and the group's relegation to a "continual headache" of terrorist acts (Al-Tamimi 2018). In this context, ideology and territorial control are prevailing drivers of outcomes that include the barring of civil activism and the erection of governance institutions—factors that civil war scholarship has indicated drive rebel behavior and governance (Kasfir 2005; Kalyvas 2006, 2015b; Suykens 2015; Arjona 2016).

In the areas of their intervention, humanitarians distribute goods, like food baskets and tent shelters. They provide services, like vaccinations and safe drinking water systems. And they promote rules, like safeguarding child protection and countering gender-based violence. Goods, services, and rules are the domains of governing authorities, even in the absence of governments (Risse 2011a). Humanitarians and other aid actors certainly do not control territories in areas of limited statehood, as rebels like the Islamic State might, but by providing goods and services and creating rules, autonomous international aid organizations engage in governance—not *over* territory, but certainly *in* it (Latham 2001). In this endeavor, they work with and through local civil actors. From Ukraine to Afghanistan, and from the 1990s to 2020s, international aid organizations, when they enjoy autonomy, enable and constrain nonviolent action in war. In the process, they create something like a civil society, which carries its own set of implications.

CONCLUSION
Contention, Civilized

Before the revolution, Zahid was prepared to leave Syria.[1] Nothing "fit" his ideas or personality except his small "book club" of friends who read literature only to discuss politics. That changed in March 2011, when Syria became a country he was "ready to die for" if his efforts could help produce a "democratic country, civil and secular, that we could live in with freedom." He says that if he wrote such a thing on Facebook six years later, it would elicit more "ha ha" than "like" reactions. With the benefit of hindsight, Zahid can see threads that would help unravel the protest movement. For one thing, the "street was not politically aware." Activists were thinking only of the goal of "bringing down the regime" and not the politics that would follow. Then came the "Islamization of the Syrian street," a development that seemed as gradual as it was shocking.

Nonetheless, Zahid continued to engage in nonviolent activism during what became a civil war. He and his friends created programs for children's mental health in rebel-held areas. They started a campaign to raise awareness against the Islamic State, but when that Islamic State took control of his Aleppo neighborhood, he and his parents fled to Turkey. In Gaziantep, Zahid wanted to remain engaged with Syria—which was easy in the bustling border town where international and Syrian organizations had converged to respond to the crisis. He found a position in a US-backed program doing M&E (monitoring and evaluation): "It wasn't very important work; the most important thing to happen in those three months was learning how to do this work." That skill set moved with him whenever his lack of a work permit, or his disinterest, became obstacles to his current job.

He next worked for a Western-funded Syrian organization promoting education, culture, and awareness in the Aleppo countryside. The substance of this work was meaningful and matched his secular principles, but now he felt strange making a comfortable income while designing programs for people from afar. Sure, he's Syrian, and "not a foreigner who doesn't know anything about Syria"; nevertheless, it felt odd that he was, remotely, "putting the plan [together], choosing how it will be coordinated and presented for people in a place I've never been in a center I've never visited." Eventually Zahid left that position, disillusioned with the idea that he could do anything to effect change.

But he couldn't bring himself to walk away from Syria altogether. He found a research position with another Western program and in this situation he "learned a lot: how to build a methodology, how to gather information, how to deal with quantitative and qualitative data, how to analyze, etc." But again, the content of the program was narrow—M&E for one governance program. Feeling that "Gaziantep took everything of me that it could," Zahid went to Istanbul: He was "running away from the revolution." That is, until he needed money, at which point he went to Gaziantep again and secured remote work.

Zahid went to secure the position he needed to make ends meet, but also to satisfy the gnawing need to stay connected to Syria despite his deepening disenchantment. He watched as others attempted the dangerous trek to Europe and he did not blame them. "I want to run away," he admits. "Syria took a lot from us—more than should have been allowed." And yet he stayed to witness, hoping to understand how it all went so wrong. He wishes for a privileged passport, for an opportunity to pursue a PhD, to analyze and explain the "really terrifying place" that Syria became.

By the luck of birth, the author of this book possesses such a passport and a PhD. I have used them not to explain how Syria became such a terrifying place, but rather to conduct research with civil activists like Zahid who acted to make it less so. In the course of this research, I found that international aid, deployed to respond to the crisis, shaped civil action in and around the war. Zahid's story does not end with the unraveling of a protest movement beset by political inexperience or Islamist armed groups. It carries on for years, across borders, through multiple organizations and endeavors, touched by international aid all along the way.

And yet international aid is deployed, adjusted, and withdrawn based on events on the ground in the countries of conflict, in those hosting aid organizations, and in donor governments. Beginning in 2017, institutions and organizations of international aid began extracting themselves from Syria's borderlands, and after 2018 the amount of aid given to Syria overall declined. In the years since, other crises have drawn international attention, and by 2024 multiple global North donors began to retrench support for aid overall. Fluctuations in aid are sometimes dramatic and cause harm in lives and livelihoods; but they are not necessarily abnormal. Arguably, aid's impermanence is built into the humanitarian system. International humanitarianism responds to "states of emergencies" with a temporality of "successive plans and missions" (Fassin and Pandolfi 2010). UN humanitarian agencies make special emergency appeals again and again because their funding is voluntary and discretionary, not mandatory or regular.

Aid's impermanence is also part of a more fundamental worldview held by humanitarians driven by "the imperative to reduce suffering." Craig Calhoun writes of humanitarianism as motivated by an "emergency imaginary" that represents "as sudden, unpredictable, and short term what are commonly gradually developing, predictable, and enduring clusters of events and interactions" (Calhoun 2008, 86). Emergency imaginaries extend to other types of crisis intervention as well. Phases are often explicitly built into international actors' strategies, be they for stabilization missions, counterinsurgency, or other forms of crisis response (U.S. Army 2006; Cole et al. 2009). Interveners shift their priorities in response to violence, domestic politics, rivalries with other intervening actors, or other factors. None of this is unreasonable. Humanitarian aid ought not to be permanent.

Yet the impermanence and endogeneity of aid matter because aid in war protects lives, and (per this book's concerns) because it does more than provide relief. International aid also supports, relies on, trains, tames, compensates, and differentiates local nonviolent actors—all in order to achieve its objectives of easing the suffering of war and making life amid violence more livable by routinizing relief. That is, aid seeks to pacify war and civilizes contention in the process. It creates something like a civil society among local actors. When aid ends—sometimes as suddenly as it arrives—it leaves that civilized society bare to violence, without a state, of which civil society is meant to be a part and a counterpart, to protect it.

On February 6, 2023, the earth raged under the feet of that civilized society in Syria's borderlands. With its epicenter about twenty miles from Gaziantep, a 7.8 magnitude earthquake shook southern Turkey and northern Syria; nine hours later, a 7.7 magnitude quake shook them again; hundreds of aftershocks followed. Tens of thousands of people perished and upward of two million people were left without a home in the middle of winter. For Turkish citizens, who suffered the greatest casualties and destruction, the tragedy was immense. For the millions of Syrians in the region already displaced and dependent on humanitarian aid for survival, "a really terrifying place" became, in an instant, even more terrible.

An imperfect response surfaced in Turkey. International search and rescue teams, aid convoys, and material support poured into the struck region, supplementing local and national efforts, but nothing entered northwest Syria for days following the quake: no international search and rescue teams, no aid convoys, no material support. The central government in Damascus was only too eager to overlook the rebel-held northwest region as it responded to the affected areas under its own control and capitalized on the opportunity to bring in more aid, achieve sanctions relief, and normalize diplomatic relations with countries in the region. Syria's civil actors were left to sort through the literal destruction of their country on their own. Days later, UN aid chief Martin Griffiths tweeted: "We have so far failed the people in northwest Syria. They rightly feel abandoned. Looking for international help that hasn't arrived."[2]

Under the circumstances, Syria's civil actors assumed the roles of "survivors and saviors" (Loveluck 2023). Themselves victims who had lost homes and loved ones, they responded with resilience developed over twelve years of hardship. Organizations that specialized in treating the war wounded, digging through bombed buildings, erecting displacement shelters, and distributing lifesaving provisions all applied their experiences in the earthquake's aftermath. They did so even as their colleagues in Gaziantep could not reach their ruined offices to communicate or manage the response; they did so without the support of search and rescue teams that only internationally recognized nation-states can call on; they did so without the "duty of care" financial provisions that donors designated to international responders suffering the same crisis; and they did so without the equipment to remove rubble in more than a small fraction of affected locations, even as they listened to desperate screams putter out from under the ruins. Eventually, cross-border operations resumed and international assistance came through to northwest Syria. For many, it seemed too little, too late. Why was an aid system that had closely interacted with local organizations for years missing in action when those local actors needed them most? And what does the answer mean for something like a civil society in war's aftermath?

Aid Comes and Goes, Activists Stay

Much that transpires in war reflects the processes of war itself. This statement seems reasonable when we consider how messy and complex some wars appear to be from the outside; thoughtful observers create analytic space for local, personal, relational, and social dynamics to understand how violence and contention unfold, again and again, throughout a conflict (Wood 2001; Kalyvas 2006; Balcells 2010; Mazur 2021; Pearlman 2021; Parkinson 2023). But often, observers try to anticipate how and why war unfolds in the way it does based on predictable, preexisting, national, or international characteristics of certain countries, actors, or narratives. By delving into repeated interactions between international and local actors and organizations, as well as into processes of change, this book has aimed to situate itself among those that analyze how violence unfolds in relation to other processes, in this case nonviolent contention and international aid. By analytically opening the borders of civil wars, it has brought to the fore several types of actors, interests, and interventions and has made it possible to see the collaboration that can manifest between refugees and civilians in rebel-held territory, between locals and international actors that intervene in nonmilitaristic arenas, and between nonviolent participants and the armed actors with whom they interact—and without whom they also act.

According to the theory of civilizing contention, interactions between international and local actors engaged in nonviolent endeavors might be expected to unfold in a condition of aid autonomy. Aid actors almost always want to help, but how, when, and where they do so autonomously is subject to the internal dynamics of conflict or other factors, like the domestic politics of donor countries. Aid, therefore, does not always pursue its objectives in partnership with local actors nor automatically affect a predictable change in civil action. Their autonomy can be touch and go; some of the processes of change they generate will be partial. Ultimately, for one reason or another, that autonomy or international involvement is likely to decline or cease and local activists will be left with their something like, not quite, a civil society.

Twelve years before the 2023 earthquake, international aid actors viewed Syria as an emergency, driving compulsions (that is, the sense that "something must be done") to intervene. The international emergency imaginary was funneled through facts on the ground, including territorial control, military dynamics, and host and donor state politics. When these various dynamics allowed for international aid autonomy, international actors and organizations interacted with local civil actors to achieve their objectives. When aid autonomy was blocked, international-local interactions were hampered. Conditions of high autonomy can transform quickly into very little autonomy at all. By the time of the earthquake, the borderlands of southern Turkey and northwest Syria were undergoing this kind of transformation. The borderlands of Jordan and southern Syria had undergone the same in the years prior. In the meantime, wartime activism itself had changed significantly in response to its interactions with international aid.

The UN's initial assumption about the situation in Syria was that it was a "human rights crisis" that would "be over quickly" (Sida et al. 2016, 19–20). When crises of needs emerged, humanitarians "originally planned . . . a short-term emergency response, in expectation of an early end to the conflict" (Integrity and Agulhas 2015). The conflict did not end early. Instead, the humanitarian response ramped up: From 2012 to 2013 total UN requirements for the internal response grew by more than 300 percent. From 2012 to 2017, Syria was the largest recipient of humanitarian aid in the world (Urquhart and Tuchel 2018). Yet short-term approaches persisted (even as some long-term ones were added) including the use of encampments for displaced people, yearly and voluntary appeals for funding, the liminal (often "guest") status of millions of refugees in host states, and the brevity of project timelines.

Compulsions to intervene were not only realized through the UN system. A large proportion of humanitarian funding was channeled bilaterally, outside of the UN appeals.[3] Even in terms of private contributions, a small but critical fraction of formal humanitarian funds, Syria was the largest recipient worldwide from 2015 to 2017 (Urquhart 2018). And Gulf states, NGOs, and individuals pledged large amounts in the early years of the crisis, much of which was also not channeled through the UN (IRIN News 2013a). Despite the persistence of needs, all of these sources of humanitarian aid eventually declined. Compulsions were also not limited to humanitarianism. Indeed, the initial political crisis prompted a multitude of donors and aid suppliers to support civil society, governance, and nonlethal aid to armed groups. These donations were also driven by an emergency imaginary that viewed these events as a state of exception, amenable to "management" by outside actors (Calhoun 2004), and thus they were also eventually retracted or replaced with different objectives.

The rapid and generous but limited approaches of the various responses functioned to shorten the time horizons of all involved, but these horizons were reduced further by their vulnerability to military and political developments. Crucially, the emergency response relied on access. From the start, the central government obstructed aid to communities in need, particularly those in opposition strongholds, some of which were under sieges imposed by that very government. When cross-border operations and the "Whole of Syria" approach were established in 2014, an appropriate humanitarian response seemed to have finally cohered, but by the second half of the 2010s, diminishing rebel-held territory in the northwest and south presented a unique challenge to cross-border operations. A UN official explained that the humanitarian space was shrinking, pushing partners and donors to look for different forms of engagement: "None of this is the result of strategy," he noted, but a matter of decreasing access.[4] Even so, OCHA continued to maintain that cross-border operations were not closing down. As late as 2019, a leader of the coordinating agency in Turkey insisted that "we need a strong and viable cross-border operation regardless of who is in control."[5]

But Syria's allies on the UN Security Council had other ideas, and they limited cross-border operations when their authorization came up for renewal. The Jordan operation was suspended altogether. Darʿa in southern Syria was, by late 2018, under Russian and Syrian control. With aid obstructed and the territory retaken, civil organizations were swiftly shut down. That is, *all* local and international work ceased, "almost overnight"; thousands of beneficiaries stopped receiving aid, hundreds of civil actors lost their employment, and the economy was paralyzed (Al Nofal and Clark 2018). Critically, in retaking territorial control, the Syrian regime "laid waste to a years-long experiment in parallel governance and aid provision in a hugely symbolic area known as the 'cradle of the revolution' to a generation of Syrian activists" (Al Nofal and Clark 2018). The same pattern had occurred in Aleppo City in 2016 and Rural Damascus in 2018, whose retakings by the government forced nonviolent actors and organizations to flee or disband. The civilized society that international aid had facilitated, formalized, and filtered lacked the state protection that civil society needs. It was disappeared by that state, instead.

The United States, the largest donor to the humanitarian response, also provided significant nonhumanitarian aid; this too followed a temporality of emergency. Indeed, to engage at all, the United States had to literally invoke emergency and contingency authorities to overcome its own bilateral sanctions on Syria (Humud and Blanchard 2020). The United States' political priorities were initially representation, civil society, and transition. These early objectives later gave way to stabilization and countering violent extremism. The shift from transition to stabilization responded to events on the ground, including al-Asad's strength following Russia's 2015 military intervention; the predominance of "proscribed" Salafi-jihadi armed groups (rather than the "moderate" Free Syria Army) in the armed insurgency; and the divided control of Syrian territory by the Islamic State, Turkey, and Kurdish armed groups. In response, the United States gradually turned away from democratic transition and toward stabilization in territories liberated from the Islamic State. It even reframed earlier efforts as competition against al-Qaeda and other Islamist groups (for example, State 2018).

The Turkish government was another consequential player for the trajectories of Syrian activists. After years of allowing for international aid autonomy that facilitated Syrians' nonviolent action, it would also eventually reduce that autonomy through shifting policies and behavior. From 2015 to 2016, Turkey was subjected to bombings by the Islamic State. In this same period, conflict between the Turkish government and a Kurdish militant group was escalating within Turkish borders while the group's counterpart organization in Syria was expanding its territorial control. Simultaneously achieving electoral majorities and surviving an alleged coup attempt, the ruling administration in Turkey rewarded itself with a mandate to pursue its real and perceived enemies. In August 2016 Turkey began construction of a 435-mile-long wall along the Syrian border and launched a military operation in northwest Syria, Operation Euphrates Shield. With US air support and Syrian armed groups on the ground, Turkey forced the Islamic State to relinquish control over numerous towns in northern Aleppo Governorate in Syria. After the military operation was declared complete, Euphrates Shield territory, extending across about a thousand square miles, was overseen by Turkey's Interior Ministry and the provincial governments along the border, like Gaziantep's. Excluding INGOs and intergovernmental agencies, Turkey proceeded to implement humanitarian, developmental, political, and religious programming through its own agencies and national organizations in the Syrian territory under its control. Local actors had to shift away from other international aid actors and adapt to the new Turkish regime.

Civil actors had to continuously adjust to these uncertainties—making decisions about how to engage as something like a civil society, without its own state. One staffer recalled the internal debate within her Syrian organization after Aleppo City was retaken by the Syrian government, as they chose between going to Turkish-held Euphrates Shield territory in Aleppo Governorate or to rebel-held Idlib Governorate. Both were outside the control of the government in Damascus, but one was led primarily by Turkey (with Syrian partners), and the other was led primarily by Syrians (with competing armed groups). "When they left Aleppo," the staffer said, "they saw that there was still a revolution going on in Idlib. Euphrates Shield wasn't revolution, it was just Turkey."[6] Despite the association of the armed groups in Idlib with the original 2011 movement (the revolution), they went to Euphrates Shield. In these areas, Turkey set up programming that mimicked that previously offered by Western donors, such as the Free Syrian Police. One former staffer of the Western-backed program noted that in some of the new stations of Turkey's police project "most of the officers came from ours, just jumped ship. . . . They swap out commanders, repaint the cars. . . . We've suspended funding."[7]

Inside Turkey, the government began to limit the autonomy it had allowed to aid actors and activists alike. Increasingly, organizations were pushed to formally register, acquire work permits for their employees, and abide by other labor regulations. Some had recognized that the status quo ante was a point of vulnerability, even if it had benefited them for years, but the switch felt sudden. In the first four months of 2017, an Italian NGO was banned, staff of a Danish organization were detained, one of the largest distributors of cross-border aid—Mercy Corps—was expelled, and employees of a US NGO were detained and deported (Cupolo 2017). Following a constitutional referendum in 2017, which received a majority "yes" vote that converted the country from a parliamentary to a presidential system, a crackdown on NGOs in Gaziantep came into force: Organizations' offices were systematically targeted and searched to ensure compliance with regulations the government had scarcely ever enforced. For months, foreigners and Syrians alike retreated to their homes rather than work in their offices.

By 2017, the emergency imaginary seemed to be closing in on Syrians' nonviolent action as aid autonomy declined. An American development contractor captured the sense of distress felt by many in Gaziantep at that moment in time: "Two years ago, [Syrian] civil society would be a different animal. Even if you took the money away, they were more focused on removing the regime and believed they had the support of the world. Today, they feel the world is against them. So now rather than unification, there's a survival mentality—each for himself. . . . There's an urgency to get money. My heart breaks for the CSOs, because if Turkey tells them to leave tomorrow, where will they go? Nowhere."[8] A civilized society with nowhere to go. By 2023, they could not even rely on the ground beneath their feet for protection.

That is, until another earth-shattering development occurred, one of immeasurable magnitude. On December 8, 2024, the Syrian regime fell, defeated in a mere eleven days by rebel forces who set ablaze a conflict that had been frozen since 2020, although active since 2011. Zahid reached out to me that very day, seven years after we last spoke, to share this message: He wasn't disenchanted anymore. Syria's something like a civil society, which had emerged from nothing and persisted against the odds of a brutal war, which had been squeezed into rebel-held territory and dispersed into the diaspora, *may* finally stand the chance to become a genuine civil society for its country, for all of Syria.

Contributions

This book makes theoretical, empirical, and methodological contributions to the study of war, particularly in the Syrian case. It offers a unifying theoretical framework for grappling with international crisis response and in the realm of local action it draws connections between nonviolent actors in refuge and within the borders of a conflict state. Empirically, it restores the nonviolent dimension of a conflict that had otherwise come to epitomize the exceptional violence of Middle Eastern wars and does so with methodological tools that elevate ethical considerations while relaying a causal story.

In it, I adopt a "unified framework" for understanding types of international aid often studied in isolation from each other (Ahmed 2019): humanitarian and nonhumanitarian aid from nongovernmental and intergovernmental organizations, all of which is deployed in response to conflict contexts. This unified framework for international aid in crisis contexts is important because it allows holistic evaluation of the effects of international actors on domestic processes. If we were only concerned with IGOs and humanitarian response, we would miss everything that transpired in the Turkey-Syria borderlands from 2011 to mid-2014, when the Security Council authorized the UN response from neighboring countries without the permission of the Syrian government. In those three years, INGOs and others with humanitarian and political agendas built such rich and substantive relationships with Syrians that a "parallel" system of aid developed that rivaled the one based in Damascus; this parallel system relied on a "new" population of local relief activists that served those people most in need (Whittall 2015). Had one missed those developments, one might have surmised that nonviolent actors associated with the 2011 uprising either vanished or took up arms, or that the local actors the UN began to rely on in mid-2014 were professional humanitarians in waiting, at the ready for an intergovernmental organization to show up and enhance their response.

The book's holistic framework for action in crisis contexts extends to local actors. Studies of civilian agency in war rarely include the agency of refugees who have escaped across borders but who engage nonviolently in conflict processes. In political science literature, refugees' nonviolent agency vis-à-vis the war at home has been overshadowed by cases of refugee violence or by transnationalism studies that attend to the conflict-related action of often distant diasporas. Yet there are reasons to expect that refugees are, potentially, poised to engage nonviolently and meaningfully in conflict processes (Khoury and Siegel 2024). Most refugees reside in the countries that border the conflict state and from where they originate. Their experiences of war can encourage mobilization, while their proximity to civilian and displaced communities creates opportunities to act on their motivations. Their activism can be enabled by sympathetic border states with geopolitical interests in the conflict and by international agencies that respond to needs among refugees and within the conflict state.

In these bordering states, refugees can engage jointly with civilians and international actors in the nonviolent processes that are at the heart of this book. For instance, civilian actors can provision public goods in rebel-held towns, while their refugee counterparts can collaborate with international development organizations in sending those goods. Syrians in Turkey have coordinated with donor states in a "complex, transnational effort to sustain wartime governance in the opposition-held 'Liberated Territories' of Syria" (Hamdan 2020). Indeed, border regions can constitute subsystems of nonviolent (if also violent) conflict processes where local, refugee, regional, and international actors enact political, diplomatic, humanitarian, development, and other objectives (Schneckener 2011). Refugee-led civil organizations emerge in these dynamic spaces, precarious though they may be.

Because of the typically bustling nature of these border regions, researchers often focus on violent conflict processes or rebel groups within them. Likewise, the study of humanitarianism and domestic processes concentrates on the former's effects on armed actor behavior or on civilian perceptions thereof. Certainly, a focus on wartime violence is crucial and natural. Our gaze turns toward the phenomenon that takes lives—by definition the most existential dimension of armed conflict. This tendency holds in the study of the Middle East in general and of Syria in particular.

The Middle East is arguably structured by violence; in Jacob Mundy's words, the "Middle East *is* violence" (2019, emphasis added). Although area studies scholars have been sensitive to essentializing formulations of the Middle East as uniquely prone to extremism and conflict, the region was in fact host to between one-third and one-half of all armed conflicts worldwide in the 2000s and 2010s, respectively. Syria had become the deadliest armed conflict of the twenty-first century by 2016 (J. Mundy 2019). Mundy argues that external actors have constituted and reproduced the region through violent practices. By activating processes of militarization, conflict exacerbation, and peace deferment, global North powers have restructured their own political and economic dominance throughout the Middle East (J. Mundy 2019).

Despite these facts, civilian and refugee-driven social and political processes precede, persist during, and are reinvented in the course of a war. To recover these nonviolent dimensions of Syria's conflict, I have sought to elevate the voices of Syrians themselves and their self-representations. Because it was not possible to safely enter Syria for field research, I am certain that important knowledge has been lost, that we have yet to grasp the localized complexities of the conflict, and that the stories and voices of people on the ground have been overshadowed by powerful military actors and master narratives. Duffield contends that research-related risk-aversion has contributed to a "growing remoteness" and a shift to computational methodologies in international and area studies. With these trends, Duffield laments, "ground truth" is lost (2014). A post-Asad Syria may allow for independent, critical, necessary research to amend substantial research gaps and to grapple with processes that took place in government-held territory, in particular.

Yet there are good reasons not to enter spaces of excessive vulnerability. Human subject researchers are responsible for doing no harm to their study participants. One way to fulfill this responsibility is to adhere to protocols like the procedural process of obtaining informed consent. However, the "dilemma of power" between researcher and researched can distort the very meaning of consent (Fujii 2012). As Daniel Masterson and Lama Mourad explain, "Even with [a researcher's] best attempts to disclose their intentions and affiliations," extremely vulnerable participants may still believe that refusal to participate could adversely affect their obtainment of benefits and thus they "may not be able to offer meaningful consent for a research project." Often, these research participants are left frustrated, disappointed, retraumatized, or fatigued, even while researchers benefit professionally from their suffering (2019; also Nayal 2013). These outcomes do not align with a "do no harm" approach (Khoury 2024).

In order to recover the nonviolent dimensions of the war, I adopted an ethnographic sensibility and approached a small number of interlocutors in the non-camp settings in which most Syrians resided in neighboring countries. I immersed with a refugee family, observing and participating in the rhythms of everyday life in displacement. At the same time, I snowball sampled research participants engaged in nonviolent action: They would connect me to other participants through their trusted social networks, which was particularly important given that their actions were sometimes sensitive and their legal situation sometimes vulnerable. I also turned my analytical lens on the organizations that structured those activists' potential: international aid organizations. I learned that expatriate humanitarian workers could be quite protective and guarded against academic researchers; they were hard to reach because they were engaged in sensitive field operations, often in competition with other organizations over projects and grants. But being hard to reach for research is distinct from being vulnerable; vulnerable research participants are in positions of weakness that raise risks of harm or exploitation. As holders of powerful passports and decision-making power over the lives of their beneficiaries and local implementing partners, most of these expatriate aid workers were not vulnerable.

Methods such as immersion, observation, and interviewing were a good fit for my purposes, which included closely tracing the processes that gave shape to Syrians' civil action, interpreting the meaning-making of the individuals engaged in it, and grappling with the everyday routines of humanitarian organizations that shaped the livelihoods of large groups of people in need through complex institutional mechanisms. The granular insights that emerge from these qualitative methods are not easy to replicate. For example, in chapter 5 I rely on the "money talk" of Syrians to understand how they enacted a resource environment structured by the ideas of international aid organizations. Parkinson conceptualizes money talk as "'everyday' discourse that uses the social meaning of money to express deeper moral critiques and judgments" (Parkinson 2016). Yet it was not until my third and fourth trips to the field that I felt comfortable engaging Syrians explicitly in money talk—by that point, I had learned enough from them that I could navigate, with sensitivity and awareness, their grievances around monetary hierarchies that were structured by aid.

Qualitative insights also made it possible to create a dataset of public Facebook pages representing formal and informal Syrian organizations. Counting NGOs in a given country at a given time is known by scholars of organizations to be "problematic" and existing strategies "all imperfect" (Watkins et al. 2012).

Directories, if they exist, often both undercount and overcount, excluding smaller organizations while including nonoperational ones (Watkins et al. 2012). These problems are amplified many times in contexts of authoritarianism, war, or both. I followed Syria's civil actors to their primary digital ecosystem after doing the bulk of my in-person fieldwork. I sought to overcome challenges of organization-counting while also accounting for a wider range of civil organizing than would otherwise exist in a context where legal registration of organizations was rarely permitted. These Facebook pages are spaces where Syrian groups represented themselves—in their own words and images—regardless of their legal or even violent operational context.

While I drew on various sources of data, including humanitarian reports, media accounts, and the social media dataset, the narratives of people in the warscape constituted the most essential components of this project. My interviewees' experiences were not mere evidence for features of a case that could check a box for my explanation, or cross off an alternative one. Rather, they allowed me to tell a whole story (Crasnow 2017), or so I hope. A broader view of process tracing than one focused on diagnostic evidence alone, as Crasnow explains, accounts for the narratives that do "cognitive work" and make "the causally salient elements of the case coherent" (Crasnow 2017). It was thanks to such cognitive work that I could see and interpret intended consequences of international aid (for example, training locals in M&E and building their organizational capacity), unintended ones (such as fomenting cleavages through technical practices like remuneration), and pathological ones (like uplifting nascent organizations and then cutting off their funding).

As Wendy Pearlman leads us to expect, those individual narratives also coalesced into a collective narrative (2016). Without understanding that collective narrative arc, I could not have made sense of it when the president of a local council in northwest Syria told me that his role was "not a political" one but rather it was to "provide services"; politics, he said, "is something else."[9] His experience represents the paradoxical arc of this story of aid and civil action: The leader of a revolutionary institution in an opposition stronghold embraced a technocratic role within an organization receiving millions of dollars in funding to counter violent extremism through services like garbage collection. What are the implications of this shift from contentious politics to civilized contention?

Implications

A straightforward takeaway of this project is that international aid, be it humanitarian or otherwise, has political effects beyond those it intends. When they enjoy autonomy, international aid actors act politically by providing services, promoting rules, and distributing goods—that is, by governing. And their actions have political effects—for our purposes, on local civil action. There is nothing terribly novel in the finding that aid is political.

At the same time, and particularly at a micro-level of analysis, international humanitarians provide relief. Few would question this fact: Aid helps individual beneficiaries, including through immediate protection and emergency provisions. Nonhumanitarian aid also achieves several of its intended objectives, such as training civil society activists in a variety of skill sets. International aid actors can do their jobs, even if most observers (and indeed participants themselves) acknowledge that they have additional effects too. What is more, in times and places where international aid organizations have not shied away from politics, they have negotiated access, pulled support from recalcitrant actors, and raised funds for people in need.

It may be that local actors could also use their political agency to better distribute aid, make and implement decisions, and even lead in aid responses if they accepted rather than disassociated from their political contexts like the rebels ruling in their areas of operation. Time and again in this text, efforts to separate civil actors from the rebels (particularly the "wrong" kind of rebels, like the Islamists) caused tensions and even dangers for those involved. If local actors could use their political agency, it might also help them better protect themselves to remain embedded in local coalitions during war and its aftermath. Impartiality and humanity—distributing relief without taking sides and with regard to needs—do not necessitate political neutrality. Neutrality, at least for local aid actors, does not amount to protection. The Asad regime persistently targeted civil actors, including humanitarians, despite it.

These conversations are critical at a time when international aid agencies are endeavoring to "localize" or even "decolonize" aid by supporting local action and leadership in crisis response, and when donors are retrenching from funding aid and seeking more efficient means of distributing it. If those efforts are to be taken seriously, international actors must accept that local actors are, like them, complex political agents, and that this fact does not make them incapable of effecting positive change in their communities or even of effectively and impartially providing relief to people in need.

If international aid continues to operate as usual, however, another implication of this study is that international aid directed at civil organizations is unlikely to pose a serious threat to existing regimes. Authoritarian governments that crack down on local actors who receive support from international aid organizations only serve to limit a source of engaged local actors who are willing to serve their communities, help meet basic needs in the population, and apply their skills and will to better the lives of others. Relatedly, those refugee host states that erect obstacles against refugees' participation in nonviolent action, for instance by precluding their employment, are undercutting responders who are eager and able to help themselves and those around them. When states fear or criminalize the activists among civilians and refugees, communities and causes suffer.

Many activists understand the processes explained in this book very well. For example, in 2021 the Sheikh Jarrah neighborhood of Jerusalem was the site of grassroots resistance against Israeli motions to remove Palestinian families from their homes. Mohammed El-Kurd, a young Palestinian activist from Sheikh Jarrah, emerged as a powerful voice of conscience and leadership for the cause. Tellingly, El-Kurd cautioned his followers against support in the form of humanitarian aid. On Twitter, he wrote: "Don't donate to any #SheikhJarrah funds that weren't endorsed by us. We are committed to keeping the fight for Sheikh Jarrah a political one—to save our homes from displacement & stop Israeli authorities from colonial expansion. It is not time for humanitarian support yet."[10] Engaging with international aid entails trade-offs that many local actors recognize, though perhaps more so for those who are seasoned in struggle. Many accept those trade-offs to achieve certain other interests, including a crucial one: engagement, especially at a large scale, and particularly of the type that can meet intensive needs. It is not for a scholar sitting at her desk to say that one approach is better than another: I only hope to have shown how local actors navigate narrow pathways for civil action in unforgiving contexts, and how international aid actors—who bring the resources and structures of their institutions to those contexts—affect their trajectories.

International aid organizations and local civil actors come from very different starting points, yet both act on behalf of communities and causes in the darkest of times and places. Wars destroy, despite their best efforts. But in the words of a Syrian working for an INGO in Lebanon, "There's still hope here."[11] As he explains:

> And I have that because I've been personally talking, through my work, to Syrian doctors in besieged areas that have seen the worst of humanity. The things they describe . . . it's just horrendous. And I always ask them if they have hope, and they always say yes. So if these guys and women have hope in the worst of situations, then in my privileged, very safe comfortable life in Beirut with my arak and NGO salary, I damn well better have hope. And this goes for everyone else—we all should have hope and start building and working. It's not over.

Acknowledgments

My deepest gratitude is to the Syrians who shared their stories with me, for their generosity and trust, and for acting on behalf of Syria against the odds. Without their voices, this project would have been neither possible nor worthwhile. Thank you to my international interviewees who aided Syrians in the darkest of days. This book cannot do justice to the fortitude of the activists and aid workers who help and serve on the front lines of violence. I hope they interpret it as testament to the import of their endeavors.

There are so many people to thank. I am ever grateful to my advisers at Northwestern University: Wendy Pearlman, William Reno, Jason Seawright, and Ana Arjona. Wendy, you strike a rare balance between rigor and humanism and you set the example for how the former furthers the goals of the latter. Thank you for being a voice of conscience for everyone who cares about the present and future of people in the Middle East. Will, your guidance through every step of my intellectual journey has consistently led me to being the kind of scholar I want to be. Jaye, your encouragement was critical to my research and to my ability to carry it out with confidence as an academic mother. Ana, you taught me how to think about civil wars and the civilians who live them, while modeling how to be a thoughtful scholar and a whole person.

At Northwestern I also thank Galya Ben-Arieh, Jordan Gans-Morse, Benjamin Page, Rachel Riedl, and Hendrik Spruyt, as well as Stephen Monteiro and Courtney Syskowski. Friends from the program have been gracious colleagues and valued companions. My thanks to Safa al-Saeedi, Rodrigo Barrenechea, Ethan Busby, D. J. Flynn, Matthew Lacombe, Sean Lee, Sarah Moore, and David Peyton. Laura García Montoya, Sasha Klyachkina, and Christa Kuntzelman have been wonderful friends and writing partners to boot.

I enjoyed the intellectual fulfillment and downright fun of an academic cohort again as a postdoctoral fellow at Princeton University's Niehaus Center. Thank you particularly to Ricky Clark and Junghyun Lim. Helen Milner and Amaney Jamal, thank you for getting me there and doing so a deferred year after the onset of the COVID-19 pandemic, and Duy Trinh and Pat Trinity for making an uncertain year so easy. Leslie Johns, Layna Mosley, Peter Rosendorff, and Jim Vreeland all provided valuable support and guidance. My special thanks to Layna, whose understanding was just right. While at Niehaus I had the great fortune of holding a workshop whose attendees had shaped my thinking for years and whose insights shaped the book into what it is today. I am still giddy that Faisal Ahmed, Noura al-Jizawi, Rawan Arar, Michael Barnett, Mark Beissinger, Sarah Bush, and Dana Moss all took the time to read and engage with the text. And a special thank you to Michael Barnett, whose input and criticism I am privileged to take personally. And thank you Hannah Kazis-Taylor for support.

In many stages, various parts of this project have also benefited from the feedback of Fiona Adamson, Marie Berry, Alex Braithwaite, Laurie Brand, Sarah Bush, Ali Hamdan, Steven Heydemann, Stathis Kalyvas, Sean Lee, Adam Lichtenheld, Marc Lynch, Lama Mourad, Sarah Parkinson, Christiana Parreira, Sam Plapinger, Justin Schon, Emily Scott, Alexandra Siegel, Macey Stapleton, Lisa Wedeen, and Yael Zeira. Thank you all.

Friends from my master's program at the Center for Contemporary Arab Studies at Georgetown University supported me in my research in Jordan and Turkey, where they had felt pulled to help Syrians in their time of turmoil. Thank you particularly to Macey Stapleton as well as Elizabeth Mohan, Thomas Osann (honorary CCAS alum), and Andrea Wegner. I am deeply indebted to Schadi Semnani, who, perhaps inadvertently, set me on my research path, opened many a door, graciously hosted me, and has been like a sister in her friendship. Thank you to her husband, Rami Nakhla, who did all these things, too.

My fieldwork in the region was supported and enriched by many others. Lina Abdel Aziz, Geraldine Chatelard, Ali Hamdan, Sean Lee, Adam Lichtenheld, and Barbara Porter were academic anchors. Thank you to Aseel Kakish and her family, whose hospitality gave me my start. I will be ever grateful to the Baradan family, who cared for me though they had unjustly little and who taught me of love though they lost so much. I so appreciate and admire my Syrian research assistants in Jordan and Turkey, Israa Sader and Mohanad Saab, who are exemplars of personal and professional growth against the odds. I have been enriched by them and their loving families. I have enjoyed the support of many others who entrusted me with their stories and facilitated connections, but whose names must be protected. Thank you again to all those Syrians who have been part of this project—you were the best of a country when it was at its worst.

The Social Science Research Council, the ZEIT-Stiftung Ebelin und Gerd Bucerius Foundation, and the American Center of Research, through the Council of American Overseas Research Centers predoctoral fellowship, were sources of financial support for the fieldwork at the heart of this research; these fellowships also generously invested in personal and academic development. At Northwestern support came from the Buffett Center, the Kellogg School of Management's Dispute Resolution Research Center, the Buffett Institute for Global Affairs, and the Department of Political Science. The University of Illinois Urbana-Champaign's Campus Research Board awarded support to complete this book and the Department of Political Science allowed me to benefit from the expertise of Laura Portwood-Stacer at Manuscript Works.

I am fortunate indeed to have landed at Illinois, where I have enjoyed the support of friends and colleagues including Asef Bayat, Jake Bowers, Cindy Buckley, Damarys Canache, Laura Goffman, Wail Hassan, Stephanie Hilger, Alyssa Prorok, Tom Rudolph, Josh Shea, Laura Wang, Nora Webb Williams, Michael Williamson, and Cara Wong. Thank you especially to Avital Livny and Matthew Winters for guidance and encouragement. Thank you also to Brenda Stamm and Abdullah Islam.

At Cornell University Press I am grateful to Jim Lance for believing in the project from first introduction to final product. Your guidance has consistently been both gentle and grounded, while your advice to stay true to my voice has been empowering. I am also grateful to two anonymous reviewers, my unsung heroes, for their thoughtful attention and support. Thank you to Karen Hwa, Marlyn Miller, and Bethany Wasik for bringing this project to fruition.

Thank you to Laura García Montoya, Schadi Semnani, and Alex Shakar, who all read the manuscript in full; to Rawan Arar and Lama Mourad, for friendship and solidarity; and to the Facebook group Academic Mamas with 2018s, for getting it. All my grandparents passed away in the course of research and writing; they have left with me distinct perspectives on, and attachments to, a beloved Syria. My parents, Wael and Sawssan Khoury, are an unwavering source of support that nurtured that attachment; my siblings, in-laws, and nephews and nieces are all wellsprings of fun and care. Alex Shakar, my life partner, has been part of this journey from the start, encouraging me with love, fortification, intellect, and a keen editorial eye (I'm sorry if I still mess up past perfect). Alex filled my heart, until we became parents, and I discovered that a heart can grow immeasurably fuller. Sumeya Shakar—my Sumi—your joy, excitement, curiosity, and cuddles are the best. You are light in a dark world. You and your daddy are my everything.

Notes

INTRODUCTION

1. Ahmed and all interviewee names are pseudonymous. Interview 54, 2016, Jordan.

2. Risse defines areas of limited statehood as "those parts of a country in which central authorities (governments) lack the ability to implement and enforce rules and decisions or in which the legitimate monopoly over the means of violence is lacking, at least temporarily" (2011a, 4).

3. For critical views, see Carpi 2018; Fiddian-Qasmiyeh 2018.

4. See Adamson 2013; Byman et al. 2001; DuBois 2018; Moss 2021; Østergaard-Nielsen 2006.

5. Fieldwork also allowed me to maintain a wider view of processes outside my immediate area of interest. In each of the three years I visited Jordan, I spent days at a time residing with a Syrian refugee family who were sheltered in the north of the country, just five kilometers away from Syria's southern border. Their modest lives (and the occasional tremors from shelling over the border) kept me from losing sight of the experiences and struggles of the wider refugee population.

6. This research was approved by Northwestern University's Institutional Review Board: STU00094852.

7. Interview data was collected in the format preferred by the participant; I preferred, in order, audio recordings, handwritten notes, or no real time note-taking at all. I took steps to protect digital files such as removing identifying material from transcripts and storing them in a password-protected cloud. I destroyed handwritten notes and removed digital files from my hard drive whenever I crossed international borders. I also took precautions to protect my research assistants, as well as steps to compensate them fairly. In addition, I trained them in certain research methods and computer software; they graciously taught me a great deal about my research context.

8. Under an Institutional Review Board waiver of documentation of consent.

9. Interview 83, 2017, Turkey.

10. The Syrian government lifted restrictions on the use of this and other social media platforms in February 2011.

11. I eliminated pages that represented business entities, conveyed violent or individual (rather than group) engagements, and had fewer than five hundred likes. This last choice was intended to limit inclusion of activities that were more aspirational than actual, though I accept that activism sometimes exists solely online.

1. HOW AID CIVILIZES CONTENTION

1. Ali is a pseudonym. Interview 77, 2017, Turkey.

2. NEA is the US State Department's Bureau of Near Eastern Affairs. OTI is the Office of Transition Initiatives at the United States Agency for International Development (USAID). DFID is the United Kingdom's Department for International Development. GIZ is the German development agency, Deutsche Gesellschaft für Internationale Zusammenarbeit.

3. As Scott contends, perceptions of risk to international aid staff do not necessarily align with actual rates of targeting (2022).

4. Barnett and Finnemore identify rules as central to four bases of bureaucratic authority: (1) rational-legal authority, (2) moral claims, (3) expertise, and (4) delegation (2004). The first three align with those I identify here. International organizations enjoy delegated authority because states have assigned it to them.

5. Paul DiMaggio and Walter Powell identify three isomorphic pressures that lead to organizational homogeneity: coercive, normative, and mimetic. Mimetic pressures mean that organizations model themselves after other organizations when their goals are ambiguous and the environment in which they find themselves is uncertain; in such a situation, they imitate organizations that they perceive to be successful or legitimate (1983). In my empirical account, mimetic pressures appear as one among other internal drivers of change in the formalization of activism.

6. Knowledge is also difficult to construct in forms of intervention that fall short of direct governance. See Foucault 1991; Mitchell 2002.

7. Of course, neither NGO and development agencies nor humanitarians are homogeneous; they disagree in their pronouncements and their practices about whether aid can or should be inextricable from politics (Weiss 1999).

8. Arguably, the dynamics of the NGO scramble extend upward to IGOs as well. UN agencies, which each operate under their own governance structures, are also under the "influence of the contract culture and market" and seeking the same donor funds; "competitiveness is built into" the UN system (Reindorp and Wiles 2001).

2. CONTENTION, CONFLICT, AND CRISIS IN SYRIA

1. Nahla is a pseudonym. Interview 87, 2017, Turkey.

2. Syrian diaspora activists enjoyed only some opportunities to voice grievances or organize from abroad. Moss explains that the regime's "transnational repression," as well as the transmission of home-country cleavages, greatly deterred their efficacy, even from abroad, prior to 2011 (2016).

3. Interview 70, Turkey, 2017.

4. Interview 14, Jordan, 2014.

5. Readers are encouraged to read Mazur's opus on the first year of the Syrian revolution to understand the causes of this geographic distribution, namely those related to state linkages and access to regime networks (2021).

6. Interview 14, Jordan, 2014.

7. Interview 49, Jordan, 2016.

8. Interviews 105 and 113, Turkey, 2017.

9. Interview 105, Turkey, 2017.

10. Interview 54, Jordan, 2016.

11. Interview 104, Turkey, 2017.

12. My interviews generally led with broad questions that encouraged Syrians to tell me their political story, during which I would ask them to expound and clarify. I refrained from asking explicitly about imprisonment, as this was a sensitive question both politically and in terms of psychological trauma. Thus, those nineteen interviewees volunteered their experiences of detention. I expect the actual number of those detained was larger.

13. Interview 103, Turkey, 2017.

14. Interview 92a, Turkey, 2017.

15. Interview 87, Turkey, 2017.

16. Interview 104, Turkey, 2017.

17. Interview 70, Turkey, 2017.

18. Interview 92a, Turkey, 2017.
19. Interview 10a, Jordan, 2014.
20. Adult Syrian men are conscripted for mandatory military service, with some exceptions.
21. Interview 10b, Jordan, 2014.
22. Quoted in Scott 2022, 6.
23. The regime's foreign policy posture in the "resistance axis" against US and Israeli domination, as well as against pro-Western Arab states, had been an element of rule and a source of domestic legitimacy (Mohns and Bank 2012).
24. Interview 87, Turkey, 2017.
25. Interview 13, Jordan, 2014.
26. Interview 29b, Jordan, 2015.
27. These entities are sometimes referred to as local administrative councils.
28. Interview 78, Turkey, 2017.
29. As Wieland points out, the content of humanitarian and nonhumanitarian aid was often indistinguishable, such as supplying medical equipment to clinics. What distinguished nonhumanitarian aid was that it could be detached from strict humanitarian principles (2020, 112).
30. Interview 85, Turkey, 2017. As chapter 1 suggests, establishing cross-border or other operations that bypass central government control has indeed occurred in past conflicts.
31. Interviews 115a–c, via Skype, 2019.
32. Interview 68, Turkey, 2017; emphasis added.
33. Interview 105, Turkey, 2017.
34. Interview 105, Turkey, 2017.
35. Interview 19, Jordan, 2015.
36. Interview 105, Turkey, 2017.
37. Interview 62, Jordan, 2016.
38. Interview 47, Jordan, 2016.

3. FILTERING PROCESS

1. Sana is a pseudonym. Interview 70, 2017, Turkey.
2. For critical views, see Carpi 2018; Fiddian-Qasmiyeh 2018.
3. As noted previously, the dataset cannot distinguish between groups that have or have not received international aid; rather, it captures trends among a large population of Syrian organizations inside and outside the country.
4. A potential concern of this finding may be that older pages were not active over the period of growth. I have analyzed the data based on the "last post date" (at the time of data collection) and found that about two-thirds of pages were actively engaging their followers through the end of 2017.
5. Interview 24, 2015, Skype.
6. The core of the Syrian Opposition Coalition (SOC) was previously the Syrian National Council and subsequently the Syrian Interim Government. These transformations are relevant to a close observer of Syria, but there was sufficient overlap to refer to them as the Opposition Coalition for simplicity's sake.
7. Interview 88a, 2017, Turkey.
8. Interview 85, 2017, Turkey.
9. Interview 84, 2017, Turkey.
10. Interview 88a, 2017, Turkey.
11. Interview 116, 2019, Skype.

12. Interview 98, 2017, Turkey.
13. Interview 94, 2017, Turkey.
14. Interview 89, 2017, Turkey
15. Interview 89, 2017, Turkey
16. Interview 54, 2016, Jordan.
17. See OCHA Financial Tracking Service, https://fts.unocha.org/, for funds and partners.
18. Interview 107b, 2017, Lebanon.
19. Interview 43b, 2016, Jordan.
20. Interview 43b, 2016, Jordan.
21. Interview 75b, 2017, Turkey.

4. FORMALIZING PROCESS

1. Rami is a pseudonym. Interview 105, 2017, Turkey.

2. A weakness of the proxy is that coding decisions are based on page content that was visible at the time they were coded (2018 to 2020) and not always on earlier content that may have been deleted or curated, or is otherwise inaccessible. Page photographs are easy to peruse because albums can be viewed within reasonable scrolling times. Nevertheless, page administrators may have deleted or otherwise curated photos. This ease in regard to photos is a contrast with page posts, which are difficult to access through manual scrolling beyond the most recent couple of dozen.

3. Islamist was used only when a political view was explicitly in favor of Islamist governance, and not on the basis of cultural markers, which were much more common, such as wishing followers a Happy Ramadan during the holiday.

4. A chi-squared test of the relationship between group orientation (inclusive of antigovernment, not visible, and the remaining "other" orientations) and year supports that this temporal trend was not the result of random chance. The χ^2 statistic was 72.58 with significance at greater than 99 percent confidence level ($p = 1.645e-08$).

5. Interview 55, 2016, Jordan.
6. Interview 61, 2016, Jordan.
7. Interview 69, 2017, Turkey.
8. Interview 88a, 2017, Turkey.
9. Aid Worker Security Database, accessed February 19, 2025, https://aidworkersecurity.org/incidents/search?detail=1&country=SY.
10. Interview 116, 2019, Skype.
11. Interview 55, 2016, Jordan.
12. Interview 77, 2017, Turkey.
13. Interview 85, 2017, Turkey.
14. Interview 115a–b, 2019, Skype.
15. Interview 100, 2017, Turkey.
16. Interview 107b, 2017, Turkey.
17. Interview 67b, 2017, Turkey.
18. Interview 72, 2017, Turkey.
19. Interview 34, 2016, country anonymized.
20. Interview 48, 2016, country anonymized.
21. Interview 92b, 2017, Turkey.
22. Interview 105, 2017, Turkey.
23. Interview 98, 2017, Turkey.
24. Interview 93, 2017, Turkey.
25. Marwan is a pseudonym. Interview 103, 2017, Turkey.
26. Bassel is a pseudonym. Interview 38, 2016, Jordan.

5. FILTERING PROCESS

1. Mustafa is a pseudonym. Interviews 88a, 88b, 2017, Turkey.
2. I thank Sarah Bush for identifying the correspondence between my data and expectations in population ecology.
3. Interview 104, 2017, Turkey.
4. "Humanitarianisms" include traditional emergency relief, medical care, and new forms of humanitarianism such as psychosocial support. Media includes formal news sites, radio, periodicals, and informal local information dissemination sites. Advocacy, politics, and justice includes human rights organizations, documenters of wartime violations, and groups engaged in political processes at local and national levels. Coordination refers primarily to those groups known as "local coordination committees" that organized resistance activities like demonstrations. Development includes such engagements as education and women's empowerment. Governance includes local and governorate councils and ministries of the opposition Syrian Interim Government. Civil society includes groups engaged in capacity-building, community centers, and coalitions of organizations.
5. In their case, the inconducive context is regulatory crackdowns on foreign-funded NGOs.
6. A separate response, outside the scope of this project, emerged for the Kurdish-held northeast.
7. Interview 95, 2017, Turkey. Emphasis added.
8. Interview 79, 2017, Turkey.
9. Interview 69, 2017, Turkey.
10. Interview 93, 2017, Turkey.
11. Interview 105, 2017, Turkey.
12. Interview 101, 2017, Turkey.
13. Interview 104, 2017, Turkey.
14. Interview 113, 2017, Skype.
15. Interview 89, 2017, Turkey.
16. Interview 88a, 2017, Turkey.
17. Interview 67b, 2017, Turkey.
18. Interview 54, 2016, Amman.
19. Interview 67b, 2017, Turkey.
20. Interview 115b, 2019, Skype.
21. Interview 88b, 2017, Turkey.
22. Interview 99, 2017, Turkey.
23. Interview 70, 2017, Turkey.
24. Interview 92b, 2017, Turkey.
25. Interview 82, 2017, Turkey.
26. Interview 76, 2017, Turkey.
27. Interview 102, 2017, Turkey. It is worth noting that many development agencies contracted by the US government are for-profit companies, whereas humanitarians are usually nonprofit.
28. Interview 92b, 2017, Turkey.
29. Interview 113, 2018, Skype.
30. On the eve of the uprising, the average monthly salary inside Syria was just $170 USD (Enab Baladi 2016).
31. Interview 94, 2017, Turkey.
32. I also break from my general practice of anonymizing the names of Syrian organizations to conduct this analysis because like other of the high-profile opposition institutions, the ACU was the subject of such immense public attention that to anonymize would be awkward and confusing.

33. Interview 76, 2017, Turkey.
34. Interview 115a, 2019, Skype.
35. Interview 76, 2017, Turkey.
36. Interview 115a, 2019, Skype.
37. Interview 76, 2017, Turkey.
38. Interview 76, 2017, Turkey.
39. Interview 107b, 2017, Lebanon. Jabhat al-Nusra would later become Hayʻat Tahrir al-Sham.
40. Interview 107b, 2017, Lebanon.
41. Interview 76, 2017, Turkey.
42. Interview 76, 2017, Turkey.
43. Interview 89, 2017, Turkey.
44. Interview 99, 2017, Turkey.
45. Interview 117, 2021, Zoom.
46. Interview 117, 2021, Zoom.
47. Interview 96, 2017, Turkey.

6. COMPARATIVE CASES

1. Prendergast and Duffield (1994) contend that the SRRA fell short in this regard because the Sudan People's Liberation Army (SPLA) lacked a public welfare mandate.

CONCLUSION

1. Interview 101, 2017, Turkey.
2. Martin Griffiths, "We have so far failed the people in northwest Syria," Twitter (now X), February 12, 2023. https://twitter.com/UNReliefChief/status/1624701773557469184?lang=en.
3. "Syrian Arab Republic Humanitarian Response Plan 2016," OCHA Financial Tracking Service, 2016. https://fts.unocha.org/appeals/501/summary.
4. Interview 85, 2017, Turkey.
5. Interview 116, 2019, Skype.
6. Interview 95, 2017, Turkey.
7. Interview 80b, 2017, Turkey.
8. Interview 69, 2017, Turkey.
9. Interview 91, 2017, Turkey.
10. Mohammed El-Kurd, "Don't donate to any #SheikhJarrah funds that weren't endorsed by us," Twitter (now X), May 9, 2021. https://twitter.com/m7mdkurd/status/1391360309609304065.
11. Interview 108, 2017, Lebanon.

References

Abbott, Kenneth W., Jessica F. Green, and Robert O. Keohane. 2016. "Organizational Ecology and Institutional Change in Global Governance." *International Organization* 70 (2): 247–77.
Abboud, Samer N. 2015. *Syria*. Polity.
Abdelwahid, Dalia. 2013. "'You Got the Stuff?': Humanitarian Activist Networks in Syria." *Humanitarian Exchange* 59, article 7, November 26. https://odihpn.org/publication/%C2%91you-got-the-stuff%C2%92-humanitarian-activist-networks-in-syria.
ACU. n.d.-a. *Annual Report 2014*. Gaziantep Assistance Coordination Unit. https://www.acu-sy.org/en/wp-content/uploads/2015/12/Annual-Report-2014-English.pdf.
ACU. n.d.-b. *Annual Report 2015*. Gaziantep Assistance Coordination Unit. https://www.acu-sy.org/en/wp-content/uploads/2017/01/Annual-Report-2015-1.pdf.
ACU. n.d.-c. *Annual Report 2017/6*. Gaziantep Assistance Coordination Unit. https://www.acu-sy.org/en/wp-content/uploads/2018/04/ACU-Annual-Report-16-17-ENG.pdf.
Adamson, Fiona B. 2013. "Mechanisms of Diaspora Mobilization and the Transnationalization of Civil War." In *Transnational Dynamics of Civil War*, edited by Jeffrey T. Checkel, 63–88. Cambridge University Press. https://doi.org/10.1017/cbo9781139179089.006.
Ahmed, Faisal Z. 2019. *The Perils of International Capital*. Cambridge University Press.
Alagappa, Muthiah. 2004. "Civil Society and Political Change: An Analytical Framework." In *Civil Society and Political Change in Asia: Expanding and Contracting Democratic Practice*, edited by Muthiah Alagappa, 25–57. Stanford University Press.
Aldrich, Howard E., and Jeffrey Pfeffer. 1976. "Environments of Organizations." *Annual Review of Sociology* 2:79–105.
Ali, Zahra. 2018. "Women's Political Activism in Iraq: Caught Between NGOization and the Struggle for a Civil State." *International Journal of Contemporary Iraqi Studies* 12 (1): 35–51.
Al Nofal, Walid, and Justin Clark. 2018. "Daraa Residents 'Paralyzed' by Economy in Recession, Collapse of Opposition-Era Civil Society and NGO Networks." *Syria Direct*, October 29. https://syriadirect.org/daraa-residents-paralyzed-by-economy-in-recession-collapse-of-opposition-era-civil-society-and-ngo-networks/.
Al-Oballi, Ayah. 2020. "Our Silenced Voices: What We Lose While Working with International 'Humanitarian' Organizations." *Hibr*, January 5. https://www.7iber.com/society/our-silenced-voices-what-we-lose-while-working-with-international-humanitarian-organizations/.
Alsarraj, Amr, and Philip Hoffman. 2020. "The Syrian Political Opposition's Path to Irrelevance." In *Contentious Politics in the Syrian Conflict: Opposition, Representation, and Resistance*, edited by Maha Yahya, 7–12. Carnegie Middle

East Center, Carnegie Endowment for International Peace, May 15. https://carnegieendowment.org/research/2020/05/contentious-politics-in-the-syrian-conflict-opposition-representation-and-resistance#the-syrian-political-oppositions-path-to-irrelevance.

Al-Tamimi, Aymenn Jawad. 2015a. "The Archivist: 26 Unseen Islamic State Administrative Documents; Overview, Translation, and Analysis." *Jihadology*, August 24. https://jihadology.net/2015/08/24/the-archivist-26-unseen-islamic-state-administrative-documents-overview-translation-analysis/.

Al-Tamimi, Aymenn Jawad. 2015b. "The Archivist: Critical Analysis of the Islamic State's Health Department." *Jihadology*, August 27. https://jihadology.net/2015/08/27/the-archivist-critical-analysis-of-the-islamic-states-health-department/.

Al-Tamimi, Aymenn Jawad. 2015c. "The Evolution in Islamic State Administration: The Documentary Evidence." *Perspectives on Terrorism* 9 (4): 117–29.

Al-Tamimi, Aymenn Jawad. 2018. "Islamic State Shifts from Provinces and Governance to Global Insurgency." *IPI Global Observatory*, September 26. https://theglobalobservatory.org/2018/09/islamic-state-shifts-provinces-governance-global-insurgency/.

Alzouabi, Zaidoun, and Khaled Iyad. 2017. *Syrian Civil Society Organizations: Reality and Challenges*. Translated by Mhd Bay. Citizens for Syria. https://citizensforsyria.org/OrgLiterature/Syrian_CSOs_Reality_and_challenges_2017-CfS_EN.pdf.

Andreas, Peter. 2008. *Blue Helmets and Black Markets: The Business of Survival in the Siege of Sarajevo*. Cornell University Press.

Angelova, Ilina. 2014. "Governance in Rebel-Held East Ghouta in the Damascus Province, Syria." Centre of Governance and Human Rights Working Papers. University of Cambridge.

Arar, Rawan. 2017. "The New Grand Compromise: How Syrian Refugees Changed the Stakes in the Global Refugee Assistance Regime." *Middle East Law and Governance* 9 (3): 298–312.

Arjona, Ana. 2016. *Rebelocracy: Social Order in the Colombian Civil War*. Cambridge University Press.

Arjona, Ana. 2017. "Civilian Cooperation and Non-Cooperation with Non-State Armed Groups: The Centrality of Obedience and Resistance." *Small Wars and Insurgencies* 28 (4–5): 755–78. https://doi.org/10.1080/09592318.2017.1322328.

Autesserre, Séverine. 2010. *The Trouble with the Congo: Local Violence and the Failure of International Peacebuilding*. Cambridge University Press.

Autesserre, Séverine. 2012. "Dangerous Tales: Dominant Narratives on the Congo and Their Unintended Consequences." *African Affairs* 111 (443): 202–22.

Autesserre, Séverine. 2014. *Peaceland: Conflict Resolution and the Everyday Politics of International Intervention*. Cambridge University Press.

Autesserre, Séverine. 2021. *The Frontlines of Peace: An Insider's Guide to Changing the World*. Oxford University Press.

Avant, Deborah, Marie E. Berry, Erica Chenoweth, et al., eds. 2019a. *Civil Action and the Dynamics of Violence*. Oxford University Press. https://doi.org/10.1093/oso/9780190056896.001.0001.

Avant, Deborah, Marie E. Berry, Erica Chenoweth, et al. 2019b. Introduction to Avant et al. 2019a, 1–31.

Aziz, Omar. 2013. "الأوراق التأسيسية لفكرة المجالس المحلية بقلم الشهيد عمر عزيز" (al-awraq al-t'sisiya li fikrat al-majlis al-mahaliya bi qalam al-shahid Amr Aziz) [The

founding documents of the idea of local councils in the words of the martyr Omar Aziz]," September 22. https://tinyurl.com/52rau8f4.
Badran, Yazan. 2020. "Strategies and (Survival) Tactics: The Case of Syrian Oppositional Media in Turkey." *Journal of Alternative & Community Media* 5 (1): 69–85. https://doi.org/10.1386/joacm_00075_1.
Badran, Yazan, and Kevin Smets. 2021. "Anatomy of a Precarious Newsroom: Precarity and Agency in Syrian Exiled Journalism in Turkey." *Media, Culture & Society* 43 (8): 1377–94. https://doi.org/10.1177/01634437211011556.
Baker, Aryn. 2013. "Savage Online Videos Fuel Syria's Descent into Madness." *Time*, May 12. https://world.time.com/2013/05/12/atrocities-will-be-televised-they-syrian-war-takes-a-turn-for-the-worse/.
Balcells, Laia. 2010. "Rivalry and Revenge: Violence Against Civilians in Conventional Civil Wars." *International Studies Quarterly* 54 (2): 291–313.
Balcells, Laia. 2017. *Rivalry and Revenge: The Politics of Violence During Civil War*. Cambridge University Press.
Balcells, Laia, and Abbey Steele. 2016. "Warfare, Political Identities, and Displacement in Spain and Colombia." *Political Geography* 51:15–29.
Banki, Susan. 2024. *The Ecosystem of Exile Politics: Why Proximity and Precarity Matter for Bhutan's Homeland Activists*. Ithaca: Cornell University Press.
Barbalet, Veronique. 2019. *Rethinking Capacity and Complementarity for a More Local Humanitarian Action*. Overseas Development Institute. https://www.odi.org/publications/11471-rethinking-capacity-and-complementarity-more-local-humanitarian-action.
Barber, Matthew. 2013. "The Raqqa Story: Rebel Structure, Planning, and Possible War Crimes." *Syria Comment*, April 3. https://joshualandis.com/blog/the-raqqa-story-rebel-structure-planning-and-possible-war-crimes/.
Barnett, Michael N. 2001. "Humanitarianism with a Sovereign Face: UNHCR in the Global Undertow." *The International Migration Review* 35 (1): 244–77.
Barnett, Michael N. 2011. *Empire of Humanity: A History of Humanitarianism*. Cornell University Press.
Barnett, Michael N. 2013. "Humanitarian Governance." *Annual Review of Political Science* 16:379–98.
Barnett, Michael N. 2021. "Humanitarian Organizations Won't Listen to Groups on the Ground, in Part Because of Institutionalized Racism." Monkey Cage, *Washington Post*, June 8. https://www.washingtonpost.com/politics/2021/06/08/humanitarian-organizations-wont-listen-groups-ground-part-because-institutionalized-racism/.
Barnett, Michael N., and Raymond Duvall. 2005. "Power in International Politics." *International Organization* 59 (Winter): 39–75.
Barnett, Michael N., and Martha Finnemore. 1999. "The Politics, Power, and Pathologies of International Organizations." *International Organization* 53 (4): 699–732.
Barnett, Michael N., and Martha Finnemore. 2004. *Rules for the World: International Organizations in Global Politics*. Cornell University Press.
Barnett, Michael N., and Jack Snyder. 2008. "The Grand Strategies of Humanitarianism." In Barnett and Weiss 2008, 143–71.
Barnett, Michael N., and Thomas G. Weiss, eds. 2008. *Humanitarianism in Question: Politics, Power, Ethics*. Cornell University Press.
Barr, Abigail, Marcel Fafchamps, and Trudy Owens. 2005. "The Governance of Non-Governmental Organizations in Uganda." *World Development* 33 (4): 657–79.

Barter, Shane Joshua. 2014. *Civilian Strategy in Civil War: Insights from Indonesia, Thailand, and the Philippines*. Palgrave Macmillan. https://doi.org/10.1057/9781137402998.

Barter, Shane Joshua. 2015. "The Rebel State in Society: Governance and Accommodation in Aceh, Indonesia." In *Rebel Governance in Civil War*, edited by Ana Arjona, Nelson Kasfir, and Zachariah Mampilly, 226–45. Cambridge University Press.

Batatu, Hanna. 1999. *Syria's Peasantry, the Descendants of Its Lesser Rural Notables, and Their Politics*. Princeton University Press.

Baum, Joel A. C., and Terry L. Amburgey. 2017. "Organizational Ecology." In *The Blackwell Companion to Organizations*, edited by Joel A. C. Baum, 304–26. Blackwell.

Bayat, Asef. 2002. "Activism and Social Development in the Middle East." *International Journal of Middle East Studies* 34 (1): 1–28.

Beach, Derek, and Rasmus Brun Pedersen. 2019. *Process-Tracing Methods: Foundations and Guidelines*. 2nd ed. University of Michigan Press.

Beals, Emma, and Nick Hopkins. 2016. "Aid Groups Suspend Cooperation with UN in Syria Because of Assad 'Influence.'" *Guardian*, September 8. https://www.theguardian.com/world/2016/sep/08/aid-groups-un-syria-concern-assad-united-nations.

Becker, Petra, and Friederike Stolleis. 2016. *The Crushing of Syria's Civil Actors: Survival of Grassroots Structures Is Crucial for Country's Future*. SWP Comments. Stiftung Wissenschaft und Politik, German Institute for International and Security Affairs.

Beckert, Jens. 2010. "Institutional Isomorphism Revisited: Convergence and Divergence in Institutional Change." *Sociological Theory* 28 (2): 150–66. https://doi.org/10.1111/j.1467-9558.2010.01369.x.

Beissinger, Mark R. 2002. *Nationalist Mobilization and the Collapse of the Soviet State*. Cambridge Studies in Comparative Politics. Cambridge University Press.

Beissinger, Mark R. 2017. "'Conventional' and 'Virtual' Civil Societies in Autocratic Regimes." *Comparative Politics* 49 (3): 351–71. https://doi.org/10.5129/001041517820934267.

Benelli, Prisca, Antonio Donini, and Norah Niland. 2012. *Afghanistan: Humanitarianism in Uncertain Times*. Feinstein International Center, Tufts University.

Bennett, Andrew. 2010. "Process Tracing and Causal Inference." In *Rethinking Social Inquiry: Diverse Tools, Shared Standards*, edited by Henry E. Brady and David Collier, 207–19. 2nd ed. Rowman and Littlefield.

Bennett, Andrew, and Jeffrey T. Checkel. 2015. "Process Tracing: From Philosophical Roots to Best Practices." In *Process Tracing: From Metaphor to Analytic Tool*, edited by Andrew Bennett and Jeffrey T. Checkel, 3–38. Cambridge University Press.

Berry, Marie E. 2018. *War, Women, and Power: From Violence to Mobilization in Rwanda and Bosnia-Herzegovina*. Cambridge University Press. https://doi.org/10.1017/9781108236003.

Betts, Alexander. 2009. "Institutional Proliferation and the Global Refugee Regime." *Perspectives on Politics* 7 (1): 53–58.

Bhungalia, Lisa. 2015. "Managing Violence: Aid, Counterinsurgency, and the Humanitarian Present in Palestine." *Environment and Planning* 47 (11): 2308–23.

Bob, Clifford. 2005. *The Marketing of Rebellion: Insurgents, Media, and International Activism*. Cambridge University Press.

Bradley, Megan, James Milner, and Blair Peruniak, eds. 2019. *Refugees' Roles in Resolving Displacement and Building Peace: Beyond Beneficiaries*. Georgetown University Press.

Brenner, David. 2018. "Inside the Karen Insurgency: Explaining Conflict and Conciliation in Myanmar's Changing Borderlands." *Asian Security* 14 (2): 83–99. https://doi.org/10.1080/14799855.2017.1293657.

Brenner, David. 2019. *Rebel Politics: A Political Sociology of Armed Struggle in Myanmar's Borderlands*. Cornell University Press.

Britannica. 2023. "Syrian Civil War." https://www.britannica.com/event/Syrian-Civil-War.

Brockett, Charles D. 2005. *Political Movements and Violence in Central America*. Cambridge University Press. https://doi.org/10.1017/cbo9780511614378.

Brooke, Steven, and Neil Ketchley. 2018. "Social and Institutional Origins of Political Islam." *American Political Science Review* 112 (2): 376–94.

Brown, Frances Z. 2018. *Dilemmas of Stabilization Assistance: The Case of Syria*. Carnegie Endowment for International Peace. https://carnegieendowment.org/2018/10/26/dilemmas-of-stabilization-assistance-case-of-syria-pub-77574.

Brynen, Rex. 1990. "The Politics of Exile: The Palestinians in Lebanon." *Journal of Refugee Studies* 3 (3): 204–27. https://doi.org/10.1093/jrs/3.3.204.

Building Markets. 2018. *Enabling a Localized Aid Response in Syria: An Assessment of Syrian-Led Organizations*. Building Markets. https://www.buildingmarkets.org/reports/enabling-a-localized-aid-response-in-syria.

Bush, Sarah. 2015. *The Taming of Democracy Assistance: Why Democracy Promotion Does Not Confront Dictators*. Cambridge University Press.

Bush, Sarah, and Jennifer Hadden. 2019. "Density and Decline in the Founding of International NGOs in the United States." *International Studies Quarterly* 63 (4): 1133–46.

Bybee, Keith J. 2021. "Law and/or/as Civility." *Annual Review of Law and Social Science* 17:1–14. https://doi.org/10.1146/annurev-lawsocsci-120920-084221.

Byman, Daniel, Peter Chalk, Bruce Hoffman, William Rosenau, and David Brannan. 2001. *Trends in Outside Support for Insurgent Movements*. RAND Corporation.

Calhoun, Craig. 2004. "A World of Emergencies: Fear, Intervention, and the Limits of Cosmopolitan Order." *Canadian Review of Sociology* 41 (4): 373–95.

Calhoun, Craig. 2008. "The Imperative to Reduce Suffering: Charity, Progress, and Emergencies in the Field of Humanitarian Action." In Barnett and Weiss 2008, 73–97.

Callahan, Mary Patricia. 2007. *Political Authority in Burma's Ethnic Minority States: Devolution, Occupation, and Coexistence*. ISEAS and East-West Center.

Campbell, Susanna P. 2018. *Global Governance and Local Peace: Accountability and Performance in International Peacebuilding*. Cambridge University Press.

Carbonnier, Gilles. 2015. *Humanitarian Economics: War, Disaster and the Global Aid Market*. Oxford University Press.

CARE. 2018. "Syria Tops the List of Deadliest Places for Aid Workers for the Second Consecutive Year." CARE International, August 15. https://reliefweb.int/report/world/syria-tops-list-deadliest-places-aid-workers-second-consecutive-year.

Carnegie, Allison, Kimberly Howe, Adam Lichtenheld, and Dipali Mukhopadhyay. 2022. "The Effects of Foreign Aid on Rebel Governance: Evidence from a Large-Scale US Aid Program in Syria." *Economics & Politics* 34 (1): 41–66. https://doi.org/10.1111/ecpo.12178.

Carpi, Estella. 2018. "Does Faith-Based Aid Provision Always Localise Aid?" *Refugee Hosts* (blog), January 22. https://web.archive.org/web/20200404190832/https://refugeehosts.org/2018/01/22/does-faith-based-aid-provision-always-localise-aid/.

Carpi, Estella, and Elena Fiddian-Qasmiyeh. 2020. "Keeping the Faith? Examining the Roles of Faith and Secularism in Syrian Diaspora Organizations in Lebanon." In *Diaspora Organizations in International Affairs*, edited by Dennis Dijkzeul and Margit Fauser, 129–49. Routledge.

Carpi, Estella, and H. Pinar Senoguz. 2018. "Refugee Hospitality in Lebanon and Turkey: On Making 'The Other.'" *International Migration* 57 (2): 126–42.

Central Bureau of Statistics. 2004. "General Census 2004." http://cbssyr.sy/index-EN.htm.

Centre for Humanitarian Dialogue. 2014. *Local Administration Structures in Opposition-Held Areas in Syria*. Centre for Humanitarian Dialogue.

Chahim, Dean, and Aseem Prakash. 2014. "NGOization, Foreign Funding, and the Nicaraguan Civil Society." *Voluntas* 25:487–513.

Chemonics International. 2016. *Syria Regional Program: Final Report*. United States Agency for International Development.

Chenoweth, Erica, and Kathleen Gallagher Cunningham. 2013. "Understanding Nonviolent Resistance: An Introduction." *Journal of Peace Research* 50 (3): 271–76.

Chenoweth, Erica, and Maria J. Stephan. 2011. *Why Civil Resistance Works: The Strategic Logic of Nonviolent Conflict*. Columbia University Press.

Clarke, Killian. 2018. "When Do the Dispossessed Protest? Informal Leadership and Mobilization in Syrian Refugee Camps." *Perspectives on Politics* 16 (3): 617–33. https://doi.org/10.1017/s1537592718001020.

Clarke, Killian, and Gözde Guran. 2016. "Mobilizing in Exile: Syrian Associational Life in Turkey and Lebanon." *Middle East Report* 278 (Spring): 20–26. https://merip.org/magazine/278/.

Cole, Beth, Emily Hsu, and Elena Brineman, et al. 2009. *Guiding Principles for Stabilization and Reconstruction*. United States Institute of Peace and United States Army Peacekeeping and Stability Operations Institute.

Collier, David. 2011. "Understanding Process Tracing." *PS: Political Science and Politics* 44 (4): 823–30.

Collier, David, James Mahoney, and Jason Seawright. 2004. "Claiming Too Much: Warnings About Selection Bias." In *Rethinking Social Inquiry: Diverse Tools, Shared Standards*, edited by Henry E. Brady and David Collier, 3–20. 1st ed. Rowman and Littlefield.

Cooley, Alexander, and James Ron. 2002. "The NGO Scramble: Organizational Insecurity and the Political Economy of Transnational Action." *International Security* 27 (1): 5–39.

Crasnow, Sharon. 2017. "Process Tracing in Political Science: What's the Story?" *Studies in History and Philosophy of Science* 62:6–13.

Cunningham, Kathleen Gallagher, Marianne Dahl, and Anne Frugé. 2017. "Strategies of Resistance: Diversification and Diffusion." *American Journal of Political Science* 61 (3): 591–605.

Cupolo, Diego. 2017. "Turkey Steps Up Crackdown on Humanitarian Aid Groups." *The New Humanitarian*, April 27. https://tinyurl.com/bn62xbev.

Cutts, Mark. 1998. "Politics and Humanitarianism." *Refugee Survey Quarterly* 17 (1): 1–15.

Dahi, Omar S, and Yasser Munif. 2012. "Revolts in Syria: Tracking the Convergence Between Authoritarianism and Neoliberalism." *Journal of Asian and African Studies* 47 (4): 323–32. https://doi.org/10.1177/0021909611431682.

Davis, Gerald F., and Christopher Marquis. 2005. "Prospects for Organization Theory in the Early Twenty-First Century: Institutional Fields and Mechanisms." *Organization Science* 16 (4): 332–43.

De Waal, Alex. 1997. *Famine Crimes: Politics and the Disaster Relief Industry in Africa*. Indiana University Press.

Dhingra, Reva. 2022. "Coordination in Practice or Performance? The Political Economy of Refugee Aid Coordination in Jordan." *Journal of Refugee Studies* 35 (4): 1472–91. https://doi.org/10.1093/jrs/feac002.

DiMaggio, Paul J., and Walter W. Powell. 1983. "The Iron Cage Revisited: Institutional Isomorphism and Collective Rationality in Organizational Fields." *American Sociological Review* 48 (2): 147–60.

Donini, Antonio. 1996. *The Policies of Mercy: UN Coordination in Afghanistan, Mozambique, and Rwanda*. Occasional Paper 22. The Thomas J. Watson Institute, Brown University.

Donini, Antonio, Larry Minear, and Peter Walker. 2004. "The Future of Humanitarian Action: Mapping the Implications of Iraq and Other Recent Crises." *Disasters* 28 (2): 190–204.

DuBois, Marc. 2018. "The New Humanitarian Basics." HPG Working Paper. Humanitarian Policy Group, Overseas Development Institute.

Duffield, Mark. 1997. "NGO Relief in War Zones: Towards an Analysis of the New Aid Paradigm." *Third World Quarterly* 18 (3): 527–42.

Duffield, Mark. 2001. *Global Governance and the New Wars: The Merging of Development and Security*. Zed Books.

Duffield, Mark. 2012. "Challenging Environments: Danger, Resilience and the Aid Industry." *Security Dialogue* 43 (5): 475–92.

Duffield, Mark. 2014. "From Immersion to Simulation: Remote Methodologies and the Decline of Area Studies." *Review of African Political Economy* 41 (S1): S75–94.

Dupuy, Kendra E., James Ron, and Aseem Prakash. 2015. "Who Survived? Ethiopia's Regulatory Crackdown on Foreign-Funded NGOs." *Review of International Political Economy* 22 (2): 419–56.

Egreteau, Renaud. 2022. "Profile: Blending Old and New Repertoires of Contention in Myanmar's Anti-Coup Protests (2021)." *Social Movement Studies* 22 (5–6): 822–29. https://doi.org/10.1080/14742837.2022.2140650.

Elhamoui, Wisam, and Sinan al-Hawat. 2015. "Civilian Interaction with Armed Groups in the Syrian Conflict." *Accord Insight* 2:30–34.

El-Helou, Zeina, and Lina Antara. 2018. *Political Participation of Refugees: The Case of Syrian Refugees in Lebanon*. International IDEA. https://doi.org/10.31752/idea.2018.11.

El Nakib, Shatha, and Alastair Ager. 2015. *Local Faith Community and Related Civil Society Engagement in Humanitarian Response with Syrian Refugees in Irbid, Jordan*. Report to the Henry Luce Foundation. Mailman School of Public Health, Columbia University.

Els, Christian, Kholoud Mansour, and Nils Carstensen. 2016. "Funding to National and Local Humanitarian Actors in Syria: Between Sub-Contracting and Partnerships." L2GP: Local to Global Protection.

Enab Baladi. 2016. "Syrian Employee Salaries: Where Are They After Five Years?" *Enab Baladi*, August 5. https://english.enabbaladi.net/archives/2016/05/syrian-employee-salaries/.

Fassin, Didier. 2012. *Humanitarian Reason: A Moral History of the Present*. Translated by Rachel Gomme. University of California Press.

Fassin, Didier, and Mariella Pandolfi. 2010. "Military and Humanitarian Government in the Age of Intervention." In *Contemporary States of Emergency: The Politics of Military and Humanitarian Interventions*, edited by Didier Fassin and Mariella Pandolfi, 5–17. Zone Books.

REFERENCES

Fast, Larissa, and Christina Bennett. 2020. *From the Ground Up: It's About Time for Local Humanitarian Action*. HPG Report. Humanitarian Policy Group, Overseas Development Institute. https://cdn.odi.org/media/documents/From_ the_ground_up_its_about_time_for_local_humanitarian_action.pdf.

Fearon, James D. 2008. "The Rise of Emergency Relief Aid." In Barnett and Weiss 2008, 49–72.

Ferguson, James. 1990. *The Anti-Politics Machine: "Development," Depoliticization, and Bureaucratic Power in Lesotho*. Cambridge University Press.

Fiddian-Qasmiyeh, Elena. 2010. "'Ideal' Refugee Women and Gender Equality Mainstreaming in the Sahrawi Refugee Camps: 'Good Practice' for Whom?" *Refugee Survey Quarterly* 29 (2): 64–84. https://doi.org/10.1093/rsq/hdq023.

Fiddian-Qasmiyeh, Elena. 2014. *The Ideal Refugees: Gender, Islam, and the Sahrawi Politics of Survival*. Syracuse University Press.

Fiddian-Qasmiyeh, Elena. 2016. "Refugees Hosting Refugees." *Forced Migration Review* 53:25–27.

Fiddian-Qasmiyeh, Elena. 2018. "Local Communities and Contextualising the Localisation of Aid Agenda." *Refugee Hosts* (blog), January 19. https:// refugeehosts.org/blog/contextualising-the-localisation-of-aid-agenda/.

Fillieule, Olivier. 2015. "Demobilization and Disengagement in a Life Course Perspective." In *The Oxford Handbook of Social Movements*, edited by Donatella della Porta and Mario Diani, 277–88. Oxford University Press.

Finkel, Evgeny. 2017. *Ordinary Jews: Choice and Survival During the Holocaust*. Princeton University Press.

Fisher, William F. 1997. "Doing Good? The Politics and Antipolitics of NGO Practices." *Annual Review of Anthropology* 26:439–64.

Foucault, Michel. 1991. *The Foucault Effect: Studies in Governmentality with Two Lectures by and an Interview with Michel Foucault*. Edited by Graham Burchell, Colin Gordon, and Peter Miller. University of Chicago Press.

Fujii, Lee Ann. 2012. "Research Ethics 101: Dilemmas and Responsibilities." *PS: Political Science and Politics* 45 (4): 717–23. https://doi.org/10.1017/ S1049096512000819.

Fujii, Lee Ann. 2018. *Interviewing in Social Science Research: A Relational Approach*. Routledge Series on Interpretive Methods. Routledge.

Fumagalli, Matteo. 2022. "The Next Swing of the Pendulum? Cross-Border Aid and Shifting Aid Paradigms in Post-Coup Myanmar." RSC Policy Paper 2022/08. European University Institute. https://tinyurl.com/ycte8reu.

Gani, Jasmine. 2015. "Contentious Politics and the Syrian Crisis: Internationalization and Militarization of the Conflict." In *Contentious Politics in the Middle East: Popular Resistance and Marginalized Activism Beyond the Arab Uprisings*, edited by Fawaz A. Gerges, 127–53. Palgrave Macmillan.

Gawfi, Iman al-, Bilkis Zabara, and Stacey Philbrick Yadav. 2020. "The Role of Women in Peacebuilding in Yemen." Center for Applied Research in Partnership with the Orient, February 27.

Gerring, John. 2004. "What Is a Case Study and What Is It Good For?" *The American Political Science Review* 98 (2): 341–54.

Gerring, John. 2008. "The Mechanismic Worldview: Thinking Inside the Box." *British Journal of Political Science* 38 (1): 161–79.

Grisgraber, Daryl, and Marc Hanson. 2013. "Aid Inside Syria: Too Little, but Not Too Late." Refugees International. https://reliefweb.int/report/syrian-arab-republic/ aid-inside-syria-too-little-not-too-late.

Gugerty, Mary Kay, and Michael Kremer. 2008. "Outside Funding and the Dynamics of Participation in Community Associations." *American Journal of Political Science* 52 (3): 585–602.

Haddad, Bassam. 2012. *Business Networks in Syria: The Political Economy of Authoritarian Resilience*. Stanford University Press.

Haddad, Saleem, and Eva Svoboda. 2017. "What's the Magic Word? Humanitarian Access and Local Organisations in Syria." HPG Working Paper. Humanitarian Policy Group, Overseas Development Institute.

Hall, Peter A., and Rosemary C. R. Taylor. 1996. "Political Science and the Three New Institutionalisms." *Political Studies* 44 (5): 936–57.

Hallaj, Omar Abdulaziz. 2017. "Geographies of Absence: Radicalization and the Shaping of the New Syrian Territoriality." *New England Journal of Public Policy* 29 (1): 1–32.

Hamdan, Ali. 2020. "Ephemeral Geopolitics: Tracing the Role of Refugees in Syria's Transnational Opposition." *Political Geography* 84:1–24, 102299. https://doi.org/10.1016/j.polgeo.2020.102299.

Hammami, Rema. 1995. "NGOs: The Professionalisation of Politics." *Race & Class* 37 (2): 51–63.

Hammodeh, Nizar, and Tania Cheung. 2013. "An Interview with Dr Nizar Hammodeh, Union of Syrian Medical Relief Organizations." *Humanitarian Exchange* 59, article 6, November 26. https://odihpn.org/publication/an-interview-with-dr-nizar-hammodeh-union-of-syrian-medical-relief-organisations/.

Hannan, Michael T., and Glenn R. Carroll. 1992. *Dynamics of Organizational Populations: Density, Legitimation, and Competition*. Oxford University Press.

Hannan, Michael T., and John Freeman. 1977. "The Population Ecology of Organizations." *American Journal of Sociology* 82 (5): 929–64.

Hauer, Neil. 2022. "Dnipro: Ukraine's Staging Ground." *New Lines Magazine*, March 21. https://newlinesmag.com/reportage/dnipro-ukraines-staging-ground/.

Healy, Sean, and Sandrine Tiller. 2013. "Out of the Spotlight and Hard to Reach: Syrian Refugees in Jordan's Cities." *Humanitarian Exchange* 59, article 10, November 27. https://odihpn.org/publication/out-of-the-spotlight-and-hard-to-reach-syrian-refugees-in-jordan%C2%92s-cities/.

Hearn, Julie. 1998. "The 'NGO-isation' of Kenyan Society: USAID and the Restructuring of Health Care." *Review of African Political Economy* 25 (75): 89–100.

Heiss, Andrew, and Judith Kelley. 2017. "Between a Rock and a Hard Place: International NGOs and the Dual Pressures of Donors and Host Governments." *Journal of Politics* 79 (2): 732–41.

Heller, Sam. 2017. "A Deadly Delusion: Were Syria's Rebels Ever Going to Defeat the Jihadists?" *War on the Rocks*, August 10. https://warontherocks.com/2017/08/a-deadly-delusion-were-syrias-rebels-ever-going-to-defeat-the-jihadists/.

Henderson, Sarah L. 2002. "Selling Civil Society: Western Aid and the Nongovernmental Organization Sector in Russia." *Comparative Political Studies* 35 (2): 139–67.

Holzer, Elizabeth. 2012. "A Case Study of Political Failure in a Refugee Camp." *Journal of Refugee Studies* 25 (2): 257–81.

Hopgood, Stephen. 2008. "Saying 'No' to Wal-Mart? Money and Morality in Professional Humanitarianism." In Barnett and Weiss 2008, 98–123.

Horst, Cindy. 2013. "The Depoliticisation of Diasporas from the Horn of Africa: From Refugees to Transnational Aid Workers." *African Studies* 72 (2): 228–45. https://doi.org/10.1080/00020184.2013.812881.

Horst, Cindy. 2019. "Refugees, Peacebuilding, and the Anthropology of the Good." In Bradley et al. 2019, 39–54.

Horstmann, Alexander. 2011. "Ethical Dilemmas and Identifications of Faith-Based Humanitarian Organizations in the Karen Refugee Crisis." *Journal of Refugee Studies* 24 (3): 513–32.

Howe, Kimberly. 2016. *No End in Sight: A Case Study of Humanitarian Action and the Syria Conflict*. Planning from the Future. Feinstein International Center, King's College London, Humanitarian Policy Group.

Howe, Kimberly, Elizabeth Stites, and Danya Chudacoff. 2015. *Breaking the Hourglass: Partnerships in Remote Management Settings; The Cases of Syria and Iraqi Kurdistan*. Feinstein International Center, Tufts University.

HPG. 2012. "Syria Crisis: The Humanitarian Response." Humanitarian Policy Group, Overseas Development Institute. https://alnap.org/documents/3136/4907-pdf.

Hulme, David, and Michael Edwards. 1997. *NGOs, States and Donors: Too Close for Comfort?* St. Martin's.

Humud, Carla E., and Christopher M. Blanchard. 2020. "Armed Conflict in Syria: Overview and U.S. Response." Congressional Research Service Report RL33487. https://crsreports.congress.gov/product/pdf/RL/RL33487.

Humud, Carla E., Robert Pirog, and Liana W. Rosen. 2015. "Islamic State Financing and U.S. Policy Approaches." Congressional Research Service Report R43980. https://crsreports.congress.gov/product/details?prodcode=R43980.

IATI. 2019. "Local Development and Small Projects Support Activity File-SY." International Aid Transparency Initiative. https://web.archive.org/web/20200718005633/https://www.iatiregistry.org/dataset/ldsps-sy.

ICG. 2011. "Popular Protest in North Africa and the Middle East (VI): The Syrian People's Slow Motion Revolution." International Crisis Group Middle East/North Africa Report 108. https://www.crisisgroup.org/middle-east-north-africa/eastern-mediterranean/syria/popular-protest-north-africa-and-middle-east-vi-syrian-people-s-slow-motion-revolution.

ICG. 2021. "The Cost of the Coup: Myanmar Edges Toward State Collapse." International Crisis Group Briefing 167. https://www.crisisgroup.org/asia/south-east-asia/myanmar/b167-cost-coup-myanmar-edges-toward-state-collapse.

Ignatius, David. 2017. "What the Demise of the CIA's Anti-Assad Program Means." *Washington Post*, July 20. https://www.washingtonpost.com/opinions/what-the-demise-of-the-cias-anti-assad-program-means/2017/07/20/f6467240-6d87-11e7-b9e2-2056e768a7e5_story.html.

Integrity and Agulhas. 2015. "DFID Syria Crisis Unit, Humanitarian Programme Process Evaluation." Agulhas Applied Knowledge. https://reliefweb.int/report/syrian-arab-republic/dfid-syria-crisis-unit-humanitarian-programme-process-evaluation-final.

Irfan, Anne. 2020. "Petitioning for Palestine: Refugee Appeals to International Authorities." *Contemporary Levant* 5 (2): 79–96. https://doi.org/10.1080/20581831.2020.1815408.

Irfan, Anne. 2023. *Refuge and Resistance: Palestinians and the International Refugee System*. Columbia University Press.

IRIN News. 2013a. "Breakdown of Syria Aid Pledges in Kuwait." *The New Humanitarian*, February 1. http://www.irinnews.org/news/2013/02/01/breakdown-syria-aid-pledges-kuwait.

IRIN News. 2013b. "Donors Pledge $1.5 Billion in Aid to Syria While Demanding More Access." *The New Humanitarian*, January 30. https://www.thenewhumanitarian.org/news/2013/01/30/donors-pledge-15-billion-aid-syria-while-demanding-more-access.
Ismail, Salwa. 2018. *The Rule of Violence: Subjectivity, Memory and Government in Syria*. Cambridge University Press. https://doi.org/10.1017/9781139424721.
Issa, Antoun. 2016. "Syria's New Media Landscape: Independent Media Born out of War." MEI Policy Paper. Middle East Institute. https://www.mei.edu/sites/default/files/publications/PP9_Issa_Syrianmedia_web_0.pdf.
Jacobsen, Karen. 2019. "Durable Solutions and the Political Action of Refugees." In Bradley et al. 2019, 23–38. https://doi.org/10.2307/j.ctvfrxq90.6.
Jad, Islah. 2004. "The NGO-isation of Arab Women's Movements." *IDS Bulletin: Institute of Development Studies* 35 (4): 34–42.
Jamal, Manal A. 2012. "Democracy Promotion, Civil Society Building, and the Primacy of Politics." *Comparative Political Studies* 45 (1): 3–31.
James, Eric. 2015. "The Professional Humanitarian and the Downsides of Professionalisation." *Disasters* 40 (2): 185–206.
Jenkins, J. Craig, and Charles Perrow. 1977. "Insurgency of the Powerless: Farm Worker Movements (1946–1972)." *American Sociological Review* 42 (2): 249–68.
Jose, Betcy, and Peace A. Medie. 2015. "Understanding Why and How Civilians Resort to Self-Protection in Armed Conflict." *International Studies Review* 17 (4): 515–35. https://doi.org/10.1111/misr.12254.
Kalyvas, Stathis N. 2006. *The Logic of Violence in Civil War*. Cambridge University Press.
Kalyvas, Stathis N. 2015a. "Is ISIS a Revolutionary Group and If Yes, What Are the Implications?" *Perspectives on Terrorism* 9 (4): 42–47.
Kalyvas, Stathis N. 2015b. "Rebel Governance During the Greek Civil War, 1942–1949." In *Rebel Governance in Civil War*, edited by Ana Arjona, Nelson Kasfir, and Zachariah Mampilly, 119–37. Cambridge University Press.
Kaplan, Oliver. 2017. *Resisting War: How Communities Protect Themselves*. Cambridge University Press.
Karim, Ataul, Mark Duffield, and Susanne Jaspars, et al. 1996. *Operation Lifeline Sudan—A Review*. Conflict Sensitivity Resource Facility, South Sudan, July 9. https://www.csrf-southsudan.org/repository/operation-lifeline-sudan-review-26/.
Kasfir, Nelson. 2005. "Guerrillas and Civilian Participation: The National Resistance Army in Uganda, 1981–86." *The Journal of Modern African Studies* 43 (2): 271–96.
Kassimir, Ronald, Robert Latham, and Thomas M. Callaghy. 2001. "Introduction: Transboundary Formations, Intervention, Order, and Authority." In *Intervention and Transnationalism in Africa: Global-Local Networks of Power*, edited by Thomas M. Callaghy, Ronald Kassimir, and Robert Latham, 1–20. Cambridge University Press.
Keck, Margaret E., and Kathryn Sikkink. 1998. *Activists Beyond Borders: Advocacy Networks in International Politics*. Cornell University Press.
Kelley, Judith G., and Beth A. Simmons. 2015. "Politics by Number: Indicators as Social Pressure in International Relations." *American Journal of Political Science* 59 (1): 55–70.
Kent, Randolph, Christina Bennett, Antonio Donini, and Daniel Maxwell. 2016. *Planning from the Future: Is the Humanitarian System Fit for Purpose?*

Humanitarian Policy Group, Tufts Feinstein International Center, King's College London.
Khaddour, Kheder. 2017. "Consumed by War: The End of Aleppo and Northern Syria's Political Order." Friedrich-Ebert-Stiftung. http://library.fes.de/pdf-files/iez/13783.pdf.
Khalaf, Rana. 2015. "Governance Without Government in Syria: Civil Society and State Building During Conflict." *Syria Studies* 7 (3): 37–72.
Khalaf, Rana, Oula Ramadan, and Friederike Stolleis. 2014. "Activism in Difficult Times: Civil Society Groups in Syria, 2011–2014." Badael Project and Friedrich-Ebert-Stiftung. https://library.fes.de/pdf-files/bueros/beirut/11162.pdf.
Khatib, Lina, and Ellen Lust. 2014. *Taking to the Streets: The Transformation of Arab Activism*. Johns Hopkins University Press.
Khoury, Rana B. 2011. "Western Sahara and Palestine: A Comparative Study of Colonialisms, Occupations, and Nationalisms." *New Middle Eastern Studies* 1 (June).
Khoury, Rana B. 2024. "Sampling Hard-to-Reach Populations." In *Doing Good Qualitative Research*, edited by Jennifer Cyr and Sara Wallace Goodman, 122–31. Oxford University Press.
Khoury, Rana B., and Emily K. M. Scott. 2024. "Going Local Without Localization: Power and Humanitarian Response in the Syrian War." *World Development* 174:106460. https://doi.org/10.1016/j.worlddev.2023.106460.
Khoury, Rana B., and Alexandra A. Siegel. 2024. "Civil Organizing in War: Evidence from Syrian Facebook Communities." *Perspectives on Politics* FirstView, 1–23. https://doi.org/10.1017/S1537592724001907.
Konyndyk, Jeremy, and Rose Worden. 2019. "People-Driven Response: Power and Participation in Humanitarian Action." CGD Policy Paper 55. Center for Global Development.
Koteiche, Rayan, Serene Murad, Michele Heisler, and Phelim Kine. 2019. *"My Only Crime Was That I Was a Doctor": How the Syrian Government Targets Health Workers for Arrest, Detention, and Torture*. Physicians for Human Rights, December. https://phr.org/wp-content/uploads/2019/12/PHR-Detention-of-Syrian-Health-Workers-Full-Report-Dec-2019_English-1.pdf.
Krause, Jana, Juan Masullo, Emily Paddon Rhoads, and Jennifer Welsh, eds. 2023. *Civilian Protective Agency in Violent Settings: A Comparative Perspective*. Oxford University Press. https://doi.org/10.1093/oso/9780192866714.001.0001.
Krause, Monika. 2014. *The Good Project: Humanitarian Relief NGOs and the Fragmentation of Reason*. University of Chicago Press.
Kreft, Anne-Kathrin. 2019. "Responding to Sexual Violence: Women's Mobilization in War." *Journal of Peace Research* 56 (2): 220–33. https://doi.org/10.1177/0022343318800361.
Lake, Milli. 2018. *Strong NGOs and Weak States: Pursuing Gender Justice in the Democratic Republic of the Congo and South Africa*. Cambridge University Press.
Latham, Robert. 2001. "Identifying the Contours of Transboundary Political Life." In *Intervention and Transnationalism in Africa: Global-Local Networks of Power*, edited by Thomas M. Callaghy, Ronald Kassimir, and Robert Latham, 69–92. Cambridge University Press.
Leenders, Reinoud, and Steven Heydemann. 2012. "Popular Mobilization in Syria: Opportunity and Threat, and the Social Networks of the Early Risers." *Mediterranean Politics* 17 (2): 139–59. https://doi.org/10.1080/13629395.2012.694041.

Leenders, Reinoud, and Kholoud Mansour. 2018. "Humanitarianism, State Sovereignty, and Authoritarian Regime Maintenance in the Syrian War." *Political Science Quarterly* 133 (2): 225–57.
Lefèvre, Raphaël. 2013. *Ashes of Hama: The Muslim Brotherhood in Syria*. Hurst Publishers.
Lichtenheld, Adam G. 2017. "Beyond Ethno-Sectarian 'Cleansing': The Assortative Logic of Forced Displacement in Syria." Project on Middle East Political Science, Elliott School of International Affairs. https://pomeps.org/beyond-ethno-sectarian-cleansing-the-assortative-logic-of-forced-displacement-in-syria.
Lichtenheld, Adam G. 2020. "Explaining Population Displacement Strategies in Civil Wars: A Cross-National Analysis." *International Organization* 74 (2): 253–94. https://Doi.org/10.1017/s0020818320000089.
Lichtenheld, Adam G., and Justin Schon. 2021. "The Consequences of Internal Displacement on Civil War Violence: Evidence from Syria." *Political Geography* 86 (April): 102346. https://doi.org/10.1016/j.polgeo.2021.102346.
Lister, Charles. 2015. *The Syrian Jihad: Al-Qaeda, the Islamic State, and the Evolution of an Insurgency*. Oxford University Press.
Loveluck, Louisa. 2023. "In Earthquake-Battered Syria, a Desperate Wait for Help That Never Came." *Washington Post*, February 10. https://www.washingtonpost.com/world/2023/02/10/syria-turkey-earthquake-aid-rescue/.
Lowe, Robert. 2006. "The Syrian Kurds: A People Discovered." Briefing Paper 06/01. Chatham House Middle East Programme. https://www.chathamhouse.org/sites/default/files/public/Research/Middle%20East/bpsyriankurds.pdf.
Lubkemann, Stephen C. 2008. *Culture in Chaos: An Anthropology of the Social Condition in War*. University of Chicago Press.
Lund, Aron. 2013. "Islamist Groups Declare Opposition to National Coalition and US Strategy." *Syria Comment*, September 24. https://www.joshualandis.com/blog/major-rebel-factions-drop-exiles-go-full-islamist/.
Lund, Aron. 2016. *Into the Tunnels: The Rise and Fall of Syria's Rebel Enclave in the Eastern Ghouta*, December 21. Report: Arab Politics Beyond the Uprisings. The Century Foundation. https://tcf.org/content/report/into-the-tunnels/.
Lund, Aron. 2017a. *How Assad's Enemies Gave Up on the Syrian Opposition*, October 17. Report: Arab Politics Beyond the Uprisings. The Century Foundation. https://tcf.org/content/report/assads-enemies-gave-syrian-opposition/.
Lund, Aron. 2017b. "The Syrian Rebel Who Tried to Build an Islamist Paradise." *Politico*, March 31. https://www.politico.com/magazine/story/2017/03/the-syrian-rebel-who-built-an-islamic-paradise-214969/.
Lund, Aron. 2020. "Stop-Gap Solutions for Syrians Without Papers." *The New Humanitarian*, August 4. https://www.thenewhumanitarian.org/analysis/2020/08/04/syria-documentation-solutions.
Lynch, Colum, and William Worley. 2023. "Exclusive: The Day the Data Died in Syria." *Devex*, May 12. https://www.devex.com/news/sponsored/exclusive-the-day-the-data-died-in-syria-105438.
Lynch, Julia F. 2013. "Aligning Sampling Strategies with Analytic Goals." In *Interview Research in Political Science*, edited by Layna Mosley, 31–44. Cornell University Press. https://doi.org/10.7591/9780801467974-004.
Lynch, Marc, Deen Freelon, and Sean Aday. 2014. *Blogs and Bullets III: Syria's Socially Mediated Civil War*. Peaceworks Report. United States Institute of Peace. https://www.usip.org/sites/default/files/PW91-Syrias%20Socially%20Mediated%20Civil%20War.pdf.

Mac Ginty, Roger. 2014. "Everyday Peace: Bottom-Up and Local Agency in Conflict-Affected Societies." *Security Dialogue* 45 (6): 548–64. https://doi.org/10.1177/0967010614550899.

Mahoney, James, and Gary Goertz. 2006. "A Tale of Two Cultures: Contrasting Quantitative and Qualitative Research." *Political Analysis* 14 (3): 227–49.

Mampilly, Zachariah. 2011. *Rebel Rulers: Insurgent Governance and Civilian Life During War*. Cornell University Press.

Mansour, Nayla. 2013. "My Name Is Kafranbel, and I Don't Need Trainings in Needs Assessment." *Al-Jumhuriya*, May 22. https://aljumhuriya.net/en/2013/05/22/my-name-is-kafranbel-and-i-dont-need-trainings-in-needs-assessment/.

March, James G., and Johan P. Olsen. 1984. "The New Institutionalism: Organizational Factors in Political Life." *The American Political Science Review* 78 (3): 734–49.

March, James G., and Johan P. Olsen. 1989. *Rediscovering Institutions: The Organizational Basis of Politics*. Free Press.

March, James G., and Johan P. Olsen. 2008. "Elaborating the 'New Institutionalism.'" In *The Oxford Handbook of Political Institutions*, edited by Sarah A. Binder, R. A. W. Rhodes, and Bert A. Rockman, 3–21. Oxford University Press. https://doi.org/10.1093/oxfordhb/9780199548460.003.0001.

Martínez, José Ciro, and Brent Eng. 2018. "Stifling Stateness: The Assad Regime's Campaign Against Rebel Governance." *Security Dialogue* 49 (4): 235–53. https://doi.org/10.1177/0967010618768622.

Masterson, Daniel, and Lama Mourad. 2019. "The Ethical Challenges of Field Research in the Syrian Refugee Crisis." *APSA MENA Politics Section Newsletter* 2 (1): 1–6.

Matelski, Maaike, Rachel Dijkstra, and Brianne McGonigle Leyh. 2022. "Multi-Layered Civil Society Documentation of Human Rights Violations in Myanmar: The Potential for Accountability and Truth-Telling." *Journal of Human Rights Practice* 14 (3): 794–818. https://doi.org/10.1093/jhuman/huac031.

Mazur, Kevin. 2019. "State Networks and Intra-Ethnic Group Variation in the 2011 Syrian Uprising." *Comparative Political Studies* 52 (7): 995–1027.

Mazur, Kevin. 2021. *Revolution in Syria: Identity, Networks, and Repression*. Cambridge University Press. https://doi.org/10.1017/9781108915274.

Mazur, Kevin, and Kheder Khaddour. 2013. "The Struggle for Syria's Regions." *Middle East Report* 269 (Winter): 2–11.

McAdam, Doug. 1999. *Political Process and the Development of Black Insurgency, 1930–1970*. 2nd ed. University of Chicago Press.

McAdam, Doug, Sidney Tarrow, and Charles Tilly. 2001. *Dynamics of Contention*. Cambridge University Press. https://doi.org/10.1017/cbo9780511805431.

McCarthy, John D., and Mayer N. Zald. 1977. "Resource Mobilization and Social Movements: A Partial Theory." *American Journal of Sociology* 82 (6): 1212–41.

McMahon, Patrice C. 2017. *The NGO Game: Post-Conflict Peacebuilding in the Balkans and Beyond*. Cornell University Press.

Menapolis. 2013. "Local Councils in Syria: A Sovereignty Crisis in Liberated Areas." Menapolis Policy Paper, Istanbul, Turkey, September.

Mercy Corps. 2023. *Understanding Ongoing Localization Initiatives and Improving the Policy and Operational Environment for Local Actors*. Humanitarian NGO Platform in Ukraine. Mercy Corps and UK Aid, December. https://reliefweb.int/report/ukraine/understanding-ongoing-localization-initiatives-and-improving-policy-and-operational-environment-local-actors-december-2023-enuk.

Mercy Corps. n.d. "Building Civil Society Through Humanitarian Assistance." MC Fact Sheet. https://tinyurl.com/tm4z29wc.

Meyer, John W., and Brian Rowan. 1977. "Institutionalized Organizations: Formal Structure as Myth and Ceremony." *American Journal of Sociology* 83 (2): 340–63.

Mitchell, Timothy. 2002. *Rule of Experts: Egypt, Techno-Politics, Modernity*. University of California Press.

Mohan, Giles, and Kristian Stokke. 2000. "Participatory Development and Empowerment: The Dangers of Localism." *Third World Quarterly* 21 (2): 247–68. https://doi.org/10.1080/01436590050004346.

Mohns, Erik, and André Bank. 2012. "Syrian Revolt Fallout: End of the Resistance Axis?" *Middle East Policy Council* 19 (3): 25–35. https://onlinelibrary.wiley.com/doi/10.1111/j.1475-4967.2012.00545.x.

Moss, Dana M. 2016. "Transnational Repression, Diaspora Mobilization, and the Case of the Arab Spring." *Social Problems* 63 (4): 480–98. https://doi.org/10.1093/socpro/spw019.

Moss, Dana M. 2021. *The Arab Spring Abroad: Diaspora Activism Against Authoritarian Regimes*. Cambridge University Press.

Mourad, Lama. 2017. "'Standoffish' Policy-Making: Inaction and Change in the Lebanese Response to the Syrian Displacement Crisis." *Middle East Law and Governance* 9 (3): 249–66.

MSF. 2015. "Working Underground—Supporting Syrian Doctors in Besieged and Intense Conflict Areas." Voices from the Field. Médecins Sans Frontières, March 13. https://www.msf.org/syria-working-underground-%E2%80%93-supporting-syrian-doctors-besieged-and-intense-conflict-areas.

MSF. 2020. "Extreme Conditions in Syria: How MSF Provides Remote Support When Necessary." Médecins Sans Frontières, December 10. https://www.doctorswithoutborders.org/what-we-do/news-stories/story/extreme-conditions-syria.

Mundy, Jacob. 2015. *Imaginative Geographies of Algerian Violence: Conflict Science, Conflict Management, Antipolitics*. Stanford University Press.

Mundy, Jacob. 2019. "The Middle East Is Violence: On the Limits of Comparative Approaches to the Study of Armed Conflict." *Civil Wars* 21 (4): 539–68. https://doi.org/10.1080/13698249.2019.1664847.

Mundy, Jacob A. 2007. "Performing the Nation, Pre-Figuring the State: The Western Saharan Refugees, Thirty Years Later." *The Journal of Modern African Studies* 45 (2): 275–97. https://doi.org/10.1017/s0022278x07002546.

Munif, Yasser. 2020. *The Syrian Revolution: Between the Politics of Life and the Geopolitics of Death*. Pluto Press.

Murshid, Navine. 2013. *The Politics of Refugees in South Asia: Identity, Resistance, Manipulation*. Routledge. https://doi.org/10.4324/9781315890142.

Nasser, Rabie, Ramia Ismail, Omar Dahi, and Nabil Marzouk. 2020. *Syria: Justice to Transcend Conflict*. Impact of Syrian Conflict Report. Syrian Centre for Policy Research, May 27. https://scpr-syria.org/justice-to-transcend-conflict/.

Nayal, Moe Ali. 2013. "Palestinian Refugees Are Not at Your Service." *Electronic Intifada*, May 17. https://web.archive.org/web/20130619041548/https://electronicintifada.net/content/palestinian-refugees-are-not-your-service/12464.

Nordstrom, Carolyn. 1997. *A Different Kind of War Story*. University of Pennsylvania Press.

Norman, Kelsey P. 2020. *Reluctant Reception: Refugees, Migration and Governance in the Middle East and North Africa*. Cambridge University Press. https://doi.org/10.1017/9781108900119.

Novak, Paolo. 2013. "The Success of Afghan NGOs." *Development in Practice* 23 (7): 872–88.

OCHA. 2015. *Turkey Humanitarian Fund Annual Report 2015*. United Nations Office for the Coordination of Humanitarian Affairs.
OCHA. 2018. "Syria Cross-Border Humanitarian Fund." United Nations Office for the Coordination of Humanitarian Affairs, February 1.
OCHA. 2023. *Humanitarian Needs and Response Plan Ukraine*. Humanitarian Programme Cycle 2024. United Nations Office for the Coordination of Humanitarian Affairs. https://www.unhcr.org/ua/wp-content/uploads/sites/38/2024/01/Ukraine-HNRP-2024-Humanitarian-Needs-and-Response-Plan-UA-20240110.pdf.
OCHA Yemen. 2017. "2018 Humanitarian Needs Overview: Yemen." December 2017. United Nations Office for the Coordination of Humanitarian Affairs. https://reliefweb.int/report/yemen/yemen-2018-humanitarian-needs-overview-enar.
OECD. 2020. "ODA by Sector: Humanitarian Aid, Million US Dollars, 1971–2019." Organisation for Economic Co-operation and Development.
Ofteringer, Ronald, and Ralf Backer. 1994. "A Republic of Statelessness: Three Years of Humanitarian Intervention in Iraqi Kurdistan." *Middle East Report*, no. 187–88 (March–April). https://merip.org/1994/03/a-republic-of-statelessness/.
OHCHR. 2018. "UN Commission of Inquiry on Syria: The Siege and Recapture of Eastern Ghouta Marked by War Crimes, Crimes Against Humanity." Office of the United Nations High Commissioner for Human Rights, June 20. https://www.ohchr.org/en/press-releases/2018/06/un-commission-inquiry-syria-siege-and-recapture-eastern-ghouta-marked-war.
OIG. 2018. *Department of State Stabilization Programs in Syria Funded Under the Further Continuing and Security Assistance Appropriations Act, 2017*. Domestic Operations and Special Reports ISP-I-18-29. Office of the Inspector General, US Department of State.
Østergaard-Nielsen, Eva. 2006. "Diasporas and Conflict Resolution: Part of the Problem or Part of the Solution?" DIIS Brief. Danish Institute for International Studies. https://www.researchgate.net/profile/Eva_Ostergaard-nielsen/publication/241917841_Diasporas_and_Conflict_Resolution_-_Part_of_the_Problem_or_Part_of_the_Solution/links/56ea9e8408ae7858657fd281/Diasporas-and-Conflict-Resolution-Part-of-the-Problem-or-Part-of-the-Solution.pdf.
Oweis, Khaled Yacoub. 2013. "Syria's Jihadists Face Test of Government in Eastern City." *Reuters*, April 9.
Pace, Joe, and Joshua Landis. 2009. "The Syrian Opposition: The Struggle for Unity and Relevance, 2003–2008." In *Demystifying Syria*, edited by Fred Lawson, 120–42. SAQI and London Middle East Institute SOAS.
Paddon Rhoads, Emily, and Rebecca Sutton. 2020. "The (Self) Protection of Civilians in South Sudan: Popular and Community Justice Practices." *African Affairs* 119 (476): 370–94. https://doi.org/10.1093/afraf/adaa017.
Parham, Nic, Leonie Tax, Lynn Yoshikawa, and Kevin Lim. 2013. "Lessons from Assessing the Humanitarian Situation in Syria and Countries Hosting Refugees." *Humanitarian Exchange* 59, article 13, November 27. https://odihpn.org/publication/lessons-from-assessing-the-humanitarian-situation-in-syria-and-countries-hosting-refugees/.
Parker, Ben. 2013. "Humanitarianism Besieged." *Humanitarian Exchange* 59, article 1, November 26. https://odihpn.org/publication/humanitarianism-besieged/.
Parker, Ben. 2018. "US Tightens Counter-Terror Clampdown on Syria Aid." *The New Humanitarian*, September 21. https://www.thenewhumanitarian.org/news/2018/09/21/us-tightens-counter-terror-clampdown-syria-aid.

Parkinson, Sarah E. 2013. "Organizing Rebellion: Rethinking High-Risk Mobilization and Social Networks in War." *American Political Science Review* 107 (3): 418–32. https://doi.org/10.1017/s0003055413000208.

Parkinson, Sarah E. 2016. "Money Talks: Discourse, Networks, and Structure in Militant Organizations." *Perspectives on Politics* 14 (4): 976–94.

Parkinson, Sarah E. 2021. "Practical Ideology in Militant Organizations." *World Politics* 73 (1): 52–81. https://doi.org/10.1017/S0043887120000180.

Parkinson, Sarah E. 2023. *Beyond the Lines: Social Networks and Palestinian Militant Organizations in Wartime Lebanon*. Cornell University Press.

Pearlman, Wendy. 2016. "Narratives of Fear in Syria." *Perspectives on Politics* 14 (1): 21–37.

Pearlman, Wendy. 2019. "Civil Action in the Syrian Conflict." In Avant et al. 2019a, 35–63. https://doi.org/10.1093/oso/9780190056896.003.0002.

Pearlman, Wendy. 2021. "Mobilizing from Scratch: Large-Scale Collective Action Without Preexisting Organization in the Syrian Uprising." *Comparative Political Studies* 54 (10): 1786–1817.

Perthes, Volker. 1997. *The Political Economy of Syria Under Asad*. 2nd ed. I. B. Tauris.

Pfeffer, Jeffrey, and Gerald R. Salancik. 1978. *The External Control of Organizations: A Resource Dependence Perspective*. Harper & Row.

Phillips, Christopher. 2015. "Sectarianism and Conflict in Syria." *Third World Quarterly* 36 (2): 357–76.

Phillips, Christopher. 2016. *The Battle for Syria: International Rivalry in the New Middle East*. Yale University Press. https://doi.org/10.12987/yale/9780300217179.001.0001.

Phillips, Sarah G. 2020. *When There Was No Aid: War and Peace in Somaliland*. Cornell University Press.

Pierret, Thomas. 2013. "External Support and the Syrian Insurgency." *Foreign Policy*, August 9.

Pierret, Thomas. 2014. "The Syrian Baath Party and Sunni Islam: Conflicts and Connivance." Middle East Brief 77. Crown Center for Middle East Studies, Brandeis University.

Pierret, Thomas, and Kjetil Selvik. 2009. "Limits of 'Authoritarian Upgrading' in Syria: Private Welfare, Islamic Charities, and the Rise of the Zayd Movement." *International Journal of Middle East Studies* 41 (4): 595–614. https://doi.org/10.1017/s0020743809990377.

Pincock, Kate, Alexander Betts, and Evan Easton-Calabria. 2020. *The Global Governed? Refugees as Providers of Protection and Assistance*. Cambridge University Press. https://doi.org/10.1017/9781108848831.

Prendergast, John, and Mark Duffield. 1994. "Sovereignty and Intervention After the Cold War: Lessons from the Emergency Relief Desk." *Middle East Report*, no. 187–88 (March–April). https://merip.org/1994/03/sovereignty-and-intervention-after-the-cold-war/.

Reindorp, Nicola, and Peter Wiles. 2001. "Humanitarian Coordination: Lessons from Recent Field Experience." Commissioned by the Office for the Coordination of Humanitarian Affairs. Overseas Development Institute, June.

ReliefWeb. 2008. *Glossary of Humanitarian Terms*. ReliefWeb Project. ReliefWeb, August. https://reliefweb.int/report/world/reliefweb-glossary-humanitarian-terms-enko.

Revkin, Mara R. 2016. "Does the Islamic State Have a 'Social Contract'? Evidence from Iraq and Syria." Program on Governance and Development Working Paper 9. University of Gothenburg.

Revkin, Mara R. 2020. "What Explains Taxation by Resource-Rich Rebels? Evidence from the Islamic State in Syria." *Journal of Politics* 82 (2): 757–64. https://doi.org/10.1086/706598.

Rieff, David. 2002. *A Bed for the Night: Humanitarianism in Crisis*. Simon & Schuster.

Riehl, Volker. 2001. "Who Is Ruling in South Sudan? The Role of NGOs in Rebuilding Socio-Political Order." Studies on Emergency and Disaster Relief 9. Nordiska Afrikainstitutet.

Risse, Thomas. 2011a. "Governance in Areas of Limited Statehood: Introduction and Overview." In Risse 2011b, 1–37.

Risse, Thomas. 2011b. *Governance Without a State? Policies and Politics in Areas of Limited Statehood*. Columbia University Press.

Roberts, Susan M. 2014. "Development Capital: USAID and the Rise of Development Contractors." *Annals of the Association of American Geographers* 104 (5): 1030–51.

Robinson, Eric, Daniel Egel, Patrick B. Johnston, Sean Mann, Alexander D. Rothenberg, and David Stebbins. 2017. *When the Islamic State Comes to Town: The Economic Impact of Islamic State Governance in Iraq and Syria*. RAND Corporation.

Root, Rebecca L., and Lusan Nu Nu. 2023. "In Myanmar's Worsening Conflict, Health Workers Deliver Care and Dodge Death." *The New Humanitarian*, April 12. https://www.thenewhumanitarian.org/news-feature/2023/04/12/myanmar-conflict-health-workers.

Roy, Arundhati. 2014. "The NGO-ization of Resistance." Toward Freedom, September 8. https://towardfreedom.org/story/archives/globalism/arundhati-roy-the-ngo-ization-of-resistance/.

Ruiz de Elvira, Laura. 2019. "From Local Revolutionary Action to Exiled Humanitarian Work: Activism in Local Social Networks and Communities' Formation in the Syrian Post-2011 Context." *Social Movement Studies* 18 (1): 36–55. https://doi.org/10.1080/14742837.2018.1540346.

Ruiz de Elvira, Laura, and Tina Zintl. 2014. "The End of the Ba'thist Social Contract in Bashar Al-Asad's Syria: Reading Sociopolitical Transformations Through Charities and Broader Benevolent Activism." *International Journal of Middle East Studies* 46 (2): 329–49. https://doi.org/10.1017/s0020743814000130.

Salih, Mohammed A., and Marwan M. Kraidy. 2020. "Islamic State and Women: A Biopolitical Analysis." *International Journal of Communication* 14:1933–50.

Sawah, Wael, and Salam Kawakibi. 2014. "Activism in Syria: Between Nonviolence and Armed Resistance." In Khatib and Lust 2014, 136–71.

Sayigh, Yezid. 2013. "The Syrian Opposition's Leadership Problem." The Carnegie Papers. Carnegie Middle East Center, Carnegie Endowment for International Peace, April. https://carnegieendowment.org/research/2013/04/the-syrian-oppositions-leadership-problem.

Schneckener, Ulrich. 2011. "State Building or New Modes of Governance? The Effects of International Involvement in Areas of Limited Statehood." In Risse 2011b, 232–61.

Schock, Kurt. 2013. "The Practice and Study of Civil Resistance." *Journal of Peace Research* 50 (3): 277–90.

Scott, Emily K. M. 2022. "Compromising Aid to Protect International Staff: The Politics of Humanitarian Threat Perception After the Arab Uprisings." *Journal of Global Security Studies* 7 (1): 1–19, ogab024. https://doi.org/10.1093/jogss/ogab024.

Scott, James C. 1998. *Seeing Like a State: How Certain Schemes to Improve the Human Condition Have Failed*. Yale University Press.

Seawright, Jason. 2016. *Multi-Method Social Science: Combining Qualitative and Quantitative Tools. Strategies for Social Inquiry*. Cambridge University Press.
Sending, Ole Jacob, and Iver B. Neumann. 2006. "Governance to Governmentality: Analyzing NGOs, States, and Power." *International Studies Quarterly* 50 (3): 651–72.
Shehwaro, Marcelle. 2019. "The Price of a Voice." *Adi Magazine*, Winter. https://adimagazine.com/articles/the-price-of-a-voice/.
Sida, Lewis, Lorenzo Trombetta, and Veronica Panero. 2016. *Evaluation of OCHA Response to the Syria Crisis*. United Nations Office for the Coordination of Humanitarian Affairs, March. https://www.unocha.org/sites/unocha/files/dms/Documents/OCHA%20Syria%20Evaluation%20Report_FINAL.pdf.
Simmons, Erica S. 2014. "Grievances Do Matter in Mobilization." *Theory and Society* 43:513–46.
Slim, Hugo. 2015. *Humanitarian Ethics: A Guide to the Morality of Aid in War and Disaster*. Oxford University Press.
Slim, Hugo. 2020. "Reflections of a Humanitarian Bureaucrat." *Humanitarian Law & Policy Blog* (blog), January 9. https://blogs.icrc.org/law-and-policy/2020/01/09/reflections-humanitarian-bureaucrat/#_ftn2.
Slim, Hugo, and Emanuela-Chiara Gillard. 2013. "Ethical and Legal Perspectives on Cross-Border Humanitarian Operations." *Humanitarian Exchange* 59, article 2, November 26. https://odihpn.org/publication/ethical-and-legal-perspectives-on-cross-border-humanitarian-operations/.
Slim, Hugo, and Lorenzo Trombetta. 2014. *Syria Crisis Common Context Analysis*. Syria Coordinated Accountability and Lessons Learning Initiative Report. IASC Inter-Agency Humanitarian Evaluations Steering Group, May. https://interagencystandingcommittee.org/sites/default/files/migrated/2016-11/syria_crisis_common_context_analysis_june_2014.pdf.
Smirl, Lisa. 2015. *Spaces of Aid: How Cars, Compounds and Hotels Shape Humanitarianism*. Zed Books.
SNAP. 2013. "Needs Assessment Lessons Learned." Syria Needs Analysis Project, September 5. https://data.unhcr.org/es/documents/download/38107.
Soss, Joe. 2015. "Talking Our Way to Meaningful Explanations: A Practice-Centered View of Interviewing for Interpretive Research." In *Interpretation and Method: Empirical Research Methods and the Interpretive Turn*, edited by Dvora Yanow and Peregrine Schwartz-Shea, 193–214. Routledge.
South, Ashley. 2007. "Karen Nationalist Communities: The 'Problem' of Diversity." *Contemporary Southeast Asia* 29 (1): 55–76.
State. 2018. "U.S. Relations with Syria." Bilateral Relations Fact Sheet, Bureau of Near Eastern Affairs, United States Department of State. https://www.state.gov/u-s-relations-with-syria/.
Steele, Abbey. 2017. *Democracy and Displacement in Colombia's Civil War*. Cornell University Press.
Stoddard, Abby, Paul Harvey, Nigel Timmins, Varvara Pakhomenko, Meriah-Jo Breckenridge, Monica Czwarno. 2022. "Enabling the Local Response: Emerging Humanitarian Priorities in Ukraine March–May 2022." *Humanitarian Outcomes*. https://www.humanitarianoutcomes.org/Ukraine_review_June_2022.
Stokke, Espen, and Eric Wiebelhaus-Brahm. 2019. "Syrian Diaspora Mobilization: Vertical Coordination, Patronage Relations, and the Challenges of Fragmentation in the Pursuit of Transitional Justice." *Ethnic and Racial Studies* 42 (11): 1930–49. https://doi.org/10.1080/01419870.2019.1572909.
Suykens, Bert. 2015. "Comparing Rebel Rule Through Revolution and Naturalization: Ideologies of Governance in Naxalite and Naga India." In *Rebel Governance*

in Civil War, edited by Ana Arjona, Nelson Kasfir, and Zachariah Mampilly, 138–57. Cambridge University Press.

Svoboda, Eva. 2014. "Aid and the Islamic State." IRIN/HPG Crisis Brief. Overseas Development Institute and IRIN News, December.

Sweis, Rania Kassab. 2019. "Doctors with Borders: Hierarchies of Humanitarians and the Syrian Civil War." *International Journal of Middle East Studies* 51 (4): 587–601. https://doi.org/10.1017/s0020743819000643.

Swidler, Ann. 1973. "The Concept of Rationality in the Work of Max Weber." *Sociological Inquiry* 43 (1): 35–42.

Syria Untold. 2013. "Idrab al-karama: Al-hikaya min al-bidaya ila al-nihaya [Dignity strike: The story from beginning to end]." *Hikaya ma inhakat* (*Syria Untold*), April. https://tinyurl.com/4jsw4scv.

Syria Untold. 2015. "That's What the Donor Wants." *Syria Untold* (blog), July 13. https://web.archive.org/web/20200409201905/https://syriauntold.com/2015/07/13/thats-what-the-donor-wants/.

Syrian Prints Archive. 2016. "Arshif Al-Matbu'at al-Suriyya [Syrian Prints Archive]." syrianprints.org.

Tarrow, Sidney. 1993. "Cycles of Collective Action: Between Moments of Madness and the Repertoire of Contention." *Social Science History* 17 (2): 281–307.

Tarrow, Sidney. 2007. "Inside Insurgencies: Politics and Violence in an Age of Civil War." *Perspectives on Politics* 5 (3): 587–600. https://doi.org/10.1017/S1537592707071575.

Tarrow, Sidney. 2011. *Power in Movement: Social Movements and Contentious Politics*. 3rd ed. Cambridge University Press. https://doi.org/10.1017/cbo9780511973529.

TBC. 2004. "Between Worlds: Twenty Years on the Border." The Border Consortium, January. https://www.refworld.org/reference/countryrep/tbbc/2004/en/76147.

Tilly, Charles. 2015. "Public Violence." In *International Encyclopedia of the Social & Behavioral Sciences*, edited by James D. Wright. 2nd ed. Elsevier.

TIMEP. 2016. "Combating Al-Qaeda in Syria: A Strategy for the Next Administration." Tahrir Institute for Middle East Policy. https://timep.org/wp-content/uploads/2016/01/Combating-al-Qaeda-in-Syria.pdf.

Tisdall, Brian. 2013. "The Challenge of Access in Syria." *Humanitarian Exchange* 59, article 3, November 26. https://odihpn.org/publication/the-challenge-of-access-in-syria/.

TNS. 2015. "Arab Social Media Report." Arab Social Media Influencers Summit. TNS.

Torrenté, Nicolas de. 2004. "Humanitarian Action Under Attack: Reflections on the Iraq War." *Harvard Human Rights Journal* 17 (1): 1–29. https://www.doctorswithoutborders.org/what-we-do/news-stories/research/humanitarian-action-under-attack-reflections-iraq-war.

Trujillo, Catherine. 2013. "Memorandum: Survey of Selected USAID Syria-Related Activities (Report No. 6-276-14-001-S)." Office of the Inspector General, US Agency for International Development, December 1.

Tsourapas, Gerasimos. 2019. "The Syrian Refugee Crisis and Foreign Policy Decision-Making in Jordan, Lebanon, and Turkey." *Journal of Global Security Studies* 4 (4): 464–81.

Turkmani, Rim, Ali A. K. Ali, Mary Kaldor, and Vesna Dzelilovic. 2015. "Countering the Logic of the War Economy in Syria: Evidence from Three Local Areas." Civil Society and Human Security Research Unit, Department of International Development, London School of Economics and Political Science.

UNHCR. 2018. "Syria Regional Refugee Response." Operational Data Portal. Accessed December 9. https://data.unhcr.org/en/situations/syria.
UNHCR. 2019. "Global Trends: Forced Displacement in 2018." United Nations High Commissioner for Refugees.
Urquhart, Angus. 2019. *Global Humanitarian Assistance Report 2019*. Development Initiatives.
Urquhart, Angus, and Luminita Tuchel. 2018. *Global Humanitarian Assistance Report 2018*. Development Initiatives.
U.S. Army. 2006. *The U.S. Army/Marine Corps Counterinsurgency Field Manual*. U.S. Department of the Army, FM 3-24 MCWP 3-33.5, December 15.
Van Baalen, Sebastian. 2024. "Civilian Protest in Civil War: Insights from Côte d'Ivoire." *American Political Science Review* 118 (2): 815–30. https://doi.org/10.1017/S0003055423000564.
Voon, Frances. 2013. "The Syrian Refugee Crisis: Findings from a Real-Time Evaluation of UNHCR's Response." *Humanitarian Exchange* 59, article 8, November 27. https://odihpn.org/publication/the-syrian-refugee-crisis-findings-from-a-real-time-evaluation-of-unhcr%C2%92s-response/.
Walker, Peter, and Catherine Russ. 2010. "Professionalising the Humanitarian Sector: A Scoping Study." ELRHA: Enhancing Learning and Research for Humanitarian Assistance. Feinstein International Center, Tufts University, and RedR UK. https://fic.tufts.edu/wp-content/uploads/Professionalising_the_humanitarian_sector.pdf.
Walter, Barbara F. 2013. "The Four Things We Know About How Civil Wars End (and What This Tells Us About Syria)." *Political Violence at a Glance* (blog), October 18. https://politicalviolenceataglance.org/2013/10/18/the-four-things-we-know-about-how-civil-wars-end-and-what-this-tells-us-about-syria/.
Ward, Patricia. 2020. "Capitalising on 'Local Knowledge': The Labour Practices Behind Successful Aid Projects; The Case of Jordan." *Current Sociology* 69 (5): 705–22. https://doi.org/10.1177%2F0011392120905342.
Watkins, Susan Cotts, Ann Swidler, and Thomas Hannan. 2012. "Outsourcing Social Transformation: Development NGOs as Organizations." *Annual Review of Sociology* 38: 285–315. https://doi.org/10.1146/annurev-soc-071811-145516.
Wedeen, Lisa. 1999. *Ambiguities of Domination: Politics, Rhetoric, and Symbols in Contemporary Syria*. University of Chicago Press.
Weiss, Thomas G. 1999. "Principles, Politics, and Humanitarian Action." *Ethics & International Affairs* 13 (1): 1–22.
Weissman, Fabrice. 2013. "Scaling Up Aid in Syria: The Role of Diaspora Networks." CRASH: La Fondation Médecins Sans Frontières, September 6. https://www.msf-crash.org/en/blog/scaling-aid-syria-role-diaspora-networks.
Whittall, Jonathan. 2015. "The 'New Humanitarian Aid Landscape' Case Study: MSF Interaction with Non-Traditional and Emerging Aid Actors in Syria 2013-14." Technical Report. Médecins sans Frontières.
Wieland, Carsten. 2021. *Syria and the Neutrality Trap: The Dilemmas of Delivering Humanitarian Aid Through Violent Regimes*. I. B. Tauris.
Wood, Elisabeth Jean. 2001. "The Emotional Benefits of Insurgency in El Salvador." In *Passionate Politics: Emotions and Social Movements*, edited by Jeff Goodwin, James M. Jasper, and Francesca Polletta, 267–81. University of Chicago Press.
Wood, Elisabeth Jean. 2008. "The Social Processes of Civil War: The Wartime Transformation of Social Networks." *Annual Review of Political Science* 11: 539–61. https://doi.org/10.1146/annurev.polisci.8.082103.104832.

Yadav, Stacey Philbrick. 2020. "Effective Citizenship, Civil Action, and Prospects for Post-Conflict Justice in Yemen." *International Journal of Middle East Studies* 52 (4): 754–58. https://doi.org/10.1017/s0020743820001051.

Zeira, Yael. 2019. *The Revolution Within: State Institutions and Unarmed Resistance in Palestine*. Cambridge University Press.

Index

Abboud, Samer, 52
access, humanitarian, 28–29
activism, wartime. *See* civil action
Afghanistan, 135–36
agency
   and civil action in war, 24
   of refugees, 151
aid chain, 38, 108, 121. *See also* supply chain
Aleppo, 44, 46, 54, 63–64, 73, 119, 148–49
Aleppo City, 21–23, 101–2, 148, 149
Algeria, 137
Alloush, Zahran, 78
Andreas, Peter, 79
areas of limited statehood, 6, 28, 29, 30, 57, 140, 161n2
arms, use of, 48
al-Asad, Bashar, 41, 42, 43, 44, 53
al-Asad, Hafez, 43, 44
Assistance Coordination Unit (ACU), 121–25
audits, 66–67, 114
Autesserre, Séverine, 15
autonomy, 6
   acquisition of, 27–28
   of aid organizations on border with Myanmar, 129
   blocking of international aid, 16, 55, 127, 128, 138–40
   changes in conditions of, 146
   international, as scope condition, 27–30
   of international actors, 6, 30–31, 68, 80
   of international aid actors in Jordan, 61–62
   of international aid actors in Turkey, 58–60
   of international aid organizations, 68
   variation in international aid, 13, 80, 109

Baba Amr, 42
Badran, Yazan, 99–100, 115, 117
Barnett, Michael, 34, 38, 83, 162n4
Barter, Shane, 25
Ba'th Party, 45
Bob, Clifford, 138
border regions, 8
   nonviolent agency of refugees in, 151
   research on, 151–52

   as spaces of convergence for international and local actors, 127–28
   as spaces of risky engagement, 128–29
brain drain, 139
Burma. *See* Myanmar
Bush, Sarah, 39, 116

Calhoun, Craig, 144
Carpi, Estella, 85
Carroll, John, 110
"causes-of-effects" approach, 12
Cave, The, 79
Centre for Humanitarian Dialogue, 94
charities, 43–44
child protection, 81–83
Citizens for Syria, 67
civil action
   in absence of international aid, 138–40
   conditions for connection between international aid and, 27–30
   emergence of, during Syria's war, 2–3
   history of, in Syria, 43–45
   international aid as facilitating participation in, 65
   international aid as shaping, 3–4, 30–32
   international aid relations as facilitating, 32–34
   international aid resources as filtering, 37–40
   international aid rules as formalizing, 34–37
   scholarship on, 7–8
   Syrians' participation in, 66–67
   in Ukraine, 134
   in war, 24–25
   without rules of international aid, 100–104
   See also facilitating process; filtering process; formalizing process
civilizing, 9–10
civilizing contention
   defined, 24
   interactions between international and local actors according to, 146
   Myanmar as case study for, 128–32
   Sudan as case study for, 132–38
   theory of, 5–6, 127
   See also facilitating process; filtering process; formalizing process

INDEX

civil society
  and civilized contention, 6, 10
  components of, 165n4
  decoupled from humanitarianism, 93
  and facilitating, formalizing, and filtering processes, 80, 125–26
  formation of almost- in Myanmar, 131, 132
  formation of almost- in southern Sudan, 133
  formation of almost- in Syria, 2–3, 150
  and ideational resources, 117–18
  and international aid, 4, 144
  in Ukraine, 134
  and uncertainties of civil actors, 149
civil society organizations (CSOs), 67, 135, 150
coalitions, 116–17, 122
coercive pressures, 34–35, 36, 91, 94, 96–97, 100
compensation, 39, 75, 108, 118–21
competitive learning, 39, 116–17, 125
contracted resources, 38, 108–9, 112–17
Cooley, Alexander, 38
countering violent extremism (CVE), 96, 102, 123–25
Crasnow, Sharon, 12, 154
cross-border operations
  and humanitarian aid to Syria crisis, 57–58
  and infrastructural relations between international aid actors and Syrians, 71–73
  and international autonomy, 29
  Jordan as origin point of, 61
  limitation of, 147–48
  maintained by OCHA, 147
  into Myanmar, 129–31
  and OCHA's knowledge production, 90

"Damascus Declaration" (2005), 44–45
"Damascus Spring" (2000–2001), 44–45
Darʿa, 45–46, 49, 61, 62, 147–48
data collection, 92, 102
Days of Freedom campaign, 47
Deir ez-Zor, 46
demonstrations, 1–2, 41–42, 46–48, 51, 63, 101–2
de Waal, Alex, 33
diaspora organizations, 25–26, 69
Dignity Strike, 47
DiMaggio, Paul, 162n5
displacement, 25, 53–54. *See also* refugees
Doctors Without Borders (MSF), 49, 57, 69, 79
"do no harm" approach, 152–53
donor funding, 33–34, 39

Douma Four, 78
Duffield, Mark, 26, 152, 166n1
Dupuy, Kendra, 110–11

earthquake (2023), 144–45
Eastern Ghouta, 78–80
"effects-of-causes" approach, 12
Elias, Norbert, 10
El-Kurd, Mohammed, 156
emergency imaginary, 144–50
enactment, 39, 118
English competency, 99
Eritrea, 79
evaluations, and resource distribution, 114
expertise, as basis of authority among international organizations, 36

Facebook, 17
  establishment of pages associated with nonviolent actors, 67, 68*f*
  and organizational growth, 110, 111*f*
  page creations by political orientation, 86–88, 89*f*
  pages representing formal and informal Syrian organizations, 153–54
  spikes in pages representing governance institutions following Opposition Coalition establishment, 76, 77*f*
  Syrian organizations active inside Syria based on information from, 49, 50*f*
facilitating process, 34, 63–66, 80
  besiegement of Eastern Ghouta, 78–80
  facilitation of relations, 68–76
  participation in civil action in Syrian war, 66–68
  and Russian invasion of Ukraine, 134–35
  in Sudan, 72
Fassin, Didier, 35
Ferguson, James, 27
Fiddian-Qasmiyeh, Elena, 85, 137–38
filtering process, 106–9
  and Assistance Coordination Unit (ACU), 121–26
  and nonviolent survival in Syrian war, 109–11
  and resource distribution, 111–21
  and Sahrawi refugees, 137–38
Financial Tracking Service, 66–67
Finnemore, Martha, 34, 83, 162n4
formalizing process, 81–84, 104–5
  in Afghanistan, 135–36
  and informal activism without rules, 100–104
  and moralistic rules, 93–97

and politics of nonviolent action in Syrian war, 84–88
and professional rules, 97–100
and rational rules, 89–93
in Sudan, 72
Free Syrian Army (FSA), 2, 51
Free Syria Police, 61

Gaziantep, Turkey, 59–60, 64, 71, 107
gender roles, 25
Ghouta. *See* Eastern Ghouta
government-organized NGOs (GONGOs), 44
Griffiths, Martin, 145

Hama, 44, 45
Hamdan, Ali, 71, 89
Hannan, Michael, 110
Hay'at Tahrir al-Sham (HTS), 54–55. *See also* Jabhat al-Nusra
Heydemann, Steven, 46
Homs, 41–42, 46, 49
hope, 156
Howe, Kimberly, 91–92
humanitarian aid
  donor funding for, 33–34, 147
  and international aid in war, 26–27
  versus nonhumanitarian aid, 163n29
  overview of, 8–9
  during Sudanese civil war, 132–33
  during Syrian uprising, 48, 49, 56–57
  from Turkey, 59
  for Ukraine, 134
  See also international aid
humanitarianism
  fluctuations in, 144
  as marginal to Syrian civil organizations' original missions, 117
  and moralistic rules in formalizing process, 93–94, 95, 96
humanitarianisms, 165n4
Humanitarian Needs Assessment Programme (HNAP), 90

ideational resources, 39–40, 107–9, 117–21
Idlib, 46, 54, 73, 74–75, 106–7, 149
information collection, 35
Information Management Unit, 122, 125
infrastructural relations, between international aid actors and Syrians, 71–74, 79
institutions, 31, 37–40
internally displaced person (IDP), 53–54
international aid
  in border regions, 8

as characterized by rules, 83–84
civil action in absence of, 138–40
civil action without rules of, 100–104
complexity of, institutions, 32–33
conditions for connection between civil action and, 27–30
effects of, 19–20
as facilitating participation in nonviolent action, 32–34, 65, 76–80, 108
impermanence of, 143–44
informational requirements and standards of, 91–92
institutional qualities of, 31–32
of intergovernmental and nongovernmental organizations, 8–9
and limitations of within-case process tracing, 14
obstruction of, 147–48
political effects of, 154–55
and politics of nonviolent action in Syrian war, 84–88
relationships as facilitating nonviolent action, 32–34
resources as filtering nonviolent action, 37–40
resources of, 108–9
response to Syrian crisis, 90
rules as formalizing nonviolent action, 34–37
scholarship on, 6
as shaping civil action in war, 3–4, 30–32
temporal variation in, 13
as threat to existing regimes, 155–56
unified framework for, 150
in war, 25–27
  See also humanitarian aid
international aid autonomy
  blocking of, 16, 55, 127, 128, 138–40
  variation in, 13, 80, 109
international aid organizations/actors
  arrive in Syria, 3
  autonomy of, 6, 27–31, 68, 80
  autonomy of, in Jordan, 61–62
  autonomy of, in Turkey, 58–60
  autonomy of, on border with Myanmar, 129
  development of relations between local actors and, 65, 68–76
  as endeavoring to "localize" or "decolonize" aid, 155
  and formalizing process, 83
  growth in, 109–10
  moral authority of, 35–36
  professionalism of, 36
  rationalism of, 35

INDEX

international aid autonomy (*continued*)
  remuneration from, 22, 23, 39, 74–75, 118–19, 121
  response to Afghanistan and Afghan refugees in Pakistan, 135–36
  response to Assistance Coordination Unit, 122
  in Ukraine, 134–35
  as working with and through local actors, 22, 23
international nongovernmental organizations (INGOs)
  autonomy of, in Turkey, 59
  on border with Myanmar, 129–30
  humanitarian aid to Syria crisis, 57
  and infrastructural relations with local actors, 79
  knowledge production of, 90
  and professional rules in formalizing process, 98
  response to Assistance Coordination Unit, 122
interviews, 15–16
Islamic State, 54, 101, 102, 138–40, 148–49

Jabhat al-Nusra, 123–24. *See also* Hay'at Tahrir al-Sham (HTS)
Jordan
  autonomy of international aid actors in, 61–62
  cross-border operations from, 57–58, 71–73
  encouragement for Syria's anti-government political opposition, 88
  refugee response without rules in, 103–4
  restrictions on border passage of activists, 119
  Syrians' participation in nonviolent action in, 66
journalism, 46–47

Karen Christian networks, 131
Karen National Liberation Army (KNLA), 130, 131
Karen National Union (KNU), 130, 131–32
Karen rebellion, 129, 130, 131–32
knowledge production, 35, 90–91, 100
Krause, Jana, 38
Kurdish struggle, 44–45, 51, 107–8

Lake, Milli, 29
learning, competitive, 39, 116–17
Lebanon, 55
Leenders, Reinoud, 46
Lichtenheld, Adam, 53

limited statehood, areas of, 29, 161n2
Local Coordination Committees (LCCs, *tansiqqiyyat*), 47, 48
local councils (*majalis mahaliyya*), 51–52, 94–95, 118
Lund, Aron, 52–53

Mansour, Nayla, 92, 93
March, James, 31
material relations, between international aid actors and Syrians, 74–76
Mazur, Kevin, 47, 162n5
Médecins Sans Frontières (MSF), 49, 57, 69, 79
Mercy Corps, 149
Middle East, as structured by violence, 152
mimetic pressures, 162n5
money talk, 39, 108, 118–21, 123, 124, 153
monitoring and evaluation (M&E), 91–92, 142–43
moralism, 35–36, 84
moralistic rules, 84, 93–97, 130
Morocco, 137
Moss, Dana M., 162n2
Mundy, Jacob, 152
Muslim Brothers (MB), 41, 44, 61
Myanmar, 83, 128–32

National Coalition for Syrian Revolutionary and Opposition Forces (the Opposition Coalition), 69, 74, 78
National Union of Sahrawi Women, 137–38
needs assessment, 65, 71, 89–92, 117, 122
networks of violence, 52
neutrality, 93–94, 96
"new humanitarianism," 26–27
NGOization, 6–7
NGO scramble, 38, 76, 114–16, 121, 162n8
nongovernmental organizations (NGOs)
  counting, 153–54
  crackdown on, in Gaziantep, 60
  formalization of grassroots organizations into, 84–85
  government-organized NGOs (GONGOs), 44
  NGOization, 6–7
  NGO scramble, 38, 76, 114–16, 121, 162n8
  and professional rules in formalizing process, 98
  registration certificate for, in rebel-held area, 85, 86f
  resource distribution to, 112–13
  survival and selection processes of, 110–11
  See also formalizing process; international nongovernmental organizations (INGOs)

nonhumanitarian aid
  government obstruction of, 55–56
  versus humanitarian aid, 163n29
  and international aid in war, 26
  Jordanian wariness of, 61
  overview of, 8–9
  provided by United States, 148
nonviolent action. *See* civil action
Nordstrom, Carolyn, 32
Novak, Paolo, 136

Al-Oballi, Ayah, 91, 93
Obama, Barack, 53
Office for the Coordination of Humanitarian Affairs (OCHA)
  "cluster" approach of, 72
  cross-border operations of, 90, 91, 147
  and financial reporting practices of humanitarian assistance agencies, 66–67
  in growing coordination superstructure, 33
  and moralistic rules in formalizing process, 93–94
  and professional rules in formalizing process, 98
  and rational rules in formalizing process, 91
  as relying on humanitarian aid organizations, 26
  response to Assistance Coordination Unit, 122
  Syria Cross-Border Pooled Fund, 73, 75, 76t, 112–13
Olsen, Johan, 31
Operation Euphrates Shield, 60, 148–49
Operation Lifeline Sudan (OLS), 132–33

Pakistan, 135–36
parallel system of aid, 151
Parkinson, Sarah E., 39, 153
Pearlman, Wendy, 154
persistence, of nonviolent activists, 63–65
Pincock, Kate, 28
Polisario Front, 137
"politics of region," 50–51
Powell, Colin, 28
Powell, Walter, 162n5
Prendergast, John, 166n1
privatization, 43–44
process tracing, 12–15, 16, 65–66, 77, 83–84, 86–88, 104, 108–9, 154
professionalism, 36, 84, 98–100
professional rules, 84, 97–100, 130
projects, and resource distribution, 38–39, 112–14

Raqqah Is Being Slaughtered Silently, 139
rationalism, 35, 84

rational rules, 84, 89–93, 130
Red Cross (ICRC), 56
refugee camps, 103–4
refugees
  agency of, 151
  as brokers between international remote managers and Syrians inside Syria, 70–71
  displacement of Syrian, 53–54
  knowledge production regarding, 90
  and professional rules in formalizing process, 99
  range of action among, 25
  response without rules in Jordan, 103–4
  Turkey's humanitarian aid for, 59
Refugees International, 98
relations
  development of, between international aid organizations and local actors, 65, 68–76
  growth in population of civil organizations as response to, 109–10
  international aid, as facilitating nonviolent action, 32–34, 65, 76–80, 108
  and international aid organizations' rules on local actors, 130
  material, between international aid actors and Syrians, 74–76
  See also facilitating process; filtering process; formalizing process
religion, and moralistic rules in formalizing process, 94
remuneration, 39, 75, 108, 118–21
resources
  contracted, 38, 108–9, 112–17
  distribution of, 34, 37–40, 131–32
  filtering of, 111–21
  ideational, 39–40, 107–9, 117–21
  as institutional quality of international aid, 108–9
Reyhanli, Turkey, 67
Riehl, Volker, 133
risk-aversion, research-related, 152–53
Risse, Thomas, 29, 161n2
Ron, James, 38
Ruiz de Elvira, Laura, 44, 49
rules
  as central to bases of bureaucratic authority, 162n4
  and formalizing process, 83–84, 89–100
  imposed on local actors, 130
  informal activism without, 100–104
  international aid, as formalizing nonviolent action, 34–37
Rural Damascus, 46, 47, 48, 49, 62, 73, 85, 148. *See also* Eastern Ghouta
Russia, 134–35

INDEX

Saharan Arab Democratic Republic, 137
Sahrawi refugees, 137–38
Salafi-jihadist armed groups, 52–53
Save the Children, 26
Scott, James C., 162n3
security vetting, 61, 114
Shehwaro, Marcel, 97
Sheikh Jarrah neighborhood, 156
Slim, Hugo, 29
Smets, Kevin, 99–100, 117
South, Ashley, 130, 132
Soviet Union, 135
Spain, 137
stabilization programs, 95, 118
Sudan, 79, 132–38
Sudan People's Liberation Army (SPLA), 166n1
Sudan Relief and Rehabilitation Association (SRRA), 133, 166n1
supply chain, 38, 124. *See also* aid chain
survival, project-based, 112–16
Swies, Rania, 96
Syria
   earthquake response in, 144–45
   fall of regime, 150
   history of civil action in, 43–45
   hope in, 156
   transnational repression by regime of, 162n2
   See also Syrian organizations; Syrian war
Syria Cross-Border Humanitarian Fund, 67
Syria Cross-Border Pooled Fund, 73, 75, 76f, 112–13
Syrian Arab Red Crescent, 56
Syrian Civil Defense, 119
Syria Needs Analysis Project (SNAP), 90
Syrian Interim Government, 163
Syrian National Council, 163
Syrian Opposition Coalition (SOC), 77f, 122, 163
Syrian organizations
   adaptation to technical tasks, 89
   audits and evaluations of, 66–67, 114
   balance between strategies and tactics in, 115
   capacity assessments of, 114
   and contract resources, 112–13
   and cross-border operations, 98
   growth in population of, 67, 107, 110
   infrastructural relations with, 71–73
   in Jordan, 61–62
   material relations with, 74
   monitoring and evaluation of, 91
   as oriented toward vertical relations with donors, 115
   professionalization of, 99
   remuneration in, 75
   resource distribution to, 112–14
   security as challenge facing, 114
   shifting toward countering violent extremism, 91
   Syria Cross-Border Pooled Fund allocations to, 113
   in Turkey, 59, 60, 85, 107
   See also Facebook
Syrian Revolution General Commission, 47
Syrian Uprising, 45–50
   and formalizing rules, 89
   international responses to, 11, 12–13, 62
   and material relations, 74
   and professional rules, 97
   and refugee response in Jordan, 103
   violent and nonviolent contention during, 43
Syrian war, 45–55
   filtering process and nonviolent survival in, 109–11
   formalizing process and politics of nonviolent action in, 84–88
   funding for, 14f, 147
   humanitarian needs and response to, 146–47
   international response to, 11, 55–62, 90
   trajectory of activists in, 21–23
   unraveling of protest movement, 142

tactical adaptation, 13, 43, 45
temporal variation, 13
territorial control, 54–55, 140, 148–49
Thai-Burma Border Consortium, 131
Thailand, 129–32
theory-building process-tracing, 16, 77
Tigray, 79
Tilly, Charles, 50
transition programs, 118
Turkey
   autonomy of international aid actors in, 55, 58–60
   as consequential player for trajectories of Syrian activists, 148–49
   cross-border operations from, 57–58, 71–73
   earthquake response in, 144–45
   encouragement for Syria's anti-government political opposition, 88
   formalizing process in, 89

marketization of civil-action work in, 120
Syrian civil society organizations in, 67
Syrians' participation in nonviolent action in, 66
See also Gaziantep, Turkey
Turkey-Syria borderlands, 101–3

Ukraine, 134–35
UN High Commissioner for Refugees (UNHCR), 59, 61
unified framework, 9, 150
United Nations
  and cross-border operations, 29
  humanitarian aid to Syria crisis, 14f, 56
  initial assumptions regarding Syrian uprising, 146
  See also Office for the Coordination of Humanitarian Affairs (OCHA)
United States
  and Assistance Coordination Unit, 122
  and moralistic rules in formalizing process, 95
  nonhumanitarian aid provided by, 148
  and stabilization programs, 118

UNRWA (United Nations Relief and Works Agency for Palestine Refugees in the Near East), 30
UN Security Council Resolution 2165 (2014), 57, 71–72, 90
US Agency for International Development (USAID), 56, 78, 133

variation, 13, 52, 56, 80, 119

wartime activism. *See* civil action
weapons, use of, 48
Western Sahara, 137–38
White Helmets, 119
"Whole of Syria" approach, 57, 72, 90, 93, 133, 147. *See also* UN Security Council Resolution 2165 (2014)
Wieland, Carsten, 56, 163n29
within-case process tracing, 12–14

Yemen, 64–65

Zaatari, 103–4
Zintl, Tina, 44

www.ingramcontent.com/pod-product-compliance
Lightning Source LLC
Chambersburg PA
CBHW031402230426
43670CB00006B/612